A Magic Shadow-show

J. P. KING
AUTOBIOGRAPHY

© 2000 J. P. King   All rights reserved.

For in and out, above, about, below,
'Tis nothing but a Magic Shadow-show,
Play'd in a Box whose Candle is the Sun,
Round which we Phantom Figures come and go.

Rubáiyát of Omar Khayyám

Introduction

A Magic Shadow show is the autobiography of a survivor of the Death Railway that was built by the Japanese during the Second World War with a labour force of Allied prisoners of war and Asiatic coolies. The death toll from tropical diseases, harsh treatment and starvation rations was terribly high.

Japan had refused to sign the convention observed by other countries which laid down the conditions under which prisoners of war were to be treated and was guilty of the most heinous cruelty in the inhuman disregard with which their helpless prisoners were treated.. This splendid personal account of what he saw and experienced is not as might be expected all gloom and desperation. As well as the tears you will inevitably be moved by, there are moments when you will laugh out loud at the comical passages. The book briefly covers childhood in a seaside town in a family of nine; time as a boy soldier and some years spent in Australia with wife and three sons as a pound a head immigrants. Be warned, you may find this book hard to put down.

.

Table of Contents

CHAPTER 1	Childhood	4
CHAPTER 2	Life After Leaving School	17
CHAPTER 3	Boy Soldier Training	20
CHAPTER 4	Posting / Voyage to Singapore	27
CHAPTER 5	Pre-War days, Singapore	34
CHAPTER 6	War Stations	43
CHAPTER 7	Fall of Singapore, early POW days	56
CHAPTER 8	Thailand Hell Camps	105
CHAPTER 9	PoW Life and Liberation	125
CHAPTER 10	Homecoming	224
CHAPTER 11	Post-War / Emigration	233
CHAPTER 12	Townsville, Australia	238
CHAPTER 13	Voyage Home	268

CHAPTER 1 Childhood

I was born on February 27th, 1922 in a terraced house in the seaside town of Eastbourne, in the county of Sussex, England.

There were, at that time, ten in our family. An eleventh member was added two years after me.

The family comprised my parents, five sisters and myself and three brothers; the eleventh member was one of the five sisters.

The house had three upstairs bedrooms and a bathroom with w.c; the lower floor had a front room (used only on special occasions), a "middle room" — as we called it — which was used as a bedroom for the boys, a small living room in which all meals were taken, and an even smaller kitchen, which had a large clothes boiler (the copper), built in one corner.

There was a small yard at the rear of the house, of bare clay (well trampled) with a strip of garden along two of the walls, a diamond shaped piece in the centre of the yard which enclosed a tea rose, and a home-built shed against the end wall beside a gate.

A roof and trellis made a lean-to along the back of the house from the kitchen door and past the outside lavatory. In summer the trellis was heavy with honeysuckle, the heavenly scent of which lingers yet in the memory.

My father did not work for a living but lived on a disability pension from W.W.1 or the Great War, as it was then called.

He had enlisted in the patriotic fever of the Boer War at the age of fifteen and had served throughout that conflict; being also in the Matabele Rebellion and the Somali Land Campaign, in which he sustained a sabre cut to one wrist. A scar which remained prominent for the rest of his life.

He volunteered again for service in the Great War and was twice wounded.
Because of his previous experience he obtained a commission in the Middlesex Regiment and served until the end of the war. In after years he did not speak much about his experiences but would happily recount the times he spent in camp concert parties.

The hallway of our house rather resembled a small military museum. From the walls there hung, a .303 rifle with bayonet, an officer's sword with scabbard, crossed "poison" daggers — allegedly taken from the Arabs. The blades had been charred in a fire. " To remove the poison," he said. I remember that the sheaves of the daggers were of soft leather and hung from handsome tasselled cords. There was also a helmet, and in the fireplace of the front room stood the nose caps of two large shells which had numbers engraved in a circular brass ring about each. There were also some big brass cartridge cases.

Other mementoes of his service days were two cups for boxing and a silver gong in a fancy frame, also an award. These stood on the lower shelf of a decorative blackwood overmantle piece. The topmost shelf (one of many), which seemed miles high to me at that time, had two delicate china figures, a shepherd and shepherdess who sat with legs dangling over the shelf edge.

Although he had been commissioned into the Middlesex Regiment, my father transferred back to his original regiment, the Royal Artillery (which thereafter became a sort of family regiment).

He was a man of short stature and square build, about 5 feet 6 inches tall with regular features. Athletic in youth he became portly in his middle years. In temperament he was subject to mood swings and was jolly or, at other times, angry, tending to violence. We were all afraid of him and not until much later in life was I to realise that it was the unspeakable horrors of the first world war that had probably made him the way he was.

Once, in the back yard, he decapitated a chicken which ran headless round the yard then part-way up the trellis from which it then hung backwards until taken down.

My mother was a small person with gentle grey eyes, and a sweet nature. Her gentleness and kindness have been second to none in my life. Like all housewives of that era she devoted her days to caring for her large family, washing and ironing on an heroic scale, cooking and cleaning. Brasses were always polished, as were lino floors; windows were cleaned, steps washed. In addition to this, two allotments were worked and all our vegetables grown. How she made ends meet on the slender income, I shall never know. But she did. We went off to school clean. We were all bathed and changed once a week, and she mended our shoes on an iron cobbler's-last with 6 penny pieces of leather bought in Woolworth's. We had no underclothes in those days and my schoolwear was a woollen jersey, shorts, knee socks and boots, and a handed-down cap.

At Christmas my mother came into her own and always produced the traditional treats of pudding (with sixpenny pieces!) iced cake, crackers, or bon-bons as we called them then, mince pies, a fire in the front room and presents for each of us.

We made our own decorations from paper chains stuck together with paste made from flour. The same flour as she used for cooking and for hanging wallpaper. We were as well looked after as any in our circumstances could be.

I attended the C of E school at the east end of town in an area that contained mainly poor families. Passing through the infants school, at which I heard my proper name for the first time, given by an older brother to the teacher who enrolled me. I was surprised it was not the one I was called at home. My mother had an affectionate diminutive for each of us. I should have enrolled on the previous day, but overcome by panic I had run away down the alley behind our house and had been permitted by my mother to postpone it until the next day.

"The Cat Sat on the Mat," are the first words I remember learning to read and write. I got my first taste for acting in tiny playlets. My teacher, a lady, toothy, who looked enormously tall to me said I liked music and should have the little ukulele which was among the toys donated to the school by some charity, but who broke the strings while demonstrating how to play it.

"Oh ! never mind. Take it home, John and get your father to mend it."

My father never mended things.

School aged 4

From the "Infants" I eventually went up into the "Big Boys' School". A building in the same complex. This happened at 7 years of age. There I began learning in earnest. There the cane was liberally applied for such awful crimes as a blot on a copy book page, smudging, talking, or any small offence.

   The headmaster, a man of saturnine, cadaverous features with long yellow teeth, exhibited a predilection for near sadism and would publicly and mercilessly flog a boy with a long thin cane. On one occasion he sent two boys off to purchase at a nearby shop the very canes with which he was about to flog them. Assembled to watch the punishment I was surprised to see the new canes tied in a tidy loop.

   The school was assembled on another occasion to witness the caning of a small boy who had refused to remove a woollen cap when ordered. The boy's head had been shaved because of ringworm.

"Let's see how your head is getting on," said the headmaster.

"No, sir," said the boy. The headmaster then tried to pull off the woollen cap. The boy, just as determined, decided to hang on to it — with both hands. He was ordered to the front of the class, and again ordered to remove the hat. Again he refused. The large partitions which separated the classrooms were folded back and the whole school assembled.

"Remove your hat," ordered the head.

"No, sir," replied the boy, now sobbing. The cane began to thwack against the top of his legs, punctuated by orders to remove the cap. The boy dropped to the floor and we witnessed the unedifying spectacle of the unfortunate child scrabbling around while the cane thrashed wildly down at him. At one time he actually crawled through the headmaster's legs. Eventually, sobbing, he was hauled to his feet, the hat dragged from his head and the head with its first sproutings of hair exposed.

"There!" crowed the headmaster exultantly.

"There's nothing there to make a fuss of." It had been a horrid spectacle and left an indelible effect on me. Needless to say we were all terrified of that awful man.

   It was during the last term of my time at that school that an experiment was tried, in which girls, previously housed in the upper part of the building, were brought in to share our class room. They sat to one side of the room, we boys on the other. The air was fairly crackling with excitement, like a fully charged battery needing only a bridge across its poles to discharge it with a blinding flash and an ear-splitting crack. Nothing happened, of course, but there was a new excitement now to every day.

It was there that I had my first, completely uneventful love affair. A note was passed to me.

It said, "Will you go out with me ?"

I asked the boy on my right who it was from.

"Audrey," he said , and pointed out a girl two seats away.

I had not noticed her before. I scribbled "No," on the note and sent it back. It was returned at once.

"Why not?" it asked. Unable to think of a suitable reply I then wrote "All right."

We met after school for a while and played together. All perfectly innocent. The "affair" did not last long, but was never forgotten.

One day, years later when we had both left school, we met again by chance near a local park. I was still quite short. She had grown quite tall. We were about 14 years old at the time. She told me that she had become an apprentice hairdresser. I had the awful impression that she felt me rather pathetic in my smallness, and shabby appearance. We never met again.

Sometimes in the gaunt old school building, punctuating the periods of anxiety, there were happy, uplifting times. For me these happened during lessons devoted to English composition and poetry.

There was one lady teacher on the staff who was most encouraging to me. A proud moment it was when I was chosen to recite Sir Henry Newbolt's poem, "Carry the Lamp," on Empire day. For the rehearsals the large between-classroom screens were folded back. "Miss" would stand at the far end of the long room and hopeful applicants were heard and eliminated one by one until only I remained.

Came the great day and in the asphalt yard between the buildings where I had played as an infant, I stood on a chair in the centre of a circle of pupils, staff and parents and confidently began my recitation. All went well. The first verse ended and then — and then the second verse failed to come. "Miss" was there in that awful moment.

"The sands of the desert, John," she hissed. "The sands of the desert."

And I was off again, plunging with gusto into the sodden wreck of the square that broke. I was disappointed that my parents did not attend.

There were magical moments too. Dusk falling on a winter afternoon . Lights on in the classroom and through the high Victorian windows I watched the snowflakes drifting and dancing down, praying the snow would settle and seeing, with a wonderful feeling of joy, the grey slates of the rooftops opposite gradually disappearing under a mantle of beautiful, beautiful white snow. Then the joy of crunching home through a thick layer, not through familiar ways but through a wild snowy landscape of vast pine forests, expecting to hear the howl of wolves at any moment, arriving rosy cheeked to a glowing kitchen range and the warm fug of home.

In my large family, as will be imagined, there was a fairly wide age range and within that range a series of fairly even gaps. The oldest of the children at my birth was a sister of 16 years of age, the next was 14, then 12; then came my oldest brother 10, another of 8, the next 6, then another sister 3. Two years after me my last sister was born.

All in turn went out to work at 14 years of age but that is another story and my part will be told later on.

In the meantime we were fortunate to grow up in a seaside town surrounded by beautiful countryside, with the South Downs at one end and a small wilderness of scrub, swamp and shingle desert at the other.

In spring we formed small groups with neighbouring children and walked by empty roads and countryside to woods and railway banks for primroses and daffodils.

In summer we roamed the rabbit-cropped grass of the great round hills among microscopic wild flowers and blue butterflies to pick toddle grass which my mother loved.

We learned to swim from the beach at the bottom of our road, and watched the beautiful old paddle steamers steaming to and from the pier: The Brighton Queen, the Brighton Belle and the Waverley, paddles chunking, spray flying, gleaming white in the sunshine.

Sometimes, a very rare treat, we would be given threepence, a boiled egg and sandwiches and sent off to spend one whole magical day on the pier with its exciting penny machines, always busy, always thronged with happy holiday-makers, young and old.

Our pocket money was one penny each a week so we were only able to watch people playing the machines, but one particular perk was ours.

Many of the machines returned the penny after the successful run of balls, into a series of holes, had been achieved, but there was an early type of crane machine which never seemed to lift any of the tempting watches or bangles displayed in its glass housing, but never failed to scoop up some of the liquorice-sweet beans heaped around the prizes. These sweets fell down into a small container at the front of the machine and were seldom collected by the person whose penny had operated it. Such sweets were a welcome prize to us and we would eagerly scoop them up as soon as the player left the vicinity.

In the autumn we collected horse chestnuts from one of the town parks which had many of the right trees. These would afford us many games of "conkers." I never managed to own a conker that reached championship standard and there were rumours that boys who had such champions had secret means of pickling them to iron hardness. However, I did often have sore knuckles!

There were bonfire "gangs" which vied with each other to build the biggest bonfire on the waste ground behind the houses on the other side of our road. These grew to half the height of a house and were made mainly from shrubs and dead bushes, brought from the Crumbles wasteland farther east, old crates and wooden boxes. They were topped on Guy Fawkes night by a "guy" made of old clothes stuffed with straw, with catherine wheel eyes, a "banger"— usually a Little Demon for a nose, and a Jumping Jack for a mouth. Never put in place until the actual night of November the fifth, for obvious reasons, they crowned the pile that had been guarded night and day against raids from rival gangs.

In ours, I remember a tunnel connected to the outside with a small inner chamber in which, in the final days some brave (or foolish!) soul sat with a hurricane lamp. A whole bonfire could disappear overnight if left unguarded.

Crowds came to watch the actual burning of these bonfires and the attendant firework displays. Such large fires were eventually stopped by the Police.

On the same wasteland, which was later made into a park, there existed a rubbish tip, acres of rusting metal and debris. We passed it daily on our way to school and it was considered very daring to actually walk across it. There were rumours of huge rats and the danger (which never materialised) of attack. It was a treasure trove of old bicycle frames and tyreless wheels from which a machine could be assembled, with metal meat skewers used for axles. A small leg passed through the frame, and some kind of ride could be achieved.

   But the biggest prize for me was the round, shallow metal bath I found one day. About 2ft. 6ins. in diameter and 6 inches deep, with a spout at one end for emptying, it seemed an ideal vessel for sailing on the swamps beyond the old wall at the edge of the wasteland.

   These swamps were also known locally as the Puddles. They were shallow, water filled depressions in the shingle areas, surrounded by blackberry bushes and grassy banks. Summer and winter alike they remained flooded and, when frozen, crowds would walk or skate on them, but the area was generally deserted and the rushes which grew along the edges gave them an exciting tropical swamp-like appearance and atmosphere, for a small boy.

   My new "boat" had a small hole in it. I found I could plug this leak with rush stalks and make an adequate seal. By kneeling in the bath and using my hands as paddles I could go where I wished about the swamp, naming the little inlets with imaginative and appropriate names, such as Dead Dog Bay, named after the corpse seen floating there!

MY FIRST BOAT

A friend found an even more useful craft. Deeper and larger, with an in-turned lip it took far longer to fill to sinking point than mine. When, as often happened a bath did sink under us, we stepped out into thigh-deep water and our feet sank into an inch or so of black ooze which swirled about our legs, turning the normally crystal clear liquid into a thick dark fog.

There were myriads of tadpoles there in the spring, minnows and sticklebacks, and lovely fan-tailed newts among the rushes. It was a magical place.

Poor as we were our surroundings gave all the happiness and adventure we could wish for.

The fishing beach nearby, with its tarred black huts and fascinating clutter of old boats, nets, discarded fish hooks and string, provided us with crude fishing lines, cork for floats, and black globules of summer-softened tar for chewing; convinced as we were by older, "wiser" children that it would , "whiten yer teef!"

We were fortunate to grow up in a town that supplied so many attractions free of charge, from the white chalk cliffs at the west end where cadmium yellow wallflowers grew, and winkles could be gathered from the miles of rocks at low tide, to the three miles of splendid promenades where "posh" people from the big hotels strolled shoulder to shoulder with straw-boatered boys from the expensive private schools; the leather-cheeked fisherman-become-boatmen for the summer season shouting of trips round the light'ouse, or out in the Channel at one shilling — a bob — a time. To the lovely old Victorian pier, the Napoleonic redoubt and Martello towers — it was all very much of a wonderland and our legs grew strong from the daily miles of walking to, from, and about such wonders, from our earliest days.

Came the day when the results of the school examinations taken at eleven years of age arrived.

I remember my mother quietly saying, "I knew you would pass for Bedewell, Jackie." This surprised me because I had not given the matter much thought and had probably not realised the importance of the exam.

I was following all four older sisters and two brothers who had attended the same secondary school. The brother nearest me in age had not passed and was sent to what was designated a senior school; he seemed quite happy there.

For my new school I was bought a new badge for my cap, and one for my jacket pocket (my jersey being no longer acceptable wear), a school tie, which was banded dark blue and green, and socks of the same colours with two rings around the turndown cuffs.

"The others had them," Mum said , "so you're going to have them." Even these small items were a struggle for her to provide.

I was not happy at my new school. The day began with a military style parade in class groups in the playground, under the command of the dapper, birdlike figure of the headmaster. From there we were marched in file to our classrooms. The orders were to walk on tiptoe once inside the hall door, because — we were solemnly warned, "The floors are hollow." I immediately imagined egg-shell like floors over a great chasm, and had no hesitation in obeying this order.

While at that school I was imbued with a fear and hatred of mathematics by a cold-eyed, bloodless master (B.Sc. Cantab), a similar loathing (after a promising and excited start) of French and French verbs by a beak-nosed, bun-haired, pigeon-bosomed, unmarried middle-aged lady who affected Breton peasant blouses and earrings.

Because of her nose she had been dubbed Polly by the boys, the fact that her surname was Virgin gave rise to all kinds of risible schoolboy jokes.

Polly Virgin gave my face a resounding, and completely unexpected, slap one day when I presented my exercise book with drawings of muscular cavemen on the cover. "Your head is too full of this muck!" she stormed.

The slap was unlawful because in that school the proper procedure was to file a report. Such reports were shown in a special box on the end of term report which one took home to one's parents and which required a signature of one of them. Three reports and a visit to the headmaster's study was mandatory, and there a caning followed.

I had the cane once only during my three years at the school, quite a gentle one after the previous school. My crime? I had forgotten to bring 1½ pence, the milk money for one week and the only time it had ever happened.

In contrast to Maths and French, literature was made enjoyable for me by a kind, elderly teacher by the name of Mister Glover. An old fashioned figure with his pince-nez spectacles and high-winged collar. He, unlike Miss Virgin, had quite enjoyed my drawings on the covers of my exercise books and had made jocular and appreciative remarks about the "splendid physique."

He had such faith in me that he encouraged me to write, direct, and act in a small play which was performed on the stage in the science classroom. He also encouraged my attempts at poetry and at eleven years of age I had the following simple poem published in the school magazine:

<u>To a Bird</u>
Oh pretty thing upon the wing,
What makes you fly, what makes you sing?

You cross the wheatfields, yellow and brown,

You cross the moors where the great crags frown,

So tell, oh tell me, bird on high,
That flutters and twitters up there in the sky,

Oh pretty, pretty little thing,

How can you fly?
How can you sing?

Mr Glover also cast me as Bob Cratchit in the school production of Charles Dickens' "A Christmas Carol" at the Town Hall theatre in Eastbourne. The play was well-received and I was disappointed that my parents did not attend.

My school reports showed me often near the bottom of my class, and near or at the top according to the subjects liked or disliked.

I won a scholarship to the local School of Arts and Crafts, learning little while I was there.

CHAPTER 2   Life After Leaving School

At 14 I left school and was sent out to find a job. Hoping to use whatever artistic ability was mine I found a job at a local sign and poster writing establishment.

I should have been warned by the man's cold eyes, but I wasn't, instead I took the job at seven shillings a week, with two pence deducted for insurance, and was put to work in a dingy workshop, down a short passage-way off a street near the Town Hall, the windows of which looked out through grimy panes into a dismal yard.

There I was put to filling in the letters on cinema and other posters and sales tickets, all written by the poster writers. For this I had to buy a set of my own brushes, which cost me dear at an art shop and, in the event, proved to be useless for the work in hand. I swept the floors, ran errands and, at the end of the day, was responsible for cleaning all the brushes used.

Being on my feet all day from 8a.m. to 5.30p.m. was proving very painful, and I grew to detest the chiming of the Town Hall clock which marked the quarters, halves, three-quarters and hours of the dragging, stultifying day.

One morning when opening a tin of printers ink the penknife slipped and went under a thumbnail. Whereupon I fainted. When I came to I became conscious of those cold eyes.
"If you faint because of a small thing like that, Jim," he growled, "what will you do if you get a man's brains blown in your face?"
He must have been in the Great War, but that does not excuse his callousness. Apparently he called all the boys who came to work for him "Jim". And it turned out that he kept them for a year then sacked them and took on a new school-leaver at the same low wage. Indeed, my turn came in the fullness of time and one year after starting, I was called into his office, quite unaware of this practice.
"You'll 'ave ter pull yer socks up, Jim. Or yer'll 'ave to go."
The fear of the sack in those hard times was a real and terrifying thing. There was a kind of roaring in my ears and a red mist closed in causing the room to disappear leaving only his hard features in a small circle at the very centre of my vision. I went home in a daze and told my mother. My father was angry but Mum was understanding and said as I wasn't happy there anyway, a change would do me good.

So off I went and found work as an errand boy at a dry cleaners, at 14 shillings and sixpence a week, more than twice the amount I had been earning. That meant more for my mother and more for me. I now gave her ten shillings a week instead of 3/8d and had four and six for myself.

Thus, _if_ I saved up for a few weeks I would be able to buy a pair of shoes to wear in place of those discarded by a brother- in- law, and which I had been wearing to work despite their being several sizes too large.

I gave my notice (one week's) to the cold-eyed boss and was very pleased to do so, and took up work on a trade bike: A change, far greater than I could envisage, was beginning in my life, and it was to make, in later years, the remark about a man's brains in my face seem like an inspired prophecy.

Often in life a new chapter opens in the most unexpected of ways, and so it was with me.

I had been working as an errand boy for several weeks pedalling around town with a heavily laden basket on the front of my machine, pushing up the steep hills in the wealthy western area of the town, which was where most of the customers lived, being the only ones who could afford dry cleaning.

In between times I was employed in the cleaning of shop floors, polishing light switches (brass ones of great age) and washing down the shop front.

I had over me a vinegary lady, who was beginning to make me feel that I was unlucky in my choice of employers, and I was really not much happier than I had been in the previous job.

Then one day in the town centre I came upon a small soldier. Very smart, he looked, in Royal Artillery uniform, well-fitted tunic, riding breeches, puttees, shining boots with spurs.

He was tapping one calf with a leather-bound, silver topped riding whip, and I saw with amazement that he was a boy with whom I had been at school. We exchanged greetings and he explained that he had joined the Army as a boy entrant and was learning to be a trumpeter.

He had been in three months and was home on a month's leave. My astonishment was so great I could hardly believe what he said. A whole month of leave after only three months of service? and here was I after almost eighteen months' work with no holidays at all !

I am ashamed because I must admit that that reason alone was sufficient to cause me to make one of the most important decisions of my life and on returning home that day I told my father of my intention. He was pleased . The "nest" was emptying .

My two eldest brothers had joined the Army, the Royal Artillery about six years before . The one nearer to me in age had done the same thing two years ago. The three senior sisters had married . Of the other two, one was in service, the one younger than I was still in school.

The very next day I went to the recruiting office to make enquiries. I later had a medical examination and sat a written examination under the supervision of the recruiting sergeant, who at one point had to help me with one of the questions. He explained to me that π (pi) was the constant of a circle used in working out the area etc. He obviously did not want me to fail.

In all events, in the fullness of time I was informed that I had passed and was accepted as a boy entrant.

There were some months before the next intake, which would be in September. My father said he was very proud, he now had four sons in the service of the King. My mother said little, but made no objection, no doubt thinking the while of her own brother who had been killed in the last war.

CHAPTER 3   Boy Soldier Training

And on 21st September, 1937 I reported to the recruiting office to be enlisted. One other local boy was present for the same reason.

An Army captain swore us in, gave us one shilling each and said "And from now until twelve years time your souls are no longer your own."

Words which gave me a moment or two of foreboding. The words were, presumably, said facetiously, but contained an element of truth and portended a future containing experiences beyond the captain's, or any normal person's imaginings.

So it was at 15 years of age I found myself at the railway station with a travel warrant for a journey into the unknown ahead. I was not really disappointed that my parents were not there to see me off. I no longer had any expectations in that direction.

I was about to set off on my first railway journey ever, in itself a great excitement, and to a new life.

The new life began at the Grand Depot, Royal Artillery, Woolwich S.E.18. September 21st, 1937.

We climbed the hill from the railway station along a grey street of sad houses and small shops and eventually saw before us a grim, encircling wall. High, it was, caked in black soot and topped with wicked-looking broken glass.

On approaching a large gate at the lower end of the forbidding structure we were directed by a sentry to one farther up the hill. There we were admitted; particulars taken at a guard room situated to one side of the entrance to a large hall in a tall building, black as the wall and disclosing signs of great age by the strips of glass cemented across cracks in its exterior walls.

There the other boy and I were parted. He was posted to 1st Boys Battery R.A., I to 2nd Boys Battery R.A.

I was shown to a dining hall, given a plate of stew, ladled out by an elderly man at a metal-topped serving point just inside the door, and joined other boys at a scrubbed deal table. The other boys were dressed in shapeless brown suits of a canvas material, not at all like the smart lad I had met in Eastbourne. I was not hungry but ate a mouthful of the hash. I became aware of the intent gaze of a boy opposite me.

"You don't 'ave to eat that if yer don't want it, mate," he said.

I pushed the plate away with a sense of relief. In a flash the boy's hands shot across the table before any of the others could move, and began shovelling the food into his mouth. It was not long before I myself developed an appetite as keen as the one he displayed.

The Boys' Depot was enclosed, with other buildings such as mobilisation stores, a canteen and offices, within the high, glass-topped wall and was a world within a larger area which contained the men's barracks, other regimental barracks, officers' messes, quarters and a host of other establishments, with a large piece of common land close by.

There were two boys' batteries and each was divided into 3 sections, all named after famous military men. I was posted to Shrapnel Section, named ,of course after Colonel Shrapnel, who is accredited with the invention of the shrapnel shell. I was pleased to be in a section with such a military-sounding name!

Three intakes a year provided the necessary number of recruits to keep the depot up to strength and the Royal Regiment with its required number of trumpeters. The September intake was the one which completed its training in time for the start of the trooping season when overseas units were supplied with replacements for men returning home after their time overseas had expired.

Already the threads of a fate, determined by a chance meeting, were being drawn together and my unavoidable progress to an horrific experience was following its inexorable way.

At present, however, there was a new life with never an idle moment, a whole host of new acquaintances and fresh experiences. A full year of training lay ahead.

During that time there would be shocks, rough corners knocked off; hours of foot drill would change clumsy boys into a squad of automatons moving and responding with clockwork precision, obeying instantly and without question any order given. We would learn the iron discipline that still ruled the army and had sent men over the top in the Great War to face withering machine-gun fire. In short, any vestiges of boyhood were stripped from us, and we became soldiers. We had lost forever the ability to question authority.

Our instructors were a mixed bunch. To some their absolute authority brought out any tendency to bullying inherent in their natures. Others were humane, some helpful and understanding. A normal enough cross-section of humanity.

Among the boys regional accents from all parts of Britain, difficult at first to understand, became accepted as normal, and I developed the ability to tell from which part of the country they came.

Sports were compulsory and, to my great surprise, so was education and we were marched to the Army Education School each afternoon.

It was necessary to obtain two certificates during our time at the depot; the Army 3rd class Cert. of Education and the Army 2nd class Cert. of Education. In the regular army of the time a 2nd class Cert. was necessary before promotion to sergeant was possible. At the depot it was needed for qualification as a trumpeter, before successful completion of the course. Relegation followed at the end of a term for any boy who failed the exam. Discharge followed failure to obtain 2nd class completely.

We were taught to sound calls on both bugle and trumpet. The bugle, a five note instrument of higher pitch than a trumpet, was used for field calls, orders to fire, cease fire etc., and for fire alarm and general alarm.

The trumpet was used for routine calls in barracks, reveille, time warnings for parades, retreat, last post, lights out, mess calls and many others.

We were not taught to read music but learned how to obtain the notes by following the example of the Trumpet Major, always an impressive figure with the four inverted chevrons at the end of each sleeve, with crossed trumpets above. Immaculate in turnout and bearing.

Each day's session began in the drum room, a large chamber at the very top of the building. The boys formed a single rank against three of the walls, facing in to the Trumpet Major. He would demonstrate the correct way of bringing the instrument up to the lips and down to the position where the bell of the trumpet is held against the thigh. Each note is obtained by varying the pressure of the mouthpiece against the upper lip, and the volume of sound results from the strength of the air blown through it.

Having listened to a note all boys would try to achieve the same effect on the command "Sound!" Early attempts resulted in a cacophony of sounds such as you might expect when standing behind a herd of elephants that had been fed a diet of beans. Discipline broke down momentarily, as we all dissolved in a fit of laughter, and was quickly restored, but in a tolerant manner. It must have happened with every new intake. In this way the notes for bugle, and trumpet (which has seven notes) were eventually learned and the next step was to memorise the calls.

Some, the trumpet ones, are quite long, and there are many to be learnt. As an aide to memorising them each one had, over the course of time, been given a rhyme: some comic, some earthy and some downright vulgar, but all very memorable, and very helpful.

Later on when I was serving in a regiment such mnemonics were invaluable when the awful moment came, with a parade assembled and awaiting the trumpet call, a mental blank occurred, a moments panic "How does it go?", then it came to mind— the little jingle that brought it all back and the trumpet notes rang out their clarion call.

One of the longer, more complicated calls was "Officers Dress for Dinner", to be sounded outside officers' quarters at the appropriate time.

We boys were having trouble remembering it and, after several failed individual attempts, the Trumpet Major was asked if he did not have a jingle for it.

He thought this over for a moment, then, "There is one" he said, and a quiet smile played around the corners of his lips in a manner that made me think of the Pied Piper of Hamelin.

"But it's too rude," he added tantalisingly.

Shouts broke out along the line "Oh, go on sir! Tell us, tell us !"
"No. No, it's too rude," he repeated mischievously.
"Go on, sir." "Go, on !" "Tell us, sir!"
He grinned openly this time. "All right," he said, "but don't tell your mothers I taught you !"

Standing smartly at attention with trumpet to thigh and held at the correct angle he intoned:

"Polly in the garden sifting cinders
"Lifted up her clothes and farted like a man
"The echo of the fart broke fifteen windows
"And the clappers of her arse went bang-diddy-bang"

It was some time before order was restored but call and rhyme were committed to memory for ever more.

Gradually over the months we learned all we had to know. I boxed as a member of the battery team and won a small cup (much smaller than those of my father) for being the "best loser". I won another for the 440 yards relay race at an open day to which parents were invited but my parents did not come.

The gym display team counted me among its members, as did the tug-of-war team and I became bigger and stronger as the days went by.

Conditions at the depot were spartan. Beds were metal and reduced to half-size by sliding the front half into the back; mattresses were "biscuits", three square ones (coir) to each bed. Pillows were cylindrical and extremely hard. There were no sheets nor pyjamas. We slept in our shirts but I had underpants (long-johns) and vests for the first time in my life.

We washed in cold water each morning, stripped to the waist and had a hot (long) bath each week on a Friday. Latrines were out in the yard.

Meals were rough and small but eaten to the last crumb, and boys sometimes broke into the workhouse at night to steal dry bread.

Kit was cleaned every evening to a high standard of spit and polish; and brasso and boot polish (black for boots, brown for belt and chin strap) took up a sizeable portion of our weekly allowance of two shillings and sixpence.

1938, BOYS' DEPOT, MYSELF IN THE REAR

Our pay was seven shillings per week but the rest, after our allowance, was kept back for us, less stoppages for such things as barber fees and other small expenses, and we received it when we went on leave plus a ration allowance and a free travel warrant.

Tidiness and order were inculcated in us from the very beginning. Above each bed was a small locker in which our belongings were stowed and on top of which a tunic was placed, a row of (polished!) buttons to the front, and beneath the tunic, slacks and riding breeches were folded to the same exact width. Irons were never used, in fact did not exist, folding produced the required effect.

The barrack room was kept immaculate; four round metal pillars passed up from floor to ceiling and beyond, and the area within these supports was sacrosanct. Nobody was allowed to walk across it except to polish it. The floor was of polished wood kept to high shine by liberal applications of floor polish and daily, morning and evening sessions with the "bumper", a heavy polishing block hinged to a long handle. All boys had to take turns at the work and were kept at it by the senior boy, a boy Bombardier, who was in charge of the room. The fireplace had to be cleaned out each morning in the winter, the fire irons blackened, the handles burnished, and the fireplace itself had to be whitened.

We were never allowed to be idle, and the rough blankets, rock-hard pillows and the clanking of trams passing up and down the hill outside did nothing to disturb our sleep at any time.

Our working day uniform was a canvas suit with removable buttons down the front. Such suits softened to a surprising degree of comfort with laundering. The brown dye, very dark at first, faded out quickly and a pale cream suit denoted someone with a bit of service, rather than a despised raw recruit. The suits were laundered weekly and on return from the laundry were dumped in a pile on the floor inside the door. This always caused a wild rush and grabbing as each boy strove to get the palest garments. Thus it was that a small boy might be later seen in an overlarge suit and a big lad might have his trousers half-way up his calf. But no one seemed to mind.

Our "proper" uniforms were fitted by the tailor's department and were worn only for Saturday morning inspections, Sunday church parades and walking out — which we were only allowed to do after duties on Saturdays and Sundays and then only until 9.30 p.m.

Leave was generous and happened three times during the year. And how we looked forward, how we longed for it! How endless the waiting seemed, especially until the first leave.

Inevitably the day came. The night before was interminable. Not many of us slept. Some already had their beds made up and kit ready for taking up to the store room the next morning. But at last we were in front of the pay table receiving pay and warrants and were off out of the barrack gate as if there were demons at our heels.

I arrived home at the place in the country, that my parents had moved to, with the princely sum of £10 and some shillings in my pocket. To me a sum beyond the wildest of my imaginings, not so long before.

The days spent on leave remain in my memory as a very happy time. No-one met me at the railway station; which did not surprise me. I found the bus which would take me to the small village of Sandy Cross, and walked down a lovely country lane, past an old thatched farmhouse and on to the bungalow which my parents were renting.

The previous occupant had a droll sense of humour as the place was named "Whywas". So the address was "Whywas, Sandy Cross", easily remembered and, like our trumpet-call jingles, never forgotten.

Our big family had now shrunk to my parents and my younger sister who was attending a tiny village school about 5 miles away. The other unmarried sister was in service near Heathfield.

I spent all three of my leaves from the depot in that quiet place set in the lush Sussex countryside.

Successfully completing my year of training and passing out as a trumpeter entitled me to wear high on each of my jacket sleeves a badge in the form of crossed trumpets, and I felt very proud to do so.

As a fully fledged trumpeter with a year's service behind me I was posted with another boy to Blackdown camp in Surrey, an Anti-Aircraft unit where a draft was being assembled for Singapore and would leave later in the year.

Some of the draft, we two trumpeters among them, were destined to go to a coast defence unit in Singapore.

In due course we were issued with tropical kit, khaki drill clothing (which felt lovely and soft after the coarse normal-issue uniform), and an extra white kit bag to contain everything.

We had a series of inoculations which made us feel rotten, and finally were sent home on two weeks' draft leave. At the end of this leave, in the garden at the front of the bungalow where fruit trees and current bushes grew, my mother, looking sad and small, said goodbye to me, and to my great surprise, kissed me for the first time in my life.

CHAPTER 4   Posting / Voyage to Singapore

I made my way alone up the hill to where the bus stop was at the end of the lane, making efforts as I went along to impress upon my memory the beautiful landscape of fields, hedgerows and woodland,

and the one impression that seemed to imprint itself more than any other was the gold of a wheatfield. That memory still burns bright, as it did throughout the years.

I was expecting to be gone for three years, which was the time of a normal posting to Singapore. The future knew better, and I was destined for a far longer absence, in completely unimaginable circumstances, before I saw such scenes again.

The troopship H. T. Dilwara was moored at the quayside in Southampton water. Some troops were already aboard, lining the rails and looking down at the quay. To me the ship looked huge, and white, and exciting.

Once on board, my draft hurried to join the others already at the rails where we could look down on the crowded scene below. A military band played stirring marches. White faces looked up at us from far below. Friends and relatives were waved to.

I saw, with a sense of poignancy, a small woman, dressed in black, sitting leaning forward on a bollard and weeping into a handkerchief, looking up now and again at a face lost in the crowd around me.

My parents were not there and no loved one saw my going.

Then there came the sad, sad sound of the band playing Auld Lang Syne. I felt my stomach lurch at the enormity of what I had undertaken, and the widening gap as the ship drew away from the quayside, the snapping of streamers, the cheers of the crowd growing fainter all seemed a full stop at the end of a chapter and the beginning of a new one in my life.

I remained on deck as dusk gathered and in the fading light saw the unforgettable view of the white cliffs of the Isle of Wight, the Needles, and the lighthouse flashing; its beacon seeming a solemn farewell to a childhood left behind.

Our mess deck was situated about three decks down. Each small table suspended from the ceiling, a wooden form on either side, formed the mess area for parties of about eight men.

Hammocks, issued from and returned to stores daily, were simple affairs: a narrow strip of canvas with a wooden piece at each end, were hung from metal rings overhead for use overnight.

To say such decks were overcrowded would be a great understatement. They were packed and, before long were foetid, in short they stank from the press of unwashed humanity, vomit, and food spilled from mess cans in rough seas; which happened often because food was brought down in rectangular metal containers from the galley situated on the open deck above.

It was rough in the Bay of Biscay; the ship wallowed, rolled and pitched all the way from the Needles to Gibraltar.

My father had given me a good piece of advice, based on his one-time duties as a draft conducting officer during the Great War when troops were being sent to Italy.

"If you feel sick," he'd said, "get up on deck in the fresh air!"
I had been on deck after watching the Needles lighthouse until the first Channel rollers started the ship into its heaving and tossing. I went below to my mess deck, slung my hammock cheek by jowl with others already hanging there and tried to sleep.

The air down there was already foul and full of strange noises, creaks and bangings from bulkheads and companionways, and the steady thump-thump-thump of the engine.

By the early hours of the morning I was feeling seasick and decided to try to get up on the open deck. I dragged myself from the hammock, my knees gave way and my legs buckled; I fell to the floor. As nausea gripped me I had time just to pull on my greatcoat and cap (I had gone to bed in trousers and shirt) and fled up the companionway which already had prostrate moaning figures sprawled here and there all over it.

The wind was keen and fresh, the seas mountainous, white capped in the grey morning. I hung over the rail for a while to do what was unavoidable, and later on tried to return below decks to get washed and properly dressed. I got as far as the head of the companionway to the second deck down, then could go no further. The heat and foul stench rising from below turned my stomach. I turned and fled once more to the open air.

The endless, merciless motion of the ship in the rough seas spared none among the troops packed in that vessel. They lay in miserable heaps around the decks.

I had heard that amidships was the best place to be, so I found it and lay flat on my back. The rocking of the ship was such that at one point of the motion I could see sky above the tips of my plimsolls, and the next there would be only the wild sea.

At night I would crawl in among a heap of Seaforth Highlanders who lay huddled together for warmth in a covered way which ran along the side of the deck outside the officers ballroom. I went without food, snatching the odd drink of water from a tap in the ablutions, one deck down, before dashing back on deck into the fresh air.

After three days friends found me and gave me some army biscuits, which I was able to eat, and told me only half jokingly that they had been searching for me and had thought I might have gone overboard. It seemed that the authorities were quite used to this kind of situation and left the majority of us alone in our misery.

At Gibraltar however, we were marshalled into some semblance of order and were taken ashore for a route march. As we assembled on the quay I had the distinct sensation of the motion of the ship under my feet; the quayside seemed to be rising and falling. I don't suppose that mine were the only unsteady legs in that party.

The great grey mass of the Rock reared over us, giving an impression of endurance and impregnability.

I knew that my father had served there and felt that I was literally following in his footsteps. There I saw the first symbol of my new life — palm trees; not the tall and stately ones I was to know later on but rather squat little trees with thick trunks formed of stems of fronds that had been lopped. Ignorant as I then was I thought that pineapples grew on them!

The air was balmy, the grey wastes of the Atlantic and the sombre skies, wind and rain of the north were behind us, and the voyage to the Far East stretched before us in colours and patterns like an exotic carpet unrolling mile by mile.

The sun shone, the Mediterranean showed me ultramarine water, the bluest blue I had ever seen.

After the first night aboard I never slept below again during the remainder of the voyage.

There were no training sessions as there were in later years. We were very much left to our own devices and only called upon for fire picquet, guard duties and cookhouse fatigues etc.

Crown and Anchor games, completely unlawful, went on in quiet corners with lookouts posted strategically.

We were rousted from the decks in the morning by laskars, with hose and brushes, scrubbing the decks, and our days began and ended in sunshine.

The first port of call after Gibraltar was Malta. Here we anchored in Valetta harbour, busy with small craft and merchant ships; R. N. vessels; the stone buildings and surroundings giving it a fortress-like air and appearance.

We saw our first bumboats, colourful and quaint and doing brisk business by means of rope and basket with the troops lined along the deck. We were not allowed ashore here and were soon on our way again.

The days became warmer still and we changed into our tropical khaki drill. It came from the kit bags crumpled and ill-fitting, the wolsey helmets carried neither badges nor pugarees (these would come later) and we looked what any respectable sergeant major would have every right to describe as "a scruffy shower!"

Soon the pattern of our exotic carpet changed and the ultramarine gave way to muddy yellow. There was yet no land in sight but the yellow came from the Nile Delta while we were still far out to sea.

It was Christmas Eve and I had been detailed for guard duty, only one of several I had done. During one spell my post was at the head of some stairs leading down to the WO's and Sergeants' deck. There was a small board of orders for the sentry and I was reading these when a fat sergeant lurched up to me, staggered a bit then, breathing beer fumes, slurred in my face, "Tha's right son. Read 'em. Know 'em by heart." Then turning away he fell straight down the stairs.

While I was standing there wondering what to do about it but not daring to leave my post, he crawled through the door of the mess and disappeared.

This Xmas Eve was to be my last tour of guard duty for we had on board an officer who had been at the Boys' Depot. On discovering that trumpeters were being used for such details he informed the ship's R. S. M. of the illegality of boys doing night duty and we were not used again. However, it was Xmas Eve and when I came off duty on Xmas Day it was to find that shore leave had been granted and that I and the rest of the guard were free to leave the ship. There was one grave snag — my boots were missing. Aboard ship all troops wore gymshoes, that is brown plimsolls, but of course could not go ashore in them. Some kindly soul took pity on me and gave me a pair of Indian-pattern boots . These differed from the normal issue in that they had a half-moon shaped toe cap. Despite the fact that they were far too big for me and gave me a chaplinesque appearance, I was very grateful for them. My own boots, I was told, had been "flogged to a bumboat for a packet of Turkish delight." I never found the culprit.

By pooling resources my companions and I raised a few shillings and hired a huge open limousine-type taxi and driver for a tour around Port Said. The natives appeared very friendly and shouted "Merry Xmas" to us as we travelled about.

We were shown inside a huge mosque and had a hair-raising dash across a level crossing after racing a huge locomotive along a railtrack for a hundred yards or so, passing across the front of the great engine with very little time to spare. Then it was time to be back on board.

To a boy of 16 such events left indelible impressions that lasted long after later journeys and experiences faded away.

Our exotic carpet continued to unroll. Down the Suez Canal where natives shouted insults and made rude gestures from the banks, we had the strange experience of cruising through desert sands, through The Great Salt Lakes in baking shimmering heat and out into the Red Sea, as blue as any other.

Port Suez on a hot morning of motionless air, then on to the great rocky barrenness of Aden, of which my father had told me and where he had served early in the century. No shore leave here.

Then the beauty of the Indian Ocean surrounded us. I saw flying fish. Out from the shoulder of a wave they came, skimming in low flight for amazing distances before plunging back into the sparkling sea. For hours there was the fascination of lying in the bows of the ship watching the dolphins weaving and plunging so close in the bow wave, matching the ship's speed with marvellous, effortless energy of balletic beauty.

When I was quite small a friend said to me, " Want to come to the pictures this afternoon?"
"What's on?" I said.
" The Pagan Love Song," he replied.
This did not appeal to me at all. Had it been a Western with Tom Mix or Buck Jones it would have been different. I said as much . I did not want to see a soppy love story . " No, no" he said. " It's not about love. It's on an island. There's a man in the water and he gets eaten by a shark. You can see it all!"

This put a very different complexion on it. I went into the house and was given two beer bottles. These I took to the Off Licence at the end of the road and was given fourpence for the two. This was the price of admission to the Saturday afternoon matinee at the Elysium Cinema, and there for the first time in my life I saw the beauty of a tropical island, complete with waving palms, silver sands and Jon Hall picking real bananas off a tree with a sarong-clad "native" beauty at his side. At least we saw a Hollywood version of it, and yes — we did see a man eaten by a shark!

Out in the reality of the tired old grey streets the vision remained in my head, not the shark, but the revelation that there existed an entirely different world to the one I knew. I never lost that vision of tropical loveliness and later came to see it for myself, as well as another side that contained ugliness as well as beauty.

But first I was to glimpse the beauty. There it was — off the port bow! Close enough to see the trees of a tropical island, tall palms along a white sandy shore, the cream of seas over a coral reef, the viridian green of a lagoon. It was difficult to judge the distance.

Were they the *Andamans*, or *Nicobar* Islands? I didn't know. No-one else could tell. I felt a stupid, wild impulse to jump over the side and swim to shore. But the water looked so far below me, the distance too far to swim, and then, I remembered <u>that</u> shark! So, I sailed on to Ceylon with all the others.

With time to spare in *Colombo* (as it then was), we were given a route march ashore.

Khaki drill was by now so crumpled and untidy that we really ought not to have been seen in public, and we were surely a very poor example of the pomp and circumstances expected of the Raj.

There was a break for refreshments at a barrack in colonial style; behind an arched, white veranda was a cool, high-ceilinged room with large fans whirling slowly and small lizards effortlessly across the pristine expanse. Outside there was a greenery, flowers and shrubs I couldn't name, but a lushness that showed there was no shortage of rain.

I remember that the harbour was very crowded and noted especially the huge swastika flaunting its red, black and white colours at the stern of a German liner — a portent of things to come, and reviving memories of the trenches we'd dug in the woods at Blackdown during the Munich crisis of not so long before.

CHAPTER 5   Pre-War days, Singapore

The last leg of our long voyage now began. By the time we reached Singapore it would have taken six weeks and at the final stage, in the pre-dawn darkness we were nosing in between islands to Singapore harbour.

My first sight of it was the lights of "kelongs". These were fishing stations, ricketty platforms built on stilts above the sea, each with a small palm thatch shelter and a naphtha flare to lure the fish.

The ship seemed almost to scrape the land on either side as we went in, so narrow is the channel at one place, Singapore Island on the port side and the island of *Belakang Mati* to the starboard. I later learned that the narrow straight is (or was) known as the Dragon's Mouth. *Belakang Mati* has since been renamed *Sentosa Island*. Perhaps because *Belakang Mati* is Malay for Beyond the Dead; and is now a very different place to the one I knew so long ago.

But now we are back to my early youth and we have been moored for some hours at the quayside. The draft is assembled on deck, each of us with our two kit bags containing all our gear. A party has come aboard to take charge and escort us to our destination, which we learn is to be the island of *Belakang Mati*.

Accustomed as we had become to our own scruffy appearance the spectacle presented by the escort party made our jaws drop. Their K.D. was starched and pressed to perfection, belts, and leather bandoliers, badges and boots glistened and gleamed in the harsh bright sunshine. Such a high standard of "bull" was terrifying to contemplate. How would we ever achieve it?

Sergeant Sammy Mayo took charge, a short compact and dapper man in his early thirties. With his swagger stick tucked under one arm he marched us down the gangplank and along the quay to where a W.D. launch awaited us at a nearby pier. A short trip across the water to another pier on the island where we were reassembled and marched about half a mile up a hill to a barrack square.

The heat and 90% humidity soon reduced us, loaded down as we were with two heavy kit bags, to a sodden mess, perspiring freely from head to foot.

The square was surround by colonial-style barrack blocks. We were lined up in ranks and, to my chagrin, I was separated from the rest of the draft and marched off on my own to the battery office.

I stood alone with my two kit bags. My face was strawberry red from the sun on my fair skin during the voyage and the exertion of the march up the hill; my topee was filthy, my K.D. uniform crumpled and saturated with sweat. My feet were squelching inside the huge Indian-pattern boots.

The sergeant major emerged from the office. I snapped to attention. He looked me up and down. "My God!" he said. "What's this?"

Hardly an auspicious beginning to my days on the island!

The barrack room to which I was allotted was in a more recent building than the others that stood around the square. It was clean and airy and spacious, with wide verandas, and showers and toilets at one end.

The beds were the standard iron push-in type with a tall locker at the head, and above each was a mosquito net fixed to a metal ring suspended from the ceiling. Beside each bed was an individual touch: a tea chest or box of some kind upon which coloured cloths were draped to form covers; and a small rug was allowed in each floor space.

The impression was of a pleasant place with a happy atmosphere, and so it proved to be.

There was a permanent room orderly whose job it was to keep it clean and who was excused all parades to do so. Naturally such a good job was well worth looking after and was therefore always well done.

From the veranda was a magnificent view across the sports fields and shore to the sea and many islands both close and distant On certain evenings the distant islands would appear to be floating in the air.

Every barrack room had an Indian "boy" who would clean each soldier's kit, make up the beds and tidily tie up the mosquito nets and make down the beds when required. All of this he would do for fifty cents a week from each soldier. The Straits dollar of the time was worth two shillings and eight pence, so forty soldiers would give him an income of just over two pounds and thirteen shillings per week. More than most of the men, and far more than I earned, but not all men used his services, so he would, of course, earn less.

As I recall it my first day coincided with "de-bugging day" or "Queen Victoria's holiday". On this day every week no parades were held except for morning roll call, and dress was completely informal, most men wearing gym shorts and plimsolls for that, and the only work to be done was the dismantling of beds, which entailed the removal of metal pins from the legs and painting of paraffin in the corners of the frame. This was soon done and the rest of the day was free for swimming or relaxing in any way one chose.

I did not know that this was the one day a week when this routine was followed and on the following morning was idling about in my gym shorts, polo vest and plimsolls, quite ignoring the trumpet calls announcing the quarter of an hour to parade.

Neither had I noticed that there was a bustle about the place and men were dressed in parade dress. Presently one of the gunners approached me with an anxious look on his face.
"Aren't you going to get ready, Badgie?" he asked.
I was puzzled. " Ready?" I said . "I am ready."
"No, no," he replied, "that dress is only for yesterday. You wear proper dress today."
The five minutes to parade sounded and the room emptied as I made frantic efforts to get changed. The get-on-parade call had finished sounding (it is a long one, and is preceded by a unit designation call) as I dashed downstairs and out onto the parade ground to fall in, flushed and dishevelled on the right flank, the proper place for a trumpeter. The Battery Sergeant Major must have despaired over this hopeless new addition to his battery but my newness and obvious incompetence excused my failings.

The nickname given to all trumpeters was Badgie, and this became my name from now on and for many years. I was told it originated in the Indian Army and was derived from the word "*baji*" meaning bugler or trumpeter.

I was to find a whole new vocabulary in use on that small island of *Belakang Mati*, many of the words being of Indian origin and some of Malay — mostly mispronounced.

The local equivalent of *"mañana"* was *"tidak apa"*, which the troops pronounced *"teeduppa"* and it was in frequent use and mostly applied to an attitude. Someone who couldn't care less was described as *"teeduppa"*. Or it would be used more correctly to imply "it doesn't matter".

In those now far off days life on the island approached being idyllic. Reveille was at six a.m. and work stopped for the day at twelve midday. In the afternoons most men took a siesta but I did not.

Working dress was sensible and comfortable and consisted of a thick, but featherweight solar topee, a white polo vest, K.D. shorts and ankle socks rolled down over boots. Proper dress for guard duties and such was the heavy cork wolsey helmet, brass-buttoned tunic fastened at the neck, leather belt, shorts (by day) with woollen puttees from the knees to ankles, and boots. Trousers were worn at night. Dress, casual or otherwise, changed at five p.m. when long sleeves and slacks replaced shorts and short sleeves, beds had to be made down, mosquito nets let down and tucked in around mattresses. Mosquitoes were plentiful after dark but there was no malaria on the island.

As the youngest "member" of the regiment, trumpeters were generally very kindly treated and most of the men considerate and helpful to us.

I slipped easily into this way of life which seemed well suited to my nature, and after the harsh regimentation and conditions of barrack life in England it seemed hardly right to accept the sixpence a day colonial pay that was added to my income.
The fact that the dollar contained one hundred Straits cents, and each cent was the size of an old penny (an inch in diameter), pay day of a Friday, when I drew two dollars, made me feel very rich indeed.

Very soon I had made two good friends, Bombardier Leslie Bills and Gunner Tom Williams.
 Les Bills reminded me of my eldest brother, Bert, who had been very kind to me and close, despite a ten year age gap.
Tom Williams from the Welsh Borders had a sunny nature and a Welsh lilt to his speech, came from a small farm and seemed as unsuited to the military life as anyone could be.

At the training depot as a recruit he had passed between two officers, one on either side . Unsure of what to do he had saluted simultaneously with both hands while marching smartly forward with both eyes to the front. He was short and fair skinned with hair the light reddish colour often seen in Wales; his ears were large, red and stood out prominently. We argued a lot in a friendly, bantering way.

Les Bills was short and stocky and came from the north country. He was swarthy in appearance with brown eyes and dark hair. He had a rudimentary grasp of Malay and was handy about small boats. I was to wonder later on if these factors contributed to his mysterious disappearance.

Entertainment on the island consisted of sports on a fine sports field, two swimming enclosures in the sea off a sandy beach close by the barracks, and a cinema organised and run by the regiment. The swimming enclosures were formed by wooden fences, a precaution against sharks but were not proof against sea snakes or the occasional sting ray that found its way in.

An orderly, known as the *Pagar* Orderly (*pagar* from Malay: fence) had the permanent job of looking after the cleanliness of the area and searching at low tide for any interlopers. This was a plumb job with extra pay and was performed by the same man who ran the cinema, a Gunner Knight, known as "Busty" because of his physique.

The "cinema" was merely a large room above one of the barrack rooms and consisted of a projector, a screen and wicker chairs. The wicker chairs were home to bed bugs and after any visit to the cinema I would leave with many red lumps from bites on my forearms and thighs. Such fresh blood must have been a great treat to them!

On the side of the island which faced across the strait to another small island, *Pulaw Brani* (a Royal Engineers Station) and Singapore island, was an abandoned swimming enclosure. The fence there was of concrete and was ruinous and broken down in places. Some Tamils lived there in a hut and acted as guards for a few small boats owned by members of the regiment.

I had bought a half-share with Tom Williams in a sea-going canoe, known in Malay as a "*kolek*" and of a shape that was based on the Malay *prahu*, which had itself been the inspiration for the clipper ships.

The canoe had two paddles and a small leg-of-mutton sail and in that little craft I spent some of the happiest hours of my life. The waters around the island were dangerous in the extreme, with treacherous currents which raced through the narrow straits with irresistible force and great speed. Coral rocks and reefs abounded. A reef twenty feet down would appear to be just under the keel in crystal clear water. And acres of reef would be out of water at low tide.

Les Bills was a man who inspired confidence. With him in charge we set out, Tom and I, for voyages on this perilous sea with never a qualm or thought of danger. With three of us in the canoe there was hardly more than an inch of freeboard at the lowest point along the side.

We visited several of the islands in the vicinity of *Belakang Mati*, some uninhabited and little more than scrub and rock, but it was always a thrill to jump out onto a small beach, feeling like an old-time explorer. We would walk on the huge flat reef at low tide finding nothing more than the odd beche-de-mer.

On one unforgettable Sunday morning we set off to sail to a more distant
destination, a fascinating little island, a volcanic cone called *Pulau Kusu*. It stood sheer out of the sea to a height I would guess to be about 100 feet. It was covered to the pointed summit in scrubby growth, and a path wound up it to two old graves at the top, possibly the tombs of holy men and a place of pilgrimage. About its foot was a small lagoon of clear water and there was a huge boulder upon which stood a Chinese temple, tucked away and half-hidden under the overhang.

The sea was as tranquil as the proverbial mill pond as we paddled our way across it. There was not a breath of air for the sail. Suddenly as we floated over the great reef a banded sea snake came swimming towards us. It looked as if it would have no trouble in entering the boat over the low gunwale. Such snakes are deadly poisonous and had it got in there is no telling what would have happened. It was swimming on the surface, advancing rapidly with its head about two to three inches out of the water and was almost upon us when Les Bills, unhesitating, with a lightning-quick chopping stroke from his paddle caught it an inch behind the head and it sank, twisting into the depths.

We landed at the base of the island, pulled the boat up on a small beach, acknowledged the ancient monk who emerged from the temple to watch us, and swam in the crystal lagoon (strictly against Regimental Standing Orders) before climbing the steep path to the summit where we found the tombs.

On the way back the tide had changed and at one point, where we had to pass close to an island, the tide race had formed a whirlpool. We were upon it before becoming aware of its presence and could not turn back. We paddled for dear life with the rocks of the island only a foot or so, out of the water, to our left and the awful gurgling vortex of the whirlpool on our right, only yards away.

For a few horrifying moments that seemed like hours we appeared to make not an inch of progress, and the noise and strength of the whirlpool increased with the changing tide. Then slowly but surely, we edged away.

THREE MEN IN A BOAT

It was an unforgettable day, one that has lived on in dreams and memory and which never seems to fade; how often have I in dreams set out on that magical odyssey upon that halcyon sea, but always alone and never ever finding that island again.

I made my first visit to Singapore city, a kaleidoscope of colour where many races, Malay, Chinese, Indians of all types and castes, Eurasians, Europeans, and natives from the surrounding islands lived together in harmony, and the air was full of sounds and music and the clack-clack of wooden clogs; the tick-tock-tack of Chinese food vendors who trotted along with a stove and wares hanging from bamboo poles across their shoulders, tapping out their distinctive message on a wooden block and stopping wherever required; and the rich smells of food stalls, spices and other unrecognisable sauces.

As a very young and completely inexperienced trumpeter it was necessary that I make such outings escorted by a senior rank and Sergeant Mayo did this duty. He took my welfare to heart, showed me the way to achieve the highest possible shine on my leather belt and bandolier, and even wrote now and again to my parents reporting my progress. Later on when we went out in the boat together I was horrified to find out that he could not swim, and I had to become the "skipper" responsible for his safety! He was noted in the regiment for his outstanding fitness and smart appearance. Fate was waiting in the wings for all of us and had a cruel and undeserved destiny reserved for him.

The regimental tailor, a Hindu, had a well-patronised, well-staffed workshop on the island. All uniforms were fitted to perfection and civilian clothes were supplied. The civilian clothes were paid for on the instalment system and I soon owned the first tailored suit of my life; a white shirt, tie, white jacket and trousers and brown shoes. These were worn on trips to the city, a short journey from the island pier in a sampan, propelled across the smooth surface of the swiftly flowing current by a Chinese standing at the rear of the strange craft, to land at Jardine Steps on the Singapore side. It was work requiring skill and judgement because the sampan was under a strong lee-way drag, and all it cost was 20 cents a time.

Luxuries came cheap in those distant days and the transit from quayside to city centre was always made by taxi, a complete novelty to me and not one a soldier could afford in England.

Life on the island was pleasant and undemanding. In the dining hall our meals were brought to the table by Chinese "boys", who came to serve us with the query, "Cully? Sitoo?" Translated this meant, "Do you want curry or stew?" I can't remember that ever varying, but if you wanted a change you could always say, "No curry. No stew. Leggy Duff." This meant you wanted only an extra pudding, and was a request I often made. "Leggy" was the troops' corruption of *"lagi",* a Malay word meaning more or again.

<u>Singapore 1940</u>

Most mail from home took about 12 days to arrive and came by Imperial Airways flying boat. Sea mail could take many weeks. Home seemed very far away and we lived in an isolated, insular world of our own. It was a way that had long remained unchanged and seemed unchanging. But change it did, and radically so. And the change came with the declaration of war in Europe, and our lives, as with so many others, were never the same again.

CHAPTER 6 War Stations

We moved to our war stations. Civilian clothes could no longer be worn. Part of my battery went to a place several miles outside Singapore city and part remained on the island for training in a different role.

At *Buona Vista* where two 15 inch guns were situated, and the gunners who had worked on them were already housed in a permanent building, we were housed in marquees. In these large tents we remained for 18 months until barrack huts of wood with attap thatch roofs were built and changes made. Training in gun drill and all that went with it went on daily and there were no more siestas. I was a plotting room specialist and the plotting room, buried deep under a hill, contained the same fire control equipment that was used on battleships.

We followed the progress of the war in Europe by means of radios and newspapers. All troop movements of time-expired men to England ceased and no requests for transfers were granted. We felt very left out of things, but in the meantime there was nothing we could do and we adjusted to our new way of life.

Time was passing, things were changing. Because of the war the rule that trumpeters joined the ranks at 18 years of age was changed and I relinquished the appointment of trumpeter and became a gunner at 17½.

Being stationed inland there were no more boat trips and I no longer had the company of Les Bills and Tom Williams. Inevitably there were new friends, one of whom was Harry Brush, a man of about 25 years of age, very thin, almost scrawny and who could perform the amazing feat of being able to sit on the ground and cross his legs behind his neck. He was unable to look smart and moved in an ungainly way. Although he was a Bombardier his authority was not much respected, but he was among the kindest men I ever met. Like Sam Mayo, it was better for him that he could have no idea of the awful destiny that awaited him.

Many and variegated as the rich colours of the oriental carpet, were the characters and events that made up the pattern of my daily existence.
So many and so varied that I can make only brief mention of a few of these; each of which could deserve a whole chapter.
Another friend; Lofty Phillips, tall, friendly nature, of gangling limbs and a ready grin. I missed his company when he married a local girl who was a wardress in an up-country prison. They met through a correspondence column. Moved into married quarters on *Belakang Mati*, and Lofty commuted daily back and forth on military transport. Unusually, for a man in his twenties, Lofty had a full set of false teeth. He was the cause of a great shock to me later on in very different circumstances.
   Paddy Smyth was a tall, handsome Ulsterman, with a John Barrymore nose. I remember his looking into a mirror, smartly dressed, prior to going out for the evening .
"That," he remarked at the conclusion of a lengthy period of combing, "is what I call a fine head of hair!"
Indeed it was. Dense, black and gleaming, with a parting straight as a die! I was to see him shortly before he died, emaciated, completely demoralised, his head shorn.
   Busty Knight; No longer *Pagar* Orderly nor cinema operator, subject now to all parades and guard duties, perspired daily in the plotting room under the hill, muttering curses soto voce as he struggled to match mag-slip dials at one end of the fire direction table, left of the Plotting Officer, in the endless repetition of practice shoots. Busty hardly ever went to town. He saved every cent for a future he was never to enjoy.
   Mac McConnel; the puritanical Ulsterman matched mag-slip dials at the opposite end of the fire direction table to Busty Knight. Tall, cadaverous, with one crossed eye, ungainly in movement, an over-conscientious N.C.O., over-strict with his younger brother, whom he always addressed as McConnel T., probably in an attempt to show no favouritism. Would he have been kinder if he'd known his brother's end?
   McConnel T: Brother of McConnel R. I saw him die from shrapnel wounds inflicted by our own planes much later in the war.
   Butch Mitchell and Taff Mahoney: two strapping lads, loveable rogues, always broke. They borrowed money on Friday; went to

town; spent it. Paid it back at once when paid on the following pay parade, then circulated the barrack room immediately to borrow once more. Like so many others, I do not know what happened to them. But I won't forget them — ever!

Albert Storey and the Chinese Sweeper: Albert, a reservist recalled to the colours, a middle-aged, corpulent man of choleric temperament with years of service in India, was of "colourful" speech. His sentences were full of the jargon of India and liberally interspersed with four-letter words. *Roti* (bread) *burgoo* (porridge) *conner* (food) were only some of the words he would use. Possibly to keep him out of the way the Battery Sergeant Major had put him in charge of area cleanliness. To do the actual work a Chinese coolie was employed. Tall for a Chinese, thin as a lath, he had high cheekbones, angular jaws and prominent teeth. Albert, with a perverted sense of humour had named him Rastus, and ordered him about mercilessly. Perhaps having command of someone for the first time in his life was a little too much to leave Albert unaffected.

This quaint pair could be seen all around the Battery area, Albert pointing at an offending piece of paper, or cigarette end, with a small cane. "Rastus y' bastard, pick that up!" Rastus was, of course, unaware of the coarseness of this mode of address, and worked cheerfully and with a will. Rastus, it transpired had an heroic streak and will be mentioned again in this narrative. Albert Storey was another whose fate remains unknown to me.

Frank: a private of the Ordnance Corps, attached to us for duties which never materialised. He was a gentle lad, quiet and unassuming, liked by all, he bunked in a small radio shack set apart from the barrack rooms, with an "other rank" from the Corps of Signals. We went to the cinema in town together from time to time. I very much enjoyed his company and his gentlemanly sense of humour. Among the very first of the casualties we sustained, I felt the sad irony of his dying among men of a unit not his own and, in the main, barely known to him.

While all hell raged in Europe we suffered vicariously with our kin folk in England as life in the colony continued on its serene way. With constant practice we became highly efficient at sinking imaginary battleships, always Japanese, and had not the slightest doubt of our ability to deal with any trouble that might come our way. Our faith in the invincibility of British arms and the impregnability of Singapore was unshakeable. Events were to prove otherwise.

No longer a boy, I was now a young man. I had been checked on parade and ordered to get my first shave! However, I was still very inexperienced in many respects and was standing on the threshold of events that were about to change all that.

Curiosity had sent me with various companions to see the night life of Singapore City. There were, at that time, three amusement parks: The Great World, The New World, and The Happy World. The first was favoured by the Chinese community; the second by a cross-section; the third mainly by the Malays.

In The Great World I was fascinated by the Chinese theatre. Played in a band-stand like structure in the open air where people would stand and watch for a while before going on; the ancient dramas would be played in all their gorgeous costumes and colours, long marches simulated by a brisk walk around the stage, castle "gates" (poles with a banner across the top with Chinese ideographs blazoned on it), and gods, devils and generals, all to the cacophony of bamboo flutes, one-string fiddles and the clatter-bang-chonk-chunk-clash of tom toms and gongs. When a general was slain a black clad assistant would walk on from back-stage and place a cushion below him and he would sink gracefully down upon it.

Harry Brush went regularly to the Great World, but not to watch the theatre. Once he took me with him to the cabaret where he used book after book of tickets dancing with a taxidance girl. I sat at a floor-side table watching as they swept around the floor, Harry looking rather awkward, the girl an exotic butterfly in a beautiful high-necked, split-to-the-thigh *cheongsam* of shimmering silk, a picture of elegance and consummate grace.

I was such a prude at the time that I was quite disgusted when he took the girl home afterwards while I waited. He smiled at my naivete and said, "First the lady has her pleasure, and then it's the gentleman's turn". I couldn't argue with that!

I have mentioned earlier, Frank of the Ordnance Corps, and now I must tell of Bing Worsdell. Bing was a real country boy whose fate was linked with that of Frank. We had unkindly christened him Bing because he was completely unable to carry a tune, but that didn't stop him from singing, and he gloried in the name. What Bing Crosby would have thought of this I shudder to think! Our Bing had the plod of a ploughboy, a sallow skin and two protuding "goofy" teeth. That he did not lack physical courage was borne out by an unpleasant episode with a really nasty gunner from Liverpool. We were in the marquee one day, when there was a disturbance outside; a heated argument with loud shouting. Bing called out asking whoever it was to quieten things down.

"Come outside and say that!" a voice snarled.

Bing got to his feet and with an upward flick of his eyebrows, he hitched up his belt and went to go outside. To do this he had to bend down to pass through the tent opening. As he emerged he was met with a cowardly and violent head butt from the Liverpudlian. This broke off, halfway, his two front teeth, which remained embedded in the forehead of his attacker. At this point the fracas ended. Bing learned to live with his shortened teeth and pretended that he liked them better that way.

Quite a different type of Liverpudlian was Joe Lowe, who became a very good friend of mine. He had fair, almost white hair, blue eyes and a sunny disposition. His front teeth sported a large chip occasioned when raising a beer bottle to his lips too enthusiastically. He too was regularly seeing a cabaret girl, in a different part of town to the one visited by Harry Brush. For companionship I accompanied him on some of these visits and, rather than play gooseberry, would dutifully wait outside on a chair while he was occupied within. On one occasion I was sitting in a corridor waiting, when a couple came upstairs. Imagine my surprise, and Tom Willaims' chagrin (for it was he) when he saw me there. I explained why I was waiting. He flushed scarlet with drink and embarrassment, thrust some money into the girl's hand and indicated that he'd changed his mind. She shouted at him angrily in Malay, no doubt feeling very insulted, and stormed off in a huff. The reason, I suspect, for his embarrassment was my reputation. I was a non-smoker, non-drinker and never a swear word passed my lips. For good or bad that was the reputation I had, and all knew I was a virgin soldier! But I was a moth and I was circling nearer and nearer to the flame.

One of the sights of Singapore was the rickshaw parade. In one part of the city a long row of rickshaws gathered nightly, each one with a girl in attendance. Customers from all three services would go there. The charge was two dollars (less than five shillings) for a "short time". The client would hop into a rickshaw with the girl and was whipped away to some seedy hotel, or dwelling nearby. The VD figures for Singapore were very high and infection was accounted a self-inflicted injury by the military and incurred condign punishment.

   I was happy in Joe's company both in and out of barracks. He was a good companion and where I was generally quiet he could talk the hind leg off a donkey. We went to town often together. The routine was always the same: he would dance and I would watch, never having danced in my life. Then one day it happened. We entered through the bat winged door of a small smoke-filled cabaret. A band was playing a Tango, "La Cumparsita". Couples danced or sat at tables around the floor and then, I saw her .
She stood out among the sophisticated throng by her very difference. Alone at a table and looking incredibly shy, peeping out from below a hand held over her eyes. In contrast to the *Cheongsams* or European clothes of the other girls she was dressed in Malay style with *sarong* and *kebaya* (a kind of long jacket) with a red paper flower on the left of her dark hair. Devoid of makeup except for the khol around her eyes, she looked as if she'd wandered into that place by mistake. I felt pleased. I was stunned. She was so small, so beautiful, and looked so vulnerable. Joe saw the effect she'd had on me.
"Go on, ask her to dance," he prompted.
"I can't dance," I said miserably.
"Go on!" he urged, "she won't bite yer!" I went to the table and asked her; she knew what I meant but made no reply. Instead she followed me onto the crowded floor and we made an awkward attempt at dancing. She knew no more than I did and we got around with small jerky steps. Later she said that it was more like a *"joget"* (a Malay dance) than "real dancing".

   We returned to the table together and I attempted to overcome her shyness. I was delighted to find that she could not speak English. This was a very welcome discovery because to me it meant that she had had nothing to do with soldiers and was therefore a "good" girl. I used what Malay I had and we got along famously. As the evening wore on our attempts at dancing grew slightly less clumsy and in no time at all it was time to return to barracks. We hailed two rickshaws. She travelled ahead and Joe and I followed in the second

one. Our journey ended at the edge of a piece of open ground at the side of the New World amusement park. A steep flight of wooden steps led to the upper storey of a large building. She started to go up them. I followed. She turned to look at me where I stood below her, and seemed wary of me. I asked if I might see her again and arranged for a meeting the following weekend. I was reluctant to leave her and stayed talking until Joe called up from the foot of the steps, "Say goodnight
and kiss her or we'll be late back!"
Good old Joe, without his prompting I would never have dared to do it. So I kissed her quickly on the lips and fled.

Thus began what, to me, was at first to be a casual and convenient affair but which became not only my first love but a deep and consuming passion that was to tear me apart emotionally and leave me never the same again.

We met again in the large wooden building in the presence of an older woman who seemed to be some sort of aunty who was looking out for the girl. I was being discussed in what I thought was Chinese but turned out to be Thai. It was clear that some kind of business was under discussion. "Aunty" wanted to know all about me. Was I intending a long-term relationship? The girl needed support and how much per week could I contribute? I did some quick arithmetic. If I dispensed with the services of the boot boy I could manage five dollars a week, regularly. This would leave me with practically nothing for myself but seemed the least respectable amount I could offer. Smiles were exchanged all round and the girl and I left the room together and went to a smaller room on the same floor. The room was simply furnished with a bed, dressing table, chairs and a mirror and an oil lamp on one wall. A shuttered window looked over the open ground where geese honked loudly at passers by, and the plaintive five-note scale of Chinese music floated in on the air.

We talked rather awkwardly and I found out that her name was *Sumini*. "Jek" was the best she could make of my name but said that the sound of Jek King was very pleasing to the ear. The way *Sumini* said it, it was! She made me understand that before we could start our relationship she wanted me to go with her to meet and get the approval of her mother who lived in the family home in the large Malay settlement of *Geylang Serai,,* so we went there together by bus.

Sumini's mother was a small, sparrow of a woman with bright, intelligent eyes and was a full-blooded Thai. She was a widow of several years standing and spoke with *Sumini*, obviously about me, at some length. She spoke to me in Malay and seemed to gain a good impression for we left with her blessing and our affair had officially begun.

Malay has been called the Italian of the East, and so it is. It is a language I fell in love with and I took to it like a duck to water. It has no harsh sounds, no difficult grammar. It has a very rich vocabulary. The Malay is an easy-going person with a natural dignity and politeness. He will always put his language at the level of the person he is speaking to, thereby making understanding easy. But it is also a very subtle language, rich in allusions and no matter how good my vocabulary became it was never possible to understand the conversation of one Malay to another. I would be lost after a couple of sentences. I bought a book of English/Malay which never left my pocket, and consulted it at every opportunity. I already knew quite a bit when I first met *Sumini* and we always had a complete understanding of what we said to each other. It became so that I eventually had no need to translate but thought entirely in Malay whenever we were together.

Little by little I learned about *Sumini* . She was one year younger than I (18). Like most Muslim girls she was married early, in her case 14 years of age, to a man of 40, and had one child, a boy, *Ahmat,* called Mat. The man, as was common among Muslims had divorced her, leaving her with no support. She had had no schooling, could not read or write and could not tell the time, this was a great shame because she was obviously intelligent. She must have been ashamed of being unable to read, for one day I found her in a pair of wire-rimmed spectacles "reading" a book, a novel printed in Romanised Malay. I gently took the book from her and turned it the right way up. She had been reading it upside down and had no need of the spectacles, which were not hers anyway. I did not laugh at her attempt to impress me and never mentioned it again.

Sumini was a lovely girl, slender, with dark naturally wavy hair, a skin the colour of *"puteh kuning"* (creamy white), a colour highly admired by the Malays, good teeth and with eyes black as midnight, yet not black, but the deepest warmest brown. Her hands were tiny and so supple from the Siamese dance that she could bend the fingers back to touch her forearm in an elegant curve. She had a good sense of humour and a kind and gentle nature. An hour in her company was like a moment in passing. We were discussing time when she remarked that when we are small a day seems to stretch in front of us endlessly; but when we are grown up it seems so very short, that is, when we are happy. On time we thought the same way.

Sumini moved from the big wooden building to another place not far away. It was far more convenient for me to get there than to travel from my barracks to *Geylang Serai* where Mama lived. Here she had a very small room just large enough to accommodate a double bed and a trunk, much more affordable than the previous place. The room was one of several in an *attap* building that housed a Javanese family of 3; the father, a devout Muslim and a quiet, serious man who performed all the daily prayers faithfully; *Bayu* his wife, a bubbly, full-of-life woman and very friendly; and *Eh Nun* a seven-year old daughter already married but who would not be living with her husband until she reached puberty. *Sumini's* room was next to the main living room, and next to *Sumini's* room on the other side was a larger room at a slightly lower level; then came a lean-to which contained a kitchen and a *jamban* (a very basic toilet) which consisted of a removable can for night soil, with a slot for crouching over. Bathing was carried out in the kitchen by means of pouring water from a dipper over oneself from a huge earthenware vessel, known as a "*tong*". It is surprising how very refreshing this form of bathing is, for the *tong* "breathes" and the water within keeps amazingly cool.

Gradually we came to know each other, to make the sweetest love and to fall deeply in love. At our tenderest moments her eyes would literally smoke and I could lose my soul in their depths.

When bombs were falling all around and the ground shaking as we lay in each other's arms, she whispered to me, "*Mati macham ini bagus, Jek, ya?*" (To die like this would be good, Jack, yes?) There was no doubting her love for me nor mine for her.

I don't know how she did it on the small amount I was able to give her but she bought me clothes to change into after bathing, when I arrived sweating freely from a twelve-mile bike ride to see her. The clothes, a sarong and short sleeved shirt were always clean, fresh smelling , washed and pressed ready for me, whenever I came, and I came whenever I could.

Sometimes we would go to the house in *Geylang Serai*. A large, airy room at the centre with a cot swinging on long ropes from a high ceiling beam, a veranda overlooking the garden, rooms leading off; all made for a comfortable home. The walls of the rooms were papered with newspaper, an inexpensive and effective way of covering the bare timbers. The roof was of attap (palm leaf thatching), the lofty roof and shuttered windows made for a cool and airy interior.

The garden was bare earth with hibiscus hedges on either side, and a clump of tall coconut palms stood at the end where the garden bordered the lane. On the veranda was a comfortable settee and a small table with family photographs on it.

I met the other members of *Sumini's* family: her older brother, *Buari*, a *naik* (corporal) in the Malay Regiment, and his wife, dainty and petite in Malay clothes who pulled *Sumini's* leg when introduced to me, by chanting a little four-line verse, known as a *puntun*, a popular form of Malay wit in which she mentioned my full cheeks and straight nose (at least it appeared so to her. The native nose being inclined to be stubby).

Sumini had two sisters; *Kakak* (older sister) *PeO*, tall for her race and very grave in manner, well respected by the community, and *Supiah*, quite the opposite in temperate and appearance, chubby and cheerful and full of fun.

We all had a picnic in the yard before the house. Rush mats were spread on the ground in the shade of the palms and a large crystal bowl, set within a larger one of Siamese silver carved in beautiful and intricate chasing was produced. The bowl was filled with ice cubes and coconut milk and slices of tender white young coconut. The delicious cold drink and simple happiness of that day became a memory that will never fade. Those kind people had so little, yet had so much.

Sumini and I went out and about together from the small room in the Javanese house. We went to the cinema to watch Hollywood films and sometimes to a Malay cinema near *Geylang Serai* which showed only Malay language films, many made in Java. *Sumini* relied on me to tell her what was happening in the Hollywood films. I understood about 50% of the dialogue of the native films.

The cinema was a rather ramshackle building, which I was to see under very different circumstances later on.

That *Sumini*, despite a lamentable lack of schooling, was intelligent, was evinced in the many questions she asked me. One evening while out walking we came upon the statue erected in memory of Stamford Raffles.

"*Siapa orang hitam itu, Jek?*" she asked in her quiet way. (Who is that black man, Jack?"). The statue did look black in the semi-darkness. I explained who he was and his connection to Singapore.

Many, many years later I chanced upon a photograph of the statue, gleaming white now under the new government of the city-state, and it brought back the memory of that little incident with a clarity that wiped out all the long years between, as if they had never existed.

"What is there most of in the world, Jack. Land or water?"
I estimated 1/3 land and 2/3 water, which is not far off. She wanted to know so much and could have learned so much if Fate had given us the time. But it did not.

The Malays, despite their Muslim faith, were firm believers in *hantu* — ghosts! *Hantu* were the ghosts of dead people and were mostly malevolent. I learned of *Pontianak,* the ghost of a woman who had died in childbirth, who lured victims into graveyards at night and killed them in a gruesome fashion. There was also the ghost of a deformed old man who lived in peoples' houses, usually harming no-one but who could be nasty when provoked.
I was to see the power of this belief quite soon, and its effect on the victim.

I learned about *bayang* — (shadow). In normal use it would mean just that, shadow; but I also found that it had another, more subtle meaning. *Sumini* was comforting a friend who was weeping, stroking the girl's head, making soothing noises. She asked the girl, was it a *bayang?* In this sense it means the shadow, or wraith of a person who has gone away, a loved one removed. The girl nodded her head and *Sumini* persisted with her questioning.
" Is it the *bayang* of *Sami?*"
It was. It was the vision of the girl's sweetheart that appeared, or seemed to appear before her eyes.

Sumini's bayang was to follow me through the years. While we were apart I saw her everywhere. Heard her voice, saw her smile, and gesture, — everywhere.

One evening Joe Lowe, his girlfriend *Salma, Sumini* and I were all together in the room next to *Sumini's*. We were larking about and there was much laughter and boisterous horse-play. I decided to act the fool and made myself into a passable imitation of Frankenstein's monster, as played by Boris Karloff. I did this by putting under my bottom lip a hair comb with long tines. The tines were stuck up like a row of yellow teeth. I screwed up one eye until it was half-closed, pulled my hair untidily over my forehead and advanced, crouching with one shoulder hunched and one hand extended like a claw towards *Sumini*.

The effect was far more dramatic than I'd intended. She screamed in terror and fell backward in a faint.

We carried her into her own room and laid her on the bed. She showed no sign of coming round but shook and moaned convulsively. *Bayu* and *Eh Nun* appeared; *Bayu* carrying a small vessel that was giving off smoke and incense.
She waved it around the bed, "To ward off evil spirits," she said. I asked *Salma* to bring a blanket, which I spread over *Sumini*. Then *Bayu's* husband entered the room. He prayed quietly at the foot of the bed, then he told me what he thought was wrong.

"In each house," he said, "there lives the ghost of an old man. The old man is hideously ugly and is lame and deformed. He lives in the kitchen but if he hears loud laughter in the house he thinks "These people are laughing at me," and he attacks them."
He said this quietly and calmly , then felt each of *Sumini's* ankles. "There," he instructed me . "Feel that. One leg is cold, the other is warm."
I felt the ankles and it was as he'd said. One was at normal body temperature, the other was icy cold.
"That is the one," he said, "that the ghost has got hold of. We must wait quietly and he may go."

We waited quietly for a long while and he lectured me in a gentle manner on the unwisdom of boisterous behaviour in a Malay house. Eventually warmth returned to *Sumini's* leg and her breathing quietened.
"The ghost has gone," *Bayu's* husband said, and went back to his own part of the house.

To me this incident showed the strength of the grip that superstition has on the human mind, and instilled in me a greater respect for native beliefs and customs. Make of it what you will.

Salma was Joe's new girlfriend and she occupied the room next to *Sumini's*. This was convenient, for Joe and I could travel in from the barracks together and go back together at night. We had to be back by 23.59 Hrs. As I came to visit more often than Joe I would use my cycle, but when Joe came with me we would travel by "piggy bus". Piggy is a corruption of the Malay word "*pergi*", which means to go.

These buses were very small and seated only about 6 passengers each side on a bench seat at the back. The driver and conductor were always Chinese. Some of them must have had pirate ancestors because one night when we were returning to barracks, having passed Holland Village, the last village en route, the bus stopped, the driver came round the back and demanded more money, not much, about 20 cents, but we refused to pay on principle. Immediately the driver threatened to turn the bus around. We had to capitulate because we were about four miles away from barracks and would never make it for 23.59Hrs. Luckily we were able to scrape up the "ransom" money between us, and we reported in on time.

In peace time, and indeed up to this time, civilian Europeans in the colony would have nothing to do with service personnel. It was like Rudyard Kipling described, 'Tommy this, and Tommy that, and Tommy wait outside."
They wanted nothing to do with us, we were all persona non-grata.

Things changed a little later and invitations to private houses came, and a civilian concert party toured the out-stations. Their idea of what a soldier was, and what they thought his level of humour to be, was made plain, to me at least, by the coarseness of the language used and the lewdness of the jokes and sketches, they included in their show.

Scrub clearing 1941

As there had been a period known as the "phoney war" in Europe so in the East we had an era of phoney peace. It was coming to an end.

I shall not attempt to describe the war in Malaya. It has been fully written up by experts in the field. Times, places, units and movements — all of these lie beyond both my ability and the scope of these memoirs.

It is my intention to give a personal account of what I saw and heard. My own experiences in a general picture of events.

CHAPTER 7   Fall of Singapore, early POW days

The fury of the war burst upon us in the darkness of the small hours of December 7th, 1941.
The heavy drone of aero engines brought us from our beds; the sky was full of bombers, and the heavy crump-crump-crump of bombs as

the aircraft dropped their loads on the lights of Singapore City, came clearly to us across the island.

At the same time, although we learned of it only later, Pearl Harbour was being attacked. It was dawn there, and the resulting damage was far more devastating, for much of the U. S. Pacific fleet was destroyed.

Joe stood at my side.

"It's started!" I said. An obvious remark, but of course, it had. Appalled at the treachery that could permit the Japs to bomb a lighted city without warning; at last we were about to become part of the great struggle, and the perfidious and cruel nature of the Japanese was to be revealed to us and to the world.

Vichy French Indo-China had allowed Japanese forces into the country where they learned and practised jungle warfare. They were veterans, battle hardened troops from the war with China which had already gone on for several years.

For our part we had been busy digging trenches, revetted and designed to text book perfection, at points around the battery area. We never had a chance to use them! We strung barbed wire through the surrounding scrub, and did this in the firmly held belief that we could cope with anything the Japs would attempt, quite happy to have the chance to have it out with them, thereby helping, hopefully, to shorten the war.

Extra precautions came into force. For a short march from parade ground to work on our entrenchments we had to don steel helmets, carry rifles and bayonets and have anti-gas capes rolled up on our packs. All this gear would be removed so that we could do the work required. It was not long before the idiocy of this procedure was realised and we reverted to the normal practice of working in gym shorts, stripped to the waist, with polo vests tied around our heads as protection against the broiling sun. We resembled nurses, about our heads, at least!

No Japanese battleship obliged by coming to allow us to demonstrate our expertise and drop an armour piercing shell of 1940lb weight down its funnel from a distance of twenty miles. How often had we done this to the mighty battleship *Nagato* in our miniature range? No enemy warship ever appeared but the Japanese army made swift progress down the Malay Peninsula (impassable our wise leaders declared) under the able command of General *Yamashita,* the tiger of Malaya.

Their bombers bombed here, there and everywhere at will. Their modern fighter planes shot the obsolete RAF planes from the sky (those that had not been evacuated), and their torpedo bombers sank H.M. great ships, the proud Prince of Wales and Repulse. Both had gone out without air cover to attack a Japanese troop convoy off *Khota Baru.*

Things went from bad to worse and the great debacle of Singapore itself was about to begin. The north shore of the island was left unprotected when an Australian division was unaccountably withdrawn.

"Someone had blundered," <u>again</u>? Who knows?

The Japanese crossed the narrow strait from *Johore Baru* unopposed. Surely the gods were with them! How could they believe their luck? The causeway across the shallow strait had been partly demolished, but they had no need of it anyway. And night was their friend.

We were now confined to barracks, no more visits to the city. I was unable to contact *Sumini* and worried that she would think I'd abandoned her. Then a chance came my way that I could not miss. A volunteer was called for to take the last telegrams into Singapore for those who wished to send them.

I volunteered and was soon on my way on my drop-handled racing bike. The bike was still serviceable but had lost its smart appearance when I'd had to have its frame straightened by blow lamp after an accident in the blackout a week or so before.

It happened this way; I had left *Sumini's* place to cycle home. Everywhere was pitch dark in the streets. As I passed the Cathay cinema I felt my face burst something open, a flash of light and the pop of bursting glass and I was cartwheeling through the air to land two or three yards away, flat on my face on the road.

A rickshaw had pulled straight across my direction of travel. My face had hit the small oil lamp at the side of the rickshaw's hood and the sudden arrest of my forward momentum had hurled me over the handlebars, up over the top of the rickshaw in a complete somersault to land prostrate on the hard road surface with arms down at my sides. Surprisingly I was not badly hurt. There was an abrasion on my chin and my teeth had sunk into my bottom lip. The fact that it had all happened so suddenly and unexpectedly probably meant that

I was completely relaxed and had flown through the air like an empty sack. There had been no time to tense up.

I got to my feet and saw immediately what had happened. The rickshaw passenger, a Chinese gentleman in European dress was soundly berating the coolie. He was very perturbed to discover that I, the victim, was European. I assured him that I was all right and did not want to make a complaint. It was not until I made to ride off again that I found the force of the impact had bent the frame of the bike, but was greatly relieved to find that I had just enough movement of the front fork to enable me to ride back to barracks and meet the 23.59 Hrs deadline. I had had a very lucky escape, but not as lucky as the one I was to experience as I rode into Singapore with the last telegrams to leave the island.

The noise of the Japanese bombardment was all about me as I rode along. My steel helmet was on my head, my rifle slung across my back. There were low clouds about . I reached the Botanic Gardens in *Tanglin* suburb. The noise of the aircraft above the overcast grew louder and suddenly there came the whistle of falling bombs. The houses across the road began to shake.

The only other person on the road besides myself was a Chinese on a bicycle about 30 yards ahead. There was a blinding orange and red flash on the grass verge directly opposite to where I was cycling. I found myself blown through the air and landing in a shallow drain channel. My helmet was two yards away to one side. There was a large tree beside me. The next bomb fell about 30 yards in front in the centre of the road. The Chinese cyclist and cycle disappeared completely. I reached for my helmet and put it on my head and crouched back in the drain. At that precise moment a huge bough, slashed through by shrapnel, fell a few inches in front of my face. It bounced gently a couple of times, before coming to rest . Shaken, I mounted my cycle and rode into the city to send the telegrams at the General Post Office, and now nothing could stop me from riding on to *Geylang Serai* to see *Sumini*.

As I neared my destination an air raid was in progress and bombs were devastating buildings ahead of me and to my right, raising clouds of debris and dust. To my horror I saw the pattern continue across the road ahead and into the *kampong* (village). I pressed hard down on my pedals and raced down the lane between the houses until I saw the tall palm trees ahead, and I turned into the front yard of *Sumini's* house.

The family was both surprised and delighted to see me, but no more so than was I to see them. They couldn't understand how I had come through the bombing unscathed, and I explained that I had not been too close to where the bombs fell. I thought it wiser not to mention the close shave I'd had in *Tanglin*.

Not far down the lane from the house, I had passed an empty space where a dwelling had received a direct hit. Smoke was still rising and debris fluttering down as I passed. There was no trace of the house and the fronds had been blown off the nearby palm trees which now poked gaunt fingers at the sky.

Sumini told me that a *Keling* (Tamil) family lived there and that the bomb was the wrath of Allah, because they were unbelievers who worshipped idols. Religion seems to become important to some people at times of great danger!

There is a custom among Malay sweethearts in which rings are exchanged. It is called "*tukar chinchin*". Some time before, *Sumini* had given me a ring, even though I had not one to give to her. It was an exquisite little thing of suasa, an inexpensive alloy of copper and gold. Engraved on it were five miniature five pointed stars and in the centre of each was set a gem stone, three small pieces of Burmese ruby and two tiny diamonds. It could just go on my little finger on the left hand. I became greatly attached to it and wouldn't part with it for the world. It was the cause of an unpleasant incident in the days to come, of which I shall tell later.

I don't know how long I stayed at the house. I was so happy to be there and was reluctant to leave but knew that I must not be too long away from my unit.

As I made preparations to leave *Sumini* said to me, " I have something for you, Jek," and produced an amulet, which she called a *tankal*. It was a tiny linen pouch with a prayer for my safety stitched within, and a cord for hanging around my neck. She had bought it at a local shrine and believed implicitly in its effectiveness. I wore it to please her and thereafter never took it off again, wearing it until sweat and time rotted it away.

The ring also I wore constantly. In the end hard labour wore the soft metal wafer thin, the ring broke into pieces and I eventually lost them. This was something I deeply regretted and in my mind's eye I can still see that lovely little love token till this day.

A thunder clap, heavier than any bomb blast, resounded overhead and torrential rain burst forth from the heavy clouds. It drummed on the attap roof with a deafening roar, but the time had come and I had to leave. I picked up my rifle and said goodbye to Mama and the sisters. Now *Sumini* stood looking up into my face, her beautiful eyes brimming. She couldn't speak and neither could I. The magic hour was over. I rode off into the storm.

" We thought you'd had it, Badgie," they said when I got back to the Battery. But I was not quizzed on the reason for my long absence and the routine of the unit went on.

Extra guards, dawn mannings when all posts were occupied and we awaited the attack from the sea that never came.

Survivors from the Prince of Wales and the Repulse arrived in our midst and we received some Bofors guns for anti-aircraft defence. The matelots worked with a will to help us drag these to one or two high points around the battery.

"There will be no surrender."
<u>Gen Wavell had visited the island. Given the order and left.</u>

A myth grew up after the war that the big guns of Singapore could only fire out to sea. This is only partly true. Some had the ability to fire on land targets and among them the 9.2 inch guns on *Pulau Belakang Mati* fired round after round until the bores required changing.

Our two 15 inch guns, it is true, could only fire out to sea. But this was their purpose, and as the Japanese fleet never did appear, did not our guns and our proficiency achieve this effect?

A bombardment from modern capital ships allied to the ground and air assault would have amounted to nothing less than a massacre of the dense civilian population of the city.

Calamity followed calamity. On one of the gun sites there was a huge Ransom and Rapier crane which had been used in installing the 15 inch guns and machinery that went with them. It sat on the railway track, the purpose of which was the means of bringing in the ammunition supply. Its removal had been delayed and now, when it was imperative to shift it, it stuck fast about 200 yards away from the Battery when its great weight caused the track to sink, effectively blocking it. Thereby causing one more place to guard, no doubt to the delight of the myriad mosquitoes which made nights there a misery.

Each day now the thunder of gunfire grew louder and shells fell nearer as the enemy approached. Their bombers crossed and criss-crossed the sky in tidy V formations. Their fighter planes flew low, strafing. Our heavy Ack Ack guns blasted away from the direction of the city and seemed to hit nothing, and our own little Bofors guns, dragged with much sweat and toil to the tops of their small hillocks, remained unchallenged and silent.

The thunder of heavy bombing rolled in from over the hills around. I stood alone on duty in a weapons pit with an ancient Lewis gun of first war vintage mounted in the anti-aircraft role, watching the skies and wondering how effective I would be if one of the darting planes with the red disc of the Rising Sun on its wings were to decide to have a go at the Battery, when I heard a shout. A red faced, perspiring figure appeared above the sandbagged parapet.
"Badgie! Badgie! Your pusher (girl friend) is down the road and wants to see you!"
"Where down the road?"
"By the bridge."

I was stunned. Here? *Sumini?* It was completely unexpected. I <u>had</u> to go to her. But I couldn't leave my post.

"Do me a favour, Mucker," I begged, pleading desperately. " Stand in for me for a few minutes."

Grumbling reluctantly he climbed into the weapons pit. I rushed off with wings on my heels, past the Battery huts, downhill on a track through scrub. Suddenly, with no warning whatsoever I was confronted by a barrier, rolls of dannet wire which I had not known were there.

The momentum of my headlong rush down hill was such that it made stopping impossible. I charged at the wire and made a desperate flying leap, with a rush of adrenalin that carried me soaring over it to land still running, on the other side. I had never made such a jump before nor have I ever since.

I saw her at the roadside, standing before the wooden hut which was occupied by a friendly family of *Bugis* people whom we had met before. Not long ago we had discussed the possibility of renting a room there. Now it appeared deserted.

The anxiety left *Sumini's* face to be replaced by relief when she saw me coming down the hill. I felt overwhelmed at the thought that she had come alone all the way from *Geylang Serai*, braving air raids and all hazards, changing buses en route until the little piggy bus had set her down here out in *Ulu Pandan*. All that without the certainty of making contact with me at all. How long had she waited before someone from the Battery had found her there and brought her message to me?

I asked her how long. She said, "*Tidak apa*, Jek." (it doesn't matter — it is nothing).

We went to the rear of the hut to talk away from the road. I would have no acceptable excuse should I be found at that spot away from my post.

We talked tete a tete. Inconsequential things. It was sheer heaven to be together again. I held her close. I longed to kiss her but she would not agree. We were, after all, in public and modesty forbade it.

She spoke quietly. "How far away are the Japanese, Jek?"
"About half a mile, I think."
"Will they take Singapore?"
"I think they may, my love."

There was a pause, and then slowly, "What — will happen — to us?"

I thought this over for a moment and gave a guarded reply, "You are civilians, I'm sure you will be all right."

"And you, *sayang* (my love). What will they do to you?"

"Soldiers become prisoners of war," I said. "But we will come back. The British will come back and when they do I shall come and find you again!" *Sumini* managed a smile.

I asked her then, "Will you come with me to England after the war?" She shook her head, "I would die of cold in England, Jek".

"Then I shall come back here and be with you," and I meant it with all my heart.

We were both aware that these precious moments were fleeting, and soon we heard the sound of the bus passing on its way to the T-junction at the end of the road to make its turn around for the journey back to the city. This must surely be its last run, for the shells were falling not far away now.

To reassure her and with some braggadocio I said, " I will oppose them, *Sumini; I* will fight them even should I have no more than a piece of wood to hit them with. I will fight them." It sounds melodramatic but I really meant it.

We could hear the bus now approaching on its way back. I gave her what money I had in my pockets and took her to where the bus waited on the other side of the road.

There was nothing left to say, no words to express the deep emotions we felt. I watched her tiny, vulnerable figure mount the steps. She turned a tear-stained face to me and attempted a smile. The bus started and as it drew away, she waved, and was gone.

We were destined to see each other once more. But we had spoken our last goodbyes.

I hurried back to the Lewis gun pit where I was met by a barrage of furious oaths. My "few minutes" had stretched into a full hour. My abject apologies seemed very inadequate indeed!

Shells were now falling about the Battery area, but appeared to be random rather than aimed. The advance of enemy troops had caused our Indian boot boys and Chinese kitchen and canteen staff to disappear. This was understandable in view of what they could expect to happen to them in the event of capture. One Chinese who did not melt away was the one we might have thought to be least expected to remain. He was "Rastus", the sanitary coolie. He appeared dressed in a home-made copy of the uniform of a Chinese Nationalist Soldier; a dark blue jacket and trousers, a red bandana wound round his head, another about his waist, and he was, as usual bare footed.

He came to me and said in broken Malay, "Lastas want gun. Give Lastas gun and bullets. Lastas go fight Japanese." His face was a mask of honesty and determination. I took him to the sergeant major and Rastas was given a .303 rifle and two cloth bandoliers of ammunition.

Rastas strode off briskly in a "Napolionic march towards the guns". The sight of that brave lone figure, the lowest of the low, going off to do battle has remained with me undiminished by time.

The Major sent for me. I found him talking with an infantry officer. Our major was slightly deaf and usually spoke leaning forward a little, one hand cupping an ear, the other holding his pipe, with his tongue sticking out from the corner of his mouth as he strained to hear a reply.

"Bombardier," he said, "You will take one man and go with this officer. You are to stay with him and bring back any messages he may wish to send. Should you receive no messages from me during the night we will rendezvous at the Golden Bell at dawn." He looked at me intently. "Now repeat that." I did so. The Golden Bell was the name of a mansion on the seaward side of the hills not far from our Battery observation point. A good place for a rendezvous, and roughly about 6 or 7 miles away as the crow flies.

I went off to collect my haversack, shaving gear and water bottle. Had I known that I was never to see the Battery again I would have taken a few souvenirs. But I was never to return to the barrack room and so lost all my kit and personal possessions.

The man seconded to accompany me was a middle-aged reservist. A tall cockney of a complaining and unwilling nature. He had been working as a London park keeper when he was recalled to the colours. He was not at all pleased to leave the barracks and venture out into the unknown.

We followed the infantry officer down the hill and into the *belukar* (secondary jungle growth) as the swift tropical twilight came down, and were allotted a position by the Company headquarters, little more than a shallow hollow in the ground.

With darkness the sounds of small arms fire crackled all around, punctuated by bursts of heavy machine-gun fire. Red flashes pierced the blackness, whether from the Japs or our own men it was impossible to tell. I had no idea of the dispositions of the various sections but it was obvious that the struggle was furious, and very close.

The night wore on interminably. Around midnight the cockney, who had been showing more and more signs of uneasiness said to me, "I fink I'll go back to the battery."

"You'll stay here," I said, forcefully.

"They're looting the canteen up there," he whined. "I could go and get some stuff for us."

"You will stay here as ordered." I insisted. He grumbled some more but dared not leave. He must have hated having to obey a 19 year-old junior N.C.O.

At a different time in another place I happened to hear his version of this event as told to a crony.

"I wanted to go and warn the battery that the Japs were coming, but 'e wouldn't let me".

Hours passed and no word came from the Major. Neither was I given any message to take to him. The time had come for me to make a decision. I found the harassed infantry officer and reminded him of my orders — to rendezvous at the Golden Bell at dawn. If I was to keep that rendezvous I would have to start out now, for dawn could not be far off.

He gave me permission to leave and I set off with my companion to keep the appointment. Bullets whizzed about us in the darkness.

The Golden Bell at last: Dawn was in the sky, its fiery radiance painting the dense black billowing smoke from the burning oil tanks on *Pulau Bukum,* a Dutch oil depot to the south, and from the docks and buildings. The whole island seemed ablaze . Chaos reigned everywhere — except in the Golden Bell . It was vast, echoing and empty. Not a soul was there, nor did it appear that anyone had been there recently. I was rendezvouing with a vacuum!

Now what? Wait. Wait and wait. Hours crawled by. Nobody, no message came. The Regiment was just across the narrow strip of water. I took a sampan at Jardine Steps, and my detachment of one man, and made our way to the pier on the island where I had stepped ashore as a 16-year old trumpeter, what seemed like more than three centuries ago. The place, and I, were unrecognisably changed!

On *Belakang Mati* I made my report and had a meal in the mess hall with the deafening thunder of bombs falling on the nearby docks sounding as if they were just outside. In fact the Japs seemed to ignore the island and no bombs fell there. I had come for further orders; but there were none. I had come for news of the fate of the battery; but again, there was none.

The reader (if I have one!) should please excuse the confused nature of events in the narrative that follows. There were comings and goings and an orderly and strictly chronological description is not possible to write; both because of the complexity and confusion of the time and the gulf of years since passed.

So here they are; the fragments of memory!
Without sleep now for 36 hours, and footsore. Other members of the battery had turned up — enough to make up a party. Bombardier "Oppo" Hill arrived, grinning, with the news that the battery had been overrun but a counter attack had got them all out, including the plotting room operators, of whom Joe Lowe was one.

We set off to rejoin them; arriving at Jardine Steps to be immediately strafed by Jap fighter planes coming in almost at water level; marching through and magically surviving a massive rain of bombs as we passed between dockyard buildings; marching up a hill to a devastated barrack building, to fall in on a small parade square of beaten earth on which stood a marquee — probably as a replacement billet and mess hall for the bombed-out detachment. Inside the tent a fat oriental was sitting, his hands tied behind his back with field telephone cable, and ankles lashed together. On his head was a stubbly growth which looked about ten days old. His face was brutal, with heavy dark jowls; and he looked very fit and strong. He was thought to be a Japanese spy, I went to look at him. "*Tolong-lah,Towkay,*" he repeated time and time again. "Help me, boss, help me!" Just then the planes came over on another raid. Was he a Jap or Chinese as he claimed to be? I'll never know. He was left in the tent, presumably for the field security police to take away for questioning. We were ordered down a long flight of steps to a kind of control centre deep inside the hill. The Jap/Chinese was left outside in the air raid.

Here another fragment of memory comes to the fore; a piece of sun-baked ground on a hillside. There are trees scattered over the area with thicker growth below in front and to the sides.

The Major and other parties from the Battery have assembled there. We are ordered to dig in, and in no particular pattern men dug small trenches willy-nilly over the surface of the slope, mostly choosing their own pals as fellow occupants. I am sent to collect a party who have arrived farther back down the road along which we had recently marched. It is a short walk downhill. A number of R.E. Sappers is busy nearby and there is the roar of heavy engines not far off. One of the Sappers says that there are Jap tanks in the area. The jungles of Malaya were considered impenetrable to tanks, so we had none, and the Japs used the excellent metal roads the British Public Works Department had built all down the peninsular.

I did not know what the Royal Engineers were about, but I was soon to find out. The party I am to guide back to the Battery position consists of about twenty men under the command of a Troop Sergeant Major. They fall in and follow me. Confidently I lead them off the road and up the hill. Near the crest of the hill I pause. Something made me look down — I am about to tread on an anti-tank mine. The size of a saucepan with a smaller circular raised portion on top, it sat in a small pit in which, thank God, the soil had not yet been replaced. Had it been I would not have seen it and these words would never have been written.

The Troop Sergeant Major, not a happy man at the best of times, fixes me with a furious glare.
"You've been sent to guide us to the Battery and you've led us straight into a bloody minefield."
I have the feeling that my explanation that it wasn't there when I passed that way before, sounds very hollow indeed!

I am given another assignment. A company of the Malay Regiment is deployed among the trees some distance out in front of our position. I go alone this time and locate the company headquarters in a thatched hut. It is soon dark and there is much coming and going of patrols. The night is busy with sporadic exchanges of fire, and mortar bombs are hissing over, bursting in a random pattern among the trees. The Malay soldiers are quietly chatting among themselves. One is visibly shaken and I hear him say, "An inch or so nearer and it would have hit my head," and he shuddered. Later another remarked, "We must surely withdraw soon," and his words were borne out much later that night when the O.C. gave me the official order to return to my Battery and inform the Major that the Malay Regiment was moving back to regroup.

This meant that the Battery was now in the front line and confronting us was a battalion of the Japanese Imperial Guards Division.

Now I have a real problem. When I came out to find the Malay Regiment it had been daylight. Now it was pitch dark among the trees and I had to find my way back to the Battery lines. I tread cautiously and as quietly as I possibly can. The thought of running into a Jap patrol is very unpleasant. They have such enormous bayonets! I sense the general direction in which I should go. The fires from the docks and oil tanks are lighting the South in a lurid glow. I head in that direction. I keep my rifle and bayonet at the ready with the safety catch off and my finger on the trigger. Behind me the night is a solid black curtain. My nerves are stretched as tight as piano wire. I cannot see, but I <u>can</u> be seen. Then I hear it. A cough, and a low laugh. There is someone ahead, more than one for I hear talking. Then — amazingly I see the glow of cigarettes — I have stumbled upon the first shallow trenches of my own Battery and I pass through unchallenged, to make my way up the dark slope of the hill. Had the Japs attacked that night they would have had a target mapped out for them.

Having made my report to the O.C. I was given an hour or so to rest before finding myself on guard duty. With snores all around I sat on sand bags halfway up the hill to keep watch.

Silence had fallen over the trees through which I had so recently found my way. The sky to the south was providing a fitful red glare and silhouetting our hill, the trees atop it and myself at my post.

I did not hear the discharge of a firearm but there was a distinct "pwee-ing" above my head. First I did not believe my ears and minutes passed by and I thought I had been mistaken, but the same thing happened again and I had the uneasy feeling that someone out there in the pitch black wood had me in his sights. I continued my watch from well below the sand bags, looking out every now and again as duty required.

No matter how long the night there is no holding back the dawn, and when dawn came it found us on that same exposed hill flank facing the enemy near a crossroads on *Ayer Raja* road some miles to the west of Singapore City.

We received some rations, bully beef and hard tack biscuits of the same vintage as our Great War .303 Lee Enfield rifles.

Mortar bombs dropped on the area, widely spaced and with capricious results. Some men, three or four sitting beneath a rather gaunt tree; a shell hits the top and explodes in a scarlet flash and a cracking report. Debris showers down but no-one is hurt. Three men sit at the roadside their feet in a shallow ditch, their backs to the road. A bomb crashes down in the centre of the road behind them. They look at each other in amazement, without a scratch between them.

During the afternoon our hill flank is receiving small arms fire. Our men are firing blindly, there is no enemy visible. Our Major is somewhere in the rear. A Royal Engineers lieutenant rushes in from one side.

He shouts in a coarse voice, "What are you firing at? Stop firing! Let's fix bayonets and charge the little yellow bastards!"

We fix our small bayonets but, suddenly, the Royal Engineers lieutenant disappears, at least we didn't see him leave. Neither did we charge — there was nothing to charge at. The Japs now knew our exact position and the small arms fire ceased.

News began to circulate. Bing Worsdell of the plough boy gait and broken front teeth was dead; Shot through the head.

So was quiet Frank of the Royal Ordnance Corps. He died in the same trench.

Knocker West who was also there said that Frank's last words were, "They got me Knocker," and he died instantly.

Away to our left I witnessed the contemptible sight of men stampeding demoralised from the thicket, bringing with them news of Badgie Mather, a trumpeter who had served with me on *Pulau Belakang Mati* but who had joined the ranks as Gunner earlier than myself and had gone to an anti-tank section.

A mortar round had fallen at his feet, he had taken the full blast and fell forwards with his hands up saying, "Oh — my face!" and was gone. His face was bloody pulp. They left him where fell.

The defensive ring around Singapore is shrinking. We are to fall back, again, to consolidate!

A whole division of reinforcements had only recently arrived — the ill fated 18th Division. Some were among us, completely bewildered, with no time to get acclimatised to the enervating heat and humidity, and with no knowledge at all of the terrain.
"Which way is Singapore, mate?" one asked me plaintively.
"Fall in on the road." We leave the shallow scrapings on the yellow hillside and assemble in loose order ready to move off.

   All hell breaks loose. The area we have just vacated is deluged in a cataclysmic barrage of shell and mortar fire. The earth humps and heaves in a pulsating, flashing inferno of scarlet and yellow; hell fire that, had it descended only minutes earlier could have wiped out the whole Battery to a man.

   It is now dark. We join a mass of figures shambling along the road. I move over the crossroads. "Mucker" the junior N.C.O. who had stood in for me at the Lewis gun pit, is at my side. There is a crash and a bang. A shower of flame and white-hot particles shoots up between us and forms an umbrella shape overhead and cascades down all around. It is as if we are standing at the centre of and under a fireworks fountain.

My left foot is thrown forward by an invisible force. A mortar bomb has exploded at our feet and between us. We are unscathed, and I have had another incredible escape.

   The column is a lumbering, shuffling bedlam in the gloom. We are among strangers, a mish mash of units and parts of units. We carry our weapons at the trail.

The shapeless mass that is a soldier in front of me turns and says, " 'Ave you got your safety catch on, Mate ?" I assure him that I have. "Only, one of our blokes got shot in the arse earlier on," he volunteers. I tell him that he is perfectly safe.

   Shells are corkscrewing through the air above and to our flanks. One blasts into an oil tank at the roadside ahead. The tank is the shape and size of a gasometer. It is ablaze, illuminating the surrounding area. Around it there is a low parapet. By the time I pass it, blazing oil has flooded out and is brimming the top of the wall. I march warily by, trusting that it will not spill over and engulf both the road and the column.

   The scene changes. I am back in the control room under the hill. My eyes are rimmed, it feels, with cinders and I am bone weary from head to foot. The room is packed with various ranks of military personnel milling about in confusion. I take off my boots and find a space by a wall, stretch out on the floor and fall instantly asleep.

Somebody was kicking at the soles of my stockinged feet. I came to and looked up blearily. It was a fat colonel with a red and angry visage.

"Are you wounded ?" he snarled.

"No, sir."

"Then put yer boots on," and he strode off.

I replaced my boots and fell asleep again, to be awoken by a very little, very young, second lieutenant who had joined the Battery only recently. I got to my feet.

"We are to join a company of the Loyal Regiment," he informed me, "and there is to be a platoon sergeant." He paused then continued nervously. "I know you are senior but seniority doesn't come into this and it's going to be Lance Bombardier Ahern."

He regarded me as if to gauge my reaction, but I showed none (which proves the effectiveness of army training).

Paddy Ahern was an older soldier, whereas I was as young as the subaltern; Paddy was about 27 years old and had served in the Irish Free State army for some years. He had only recently been appointed Lance Bombardier; coming late in his service it had gone to his head and he had thrown his weight around, making himself unpopular in the process.

Uneasy about my seniority he decided to demonstrate his new authority and came to me and said, "You can smoke if you like, Badgie."

My reply was simple, "I don't smoke, Paddy," I said.

We were ordered to prepare to move off. Paddy left the room alone and mounted the stairs to the outside area. A short while later two gunners came hurrying down with Paddy supported between them. His hand was a bloodied mess with splintered bones sticking up tent-like through the shattered flesh.

"Snipers!" one of the gunners said. "Paddy said it was a sniper!"

A buzz ran round the chamber. However, it was quickly evident that the wound was self inflicted. Paddy had placed his right hand over the muzzle of his rifle and pulled the trigger with his left. An examination of the rifle confirmed this.

He was hustled away to Alexandra Military Hospital and was never seen again. Now a rather shame-faced subaltern had to come back to me and inform me that I was now the Platoon Sergeant.

In our new role as infantry, completely untrained and unsuited, we marched off to Gilman Barracks where we had swum so often in the outdoor pool in happier days, and there we were quartered for an hour or two in an empty canteen building.

Casualty after casualty was being brought in bandaged and bloody on stretchers. We were witnessing the real, raw side of war. The infantry officer apologised to our second lieutenant saying, "I hope this isn't upsetting your men!" It was certainly not cheering us up.

We moved to a place just south of Alexandra Military Hospital. The enemy was very close now, and pressing their assault.

Gunner "Topper" Brown received a small shrapnel wound to one shoulder. He stood grinning happily at me, waiting to be taken to the hospital, and waved cheerfully as he was led off by a medical orderly.

"So long," he called, "I'm out of it now," and off he went, to his destiny.

The advancing Japanese stormed the hospital and in a wild blood lust perpetrated wholesale murder. Walking patients were taken outside and shot. Others were bayoneted in their beds.
Bursting into the operating theatre, they bayoneted the surgeons and the patient on the table. One of the staff miraculously survived to tell the tale.

The freedom of operations enjoyed by the Japs on Singapore island was displayed most obviously by the spectacle of an old-fashioned observation balloon floating completely unmolested above the battlefield to the north. There were no planes to shoot it down, none of our ground troops were now near enough to bring small arms fire to bear, and I saw no anti-aircraft fire directed towards it. The silvery sphere with its wicker basket suspended beneath it seemed to mock us contemptuously.

From the area by Alexandra Hospital we withdrew, once more reducing the circle of defence around the city. Our field artillery was already on the shore and firing over the rooftops. There was nowhere else left for them to retreat to.

The sky was full of low-flying aircraft, machine gunning at will everything and anything that moved. Came the roar of an aero

engine flying directly towards us at tree top height. Nearby was a small trench, dug in a T shape with three shallow sections and one deep one at the junction of the T. Three of us dived for the trench. We all squeezed in but I was last and the shape allowed only two to get their heads down below ground level. There was room at the deep part for my feet and legs but no room for me to bend down. The plane roared overhead with the crimson disc of the Rising Sun gleaming on its wing tips. I felt a sudden rush of rage and blazed away at it. This was against orders which said we must not fire on enemy aircraft for fear of giving our position away.
To me the order seemed as stupid then as it still seems daft today.

On the road again, an untidy ragged column. Time and time again leaping to the side for cover as the relentless fighters ripped up the road with their fire.

The little subaltern was stumbling along under a huge cylindrical bundle. I peered into his face and asked, "What's that you're carrying, Sir?"
He was all-in drenched with sweat from head to foot, scarlet faced and panting.
"It's the Major's kit and bedroll," he gasped. I was angry.
"<u>You</u> shouldn't be carrying that," I said, and taking it from him hurled it into the undergrowth at the roadside. He said nothing.

The planes were on us again.
"My God, this is murder," he wailed. "Why doesn't somebody stop it?" His nerves had cracked completely.

We passed a large fuel dump and marched on for another mile or so. This was where we were to make a stand. A stretch of open ground, a few scattered trees, a ruined building or so and a very small copse. It was well into the afternoon by now.
I deployed my makeshift platoon about the area and selected a spot from which I could watch for the advancing Japanese. Then came a summons to attend an orders group in the copse, which was no more than a ring of scrubby bushes with a thin tree or two forming a rough circle about a bare centre.

Assembled within the ring a dozen or so of us awaited instructions.

A Regimental Quartermaster Sergeant came and counted heads then went away.

At my side, on my left and very close sat a Bombardier, a Scot who had joined the Battery very recently. Normally a pleasant, generous man he had complained to the RQMS before his departure.
"I'm an artillery man," he'd said bitterly, "not an infanteer."
The RQMS had looked at him but left without saying anything.

I was lying on my stomach on the ground. To the other side of me was a wire netting enclosure in which was one small pig. Idly I picked up a pebble and flicked it lightly at the animal. No sooner had I done it than I thought, "That wasn't very nice. How would I like it if somebody did that to me?" At that very instant in the twigs above my head a mortar round burst with an ear-shattering explosion. I felt the blast, like a giant hand, flatten me into the dirt.

A soft gasp came from the Bombardier and he fell forward without toppling over. I looked at him. He was dead. A small piece of shrapnel had pierced his right temple leaving a tiny hole that did not even bleed. He remained in a sitting posture, leaning forward, his trunk between his raised knees.

I tried to move but found I could do so only above the waist. Looking over my shoulder I saw behind my right hip a rent in my trousers, which were flooding with blood.

Once again I had had a narrow escape, but far from his native mountains and glens our Scottish soldier had made his rendezvous with Death.

The RQMS returned bringing with him a bucketful of tea. He glanced at the still figure which resembled a tired man leaning forward in an attitude of rest then made a sarcastic and callous remark, "That's the corporal who said he was not an infanteer then, is it?" He made no attempt to hide the gloating in his voice; and I hated him for it.

The young medical officer attached to the company made his appearance on the scene and made a rapid examination of the casualties among us. After a brief glance at my bloodied trousers he proclaimed it a flesh wound.

That "flesh wound" was to cause many years of pain and difficulty, culminating in six surgical operations of which four were replacement joints; and six dislocations occurred following the next-to-last replacement done in a London hospital by an eminent surgeon.

After a field dressing was applied to the wound I was tossed into the back of a small truck, becoming one of a heap of bodies. We sped away along a rough track with artillery shells straddling it on the way.

Beside me I found "Oppo" Hill. He looked at me excitedly. He had a slight flesh wound to one shoulder. His eyes were blazing.

"How many did <u>you</u> get Badgie?" he asked. "I got <u>three</u>," he was beside himself, "and they don't half scream when they're hit, don't they". "How many did you get?" Grudgingly I had to admit that I hadn't got any.

The truck stopped. I was carried on a stretcher into the Victoria Hall opposite St.Andrew's cathedral. Once a theatre it was now a casualty centre. As we entered there came the scream of bombs and the thunder of detonations. The old building shook to its foundations and my stretcher was dropped unceremoniously to the floor of the foyer as the bearers fled to cover. I felt very vulnerable left there on my own. The noise ceased and the orderlies returned. They took away my helmet, rifle and ammunition. I had two cloth bandoliers crossed on my chest and two more about my waist. I was determined not to run out of ammunition!

"Cor," remarked one of the orderlies as he removed the bandoliers, "I can see you didn't intend to give up without a fight!" He tossed a packet of cigarettes on to my chest. My trousers and underpants were swiftly cut away with a sharp pair of scissors and I was carried upstairs in the main part of the building.

It was February 15th, 1942.

At that time, of course, I did not know, but the surrender of the British garrison had already been signed at *Bukit Timah* in an office at the Ford motor works. General Percival and his aide, under the Union Jack and carrying a white flag of truce, had gone to end one of the greatest disasters of British military history. We all keenly felt the awful disgrace of it. Word of the ceasefire was going out to all units, too late to spare the life of the Scottish Bombardier and so many others like him.

The casualty station was dark, crowded and noisome, like pictures I had seen of the hospital at *Scutari* in the Crimean War. The din of battle had died away outside. A bed was found for me, jammed among many others. Now that all was quiet my youth, optimism and stupidity led me to believe, or at least hope, that the <u>Japanese</u> had surrendered. So steeped was I in the belief of the invincibility of British arms. "There's a breathless hush in the close tonight …." Such heroic poetry had as effectively brainwashed my generation of schoolboys as had Hitler's the Nazi Youth Movement.

Water was short. I felt desperately thirsty from loss of blood, and was in great pain now that the numbness of the wounding had worn off. An orderly passed among the beds with a small oil lamp. I begged him for a drink of water. He said "OK mate," but went off and did not return. The night dragged on to the accompaniment of groans and the occasional cry of pain from the wounded.

There was a Florence Nightingale among us, making the place seem even more like *Scutari* She made the rounds, stopping to give a word of comfort everywhere. She came to my bed, a little old lady in a nurse's uniform. "Do you have to lie like that ?" she asked. I explained as delicately as possible why I was not lying on my back. "Ah, well then," she murmured, "that will be much more comfortable for you!" She went away and I did not see her again. I have often wondered through the years what happened to that dear, courageous little woman.

A small, angry red swelling appeared on my right forearm and I saw that a fragment of shrapnel was lodged just below the surface and was beginning to fester. My haversack had been left with me, so I got my jack knife and used the spike to prize the tiny piece of metal out. The small wound healed rapidly.

Some days later a large piece of metal emerged from the oozing hip wound. It was about a quarter of an inch thick and was square in shape with sides about two inches long. An orderly handed it to me with the words, "Here's a souvenir for you", I returned it. "No thanks," I replied. "I've had enough of that," as I gave it back. I later wished I'd kept it. What I was not to learn until thirty years later was that a small splinter, about three quarters of an inch long and about an eighth of an inch in cross-section had been blasted into the head of the femur from behind and would cause all the trouble of later years.

Some days passed and a Japanese officer came to inspect the ward, perhaps to check that all the casualties were genuine. His party stopped at my bed and seeing me apparently uninjured, my wound being covered, asked why I was there. The British M.O. made a guess. He put a hand to my forehead and announced, "Malaria".

"Ah so. Mararia-*kah*?" said the Jap, and the party moved on. "Oh no." I thought, "not malaria too. I've got quite enough to contend with without that!" I <u>was</u> burning up with a temperature but I soon realised why the M.O. said what he did. After all there were so many cases and he could only have had time to see a small proportion of them, and had made a guess at my case.

Following that visit an order came to evacuate all the wounded to Changi barracks, the large military complex at the east end of the island. An Army Medical Corps ambulance gave me a jolting and painful ride over the fifteen or so miles. The ambulance stopped and I was lifted out and set down near a cross roads.

"Your mob is over there, mate" one of the orderlies informed me, pointing to a barrack block in the distance. The ambulance sped away and I was left standing, trouserless, at the road side.

I waited, wondering what to do next. I felt as I felt as a child in dreams in which I found myself on the way to school trouserless. But this was no dream. This was the beginning of a new life, life as a prisoner of war, and not an ordinary prisoner of war but of the Japanese; the Japanese who did not follow the Geneva Convention. The Japanese to whom we were disgraced soldiers by virtue of the surrender. The Japanese whose mindless vicious cruelties we would experience to the full in due course.

Help came to me in the form of a burly Irish T.S.M. and friend, both from a different battery of my own regiment. Seeing me standing there, helpless, in only a shirt, socks and boots, they put my arms about their shoulders, one on either side.

"Let's get dis poor little bogger to the lines," and with their arms about my waist I was swept along between them.

My soul possessions for this new start amounted to very little . Other than the items already mentioned I had only my haversack containing shaving gear, Army Book 64 part one and two, and a sepia photograph of *Sumini* and me which had been taken at a studio in the New World amusement park in happier times. *Sumini* seated, with a solemn expression on her lovely face — as she thought befitting such an occasion. I standing beside her, looking very happy, as well I might, dressed, of course in uniform, but hatless (at her request). I treasured that portrait until sweat and jungle dampness had turned it into a faded brown mist.

I was among friends again in the large barrack block which housed my unit. There were no beds, lockers or metal objects. All had been removed for the Japanese war effort. There was no furniture of any kind but there were palliasses, straw-filled. Somebody found me a pair of shorts and a palliasse. But I was a late-comer. There was little straw left and my palliasse was very thin indeed — in fact, it was wafer thin. At night when all around me were sleeping, I lay on my wafer-thin mattress on the floor in great discomfort. The pain from the wound was excruciating and seemed more so at night. One night, unable to rest I dragged myself out onto the veranda and looked over the parapet. A huge moon was flooding the square below with silver light, as bright as day. I felt a strong urge to throw myself over and end the misery. Then came the thought, "What if I wasn't killed, but badly injured, crippled even!" Then I remembered my parents at home. The blow to my poor mother who already had three other sons in the war. And *Sumini*. I <u>must</u> get back to her. No more thought of ending it all, but in its place came the determination that come what may I <u>would</u> stick it out to the end.

Soon I was able, using a broom as a crutch, to hop to the nearby medical centre that the RAMC had set up. Here my dressings were changed regularly and the wound began to heal. In the process of healing a tongue of flesh grew and protruded from the wound like a real, very pink tongue of the sort stuck out by cheeky boys. Proud flesh the MO called it, and burnt it away using copper sulphate.

It was good to be among old friends and acquaintances. Tom Williams found me. I asked him what had become of our old "shipmate", Leslie Bills.
"Nobody knows," Tom said. "Les Bills was never seen after we left *Belakang Mati*. Nobody saw the going of him."
What had happened to that likeable man? With his swarthy appearance, speaking some Malay, resourceful and handy with small boats, perhaps he had sailed off to one of the countless small islands of the *Riau* Archipelago to the south of Singapore. Many had landed on those small islands in attempts at escape.

Most, including nurses, had perished at the hands of Japanese murder squads sent to seek them out. The fate of that good friend is, and will always be a mystery to me but he remains for ever young and smiling in my memories of those happy voyages we made over sunlit seas in our little canoe.

Life in Changi Barracks was somehow surreal. For a while we were left alone by the Japs. A concert party was formed and good shows were put on in an open air theatre made for the purpose . Societies were organised for various hobbyists. Daily parades were held, which gave some semblance of normality. But the real world was still there outside.

In the real world the Japanese, as an example to us all, shot twenty-one soldiers. All had been rounded up from their hideaways in the city. British officers attended to witness the execution. One defiant private was reported to have shouted, "Tell the folks back home that I never bowed down to the little yellow bastards!" before the fusillade rang out.

A movie film for propaganda purposes, and photographs, had the PoWs lining each side of a road while a cavalcade of Jap VIPs and military drove slowly through in limousines. Our humiliation was to be put on display to the world!

Singapore was renamed *Shonan To,* sometimes the spelling *Syonan To* was used. The "The Lion City" had been shorn like a lamb.

Deprived of electricity, running water and most of the amenities of civilised living, the ingenuity that became such a vital element of our survival, began to appear. Salt was obtained by evaporating sea water exposed to the hot sun, in *kualis* (an iron vessel shaped like a wok).

Light was provided by oil lamps made from small tins with coconut oil as fuel and string for wicks . And every heavy rain shower found lines of naked men standing under the overflow from barrack roofs. The only way to take a bath!

Demands began to come for daily working parties to go into the city. These became popular because of the cigarettes, bread rolls and tinned foods that could be bought there. Men had been reduced to smoking the dried leaves of the Japanese cherry trees that grew about the area. So the opportunities afforded by such outings insured there was no shortage of volunteers. We were already very hungry.

We <u>were</u> hungry. Time is at best an imponderable quantity. More so to a PoW. We knew our imprisonment had begun; there was no way of foreseeing when it would end. There appeared no end in sight. There was no fixed term to serve and no remission of sentence available. This fact alone weighs heavily upon the human psyche.

We were <u>hungry</u>. We were <u>very</u> hungry. Our daily fare was rice, and very little else. The morning meal was a ration of rice (about a pint mug measure); just that, plain, boiled rice, and a mug of tea. Lunch was rice with a watery, meatless soup, the contents of which mostly disappeared when poured over the rice. The teatime meal was the same as the lunch time one. No wonder we were hungry. An unpleasant condition which remained with us constantly through the years of captivity.

Weeks passed. The world outside was now a closed book. Men began to long for a word from home. Something to let us know that our people were aware that we were alive. And when could we write home? When indeed? Some months were to pass before it was permitted to write a letter. This was to be of twenty words on one small square of paper. These were taken away, ostensibly to be censored. But were never seen again, in fact, were never sent. In later years, on two occasions, we were given printed cards to fill in. These had boxes to tick against items that read; I am well; I am sick; I am in a sanatorium; I am working for pay; and there was a small space towards the bottom of the card for a few words.

The Japanese did not permit the exchange of letters and receipt of parcels as was the right of PoWs in all the other countries. They made exceptions on only very few occasions. Two brief letters reached me in the jungle during the rest of the war. One was from my father. The other was from a penfriend of boyhood days, and to whom I became engaged for a short while after release from captivity. As well as these unwarranted deprivations the Japanese provided no clothing, no bedding, no mosquito nets and no furniture of any kind. I must add, also, that the two letters already mentioned were over two years old when I got them.

We were accepting and adapting to this harsh new existence. The rice diet had already claimed its first victim. Busty Knight our cinema operator and swimming *pagar* orderly, who had spent so many hours on that sunny beach, and had saved so diligently for his future, died raving about the row of shops he would open when he got home. Dysentery is no respecter of ambition. If there is any consolation to be found in this death so early in the game, it is that he was at least spared the horrors and hardships that were to be the lot of those of us left behind.

People are remembered, often for little inconsequential things. The old song "Oh, Mr.Porter," always brings Busty to my mind. He had his own version of it and I can see him still, a mug of tea in his hand, a sweat towel about his neck, singing, "Put me on the next train, quickly as you can. Oh, Mr.Porter what a sloppy bitch I am!"

I was now able to limp around the area quite well and found my way down to a small cluster of Malay huts near the sea shore. The Malays were very friendly despite the great change in circumstances. In Singapore city every house had the red and white Rising Sun flag poking out of the upstairs window. Here I saw none. Life, for the time being, anyway, was going on unchanged. One elderly man told me that he would not change his allegiance, for, he said, "We have eaten British rice, and they have never disturbed us."
"For over 100 years," I ventured.
Gently he corrected me. "For one hundred and twenty-three years." He paused, "And the British will come back."

I became friendly with a younger man and soon felt confident to ask him if he would take a message to *Geylang Serai* to let *Sumini* know that I was still alive, and to find out how she fared. He readily agreed. I told him the address, Number 699 Q, and described the house with its clump of palm trees.

Some days later I saw him again when he had accomplished his mission.
"I would have found the house more easily," he explained, "if you had told me that her brother was in the Malay regiment. I know him well."

Sumini and all members of the family were unharmed and had food.
"I told them you were *tempang* (lame)," he said, "They were very sorry, and worried for you ." There was no other message. This is understandable . Communication with a British soldier would have been very dangerous for them. In various places around Singapore the heads of Chinese had been hoisted on poles. There was no mistaking the message, nor was there any possible doubt as to who was master here.

One day my friend Joe said that he had volunteered to go on a working party. Not one of the daily ones, but as part of a detachment that would be working in the city area from a new camp. I was sorry to lose his companionship but his reason for going was the possibility of finding more food and cigarettes. A long time was to elapse and conditions would be very different before we were to meet again.

In the meantime my wound had healed and I was walking quite well, with only a slight limp. Now many working parties were being called for and men had to be detailed to fill them. Inevitably my turn came, and the change alone seemed welcome. After weeks of confinement it would be good to see something of the outside world.

While waiting to leave on the transport provided I was approached by the RQMS who had previously been our BSM. An old regular soldier, he had been a German PoW in the first world war. He said that he did not remember much about it, but added that "It wasn't like this!" He gave me money and asked if I would try to buy some bread while I was in town.

I was able to buy a number of long, fresh crusty rolls. They smelled heavenly. The nearly forgotten fragrance tormenting my senses beyond constraint. My control snapped. I ate one — It tasted delicious, delectable, delightful, pleasant, pleasing, palatable. Utterly, absolutely, irresistible. I was lost. I wolfed another. Standing in the back of the truck on our way back to Changi, I ate another, and another. I had destroyed at least six of those tempting morsels by the time I had myself under control again. The bag was only half as full as when I started, but RQMS J.Congdon was delighted when I handed it over to him, and I assured him that I had already eaten my reward.

While out on a working party I had a graphic example of Japanese brutality. I witnessed a soldier punishing an aged Chinese woman and a young Indian boy. Caught trading with PoWs they were being forced to do press-ups. While they were struggling to do this he walked from one to the other beating them on the buttocks with a spade. The little boy's arms were trembling uncontrollably and his cotton shorts were blood soaked. The pathetic old woman could not manage the press-ups at all but lay there moaning piteously as the young thug rained blows on her. I felt sickened by the sight and felt terribly angry and ashamed that I could do absolutely nothing about it.

One trait in the Japanese character was impossible to comprehend. It was their utter unpredictability. One day trading would be severely punished. Another it could be tolerated, or even encouraged. It varied from individual to individual, and sometimes the same guard could act both ways inside an hour.

Work on these parties was always hard labour. Some days we toiled all day long, moving full 40 gallon drums of oil down on the docks. Once we were put to clearing a bombed-out shop of sacks of lime. Lime covered the floor an inch deep where it had spilled from burst sacks. The atmosphere in the shop was soon a dense fog which burnt the eyes and skin, and coated our sweating bodies in a thick layer of white.

Some of the work party had "rescued" small items that were lying around, such as safety razors and packets of blades. Useful items of barter. We were unfortunate in having a particularly nasty guard that day. He lined us up on the pavement, searched us none to gently, and heartily enjoyed himself by energetically beating up anyone he found with anything in their pockets. I had "won" a safety razor which I had craftily hidden in one of my socks. He didn't find it, so I didn't get bashed! I'd had some luck for once.

On one of these working parties I found myself quite by chance at the big, old wooden cinema where I used to go to watch films with *Sumini*. Some baulks of timber were being collected from the rear of the building. The place was very nostalgic for me, for it held so many happy memories.

The vehicle was loaded and we drove away. It was an open truck and I was sitting in a corner at the back. Opposite me sat the Jap guard with his rifle and bayonet. Suddenly I had the surprise of my life. I was stupefied. There, walking on the pavement were two figures, *Sumini* and her sister, *Supiah*. My heart flipped a somersault. I froze for an instant, then I waved frantically. *Sumini* glanced quickly at her sister. She had recognised me! There was the brief wave of her small hand, then distance swallowed her up, and I could see her no more.

This was my last sight of *Sumini*. I was never to see her again. But I would hear of her, not once but twice more.

The guard had seen me wave. He looked from me to the two girls, then back at me. Apart from a look of puzzlement and momentary frown, he said and did nothing.

On another occasion the day's work was at a railway goods yard by the docks. It was the usual sweltering, steamy Singapore day, and time for a brief midday break. Present were Indian troops who had transferred their allegiance to the Japanese as part of Chandra Bose's army, whose object was the overthrow of the British Raj. On the front of their British uniforms they were wearing the small red and white symbol of the Rising Sun.

They lay around the railway yard in patches of shade, out of the midday sun. With no warning of any kind there came the clank and rattle of shunted box cars, immediately followed by a blood-curdling scream and loud shouts. Showing no common sense whatsoever, some had actually lain between and under the wagons.

One man, his face a mask of pain and misery, lay on his side beside the track. One buttock had been pinched off cleanly between rail and wheel. Another moaned nearby, his trunk rolling in agony from side to side, his legs and feet stretched out unmoving in front of him, joined to his torso by two ribbons of skin.

It was a gruesome sight but I was unmoved by it. The sight of the Rising Sun on British uniforms and the knowledge that Indian troops had treacherously murdered their British officers on Christmas Island (an outstation of our Regiment) rendered me impervious to pity.

Changi Barracks had become a labour pool, and it was being drained. My turn to leave came when a large exodus of PoWs was ordered for a march to new camps and my name was on the list.

I said goodbye to RQMS Congdon, a man who had shown me kindness and consideration and who had been instrumental in getting me my first stripe, an appointment that had been opposed by others on the grounds that I was too young.

I never saw him again and later I learned that he had died on one of the death marches in Borneo. A sad and miserable end to a decent man, who, but for the war, would by now have been retired with a pension.

We set off on the march early one morning with our belongings on our backs. I now owned more than I had started with, but it was still a very light load.

The march turned out to be 17 miles, and the guards did not bother us much. There were few of them and they had to cover the same distance as the rest of us!

All along the route the locals would talk with us and pass small presents of food and drink. There was obviously a lot of goodwill towards us.

A sad sight en route came as we passed Changi prison. The grim building, so reminiscent of a Hollywood gangster movie, housed women and children internees, and at every window that could be seen above the encircling wall, handkerchiefs waved. It was deeply moving and many a man's eye blinked back tears as we marched past.

Farther along the route, as we entered the city area there was a military checkpoint. In front of a sentry box a Japanese soldier stood, his bayonet tip reaching well up over his head. Natives were shuffling past in an orderly queue (a phenomenon never seen before in Singapore city). As they came abreast of the sentry each stopped and bowed low; all the rich mixture of races that formed the population; men, women and children.

The British had never demanded this, and it showed quite plainly the place of the common people in the much vaunted Greater East Asia Co-prosperity Sphere. The Sphere that was to brutalise, ravage and kill countless thousands throughout the Far East; that would drain the countries of all commodities useful to the homeland and war effort, and would wreck economies by issuing worthless notes of Japanese scrip, printed wherever needed, and not one with a serial number.

The populace had already found they had a tiger in their midst!

Towards the end of the afternoon we traipsed footsore into our new quarters which were situated in Havelock Road, to the west of the city, on flat, marshy ground set well back behind a row of tall buildings and a high wooden fence.

The rows of palm-thatch huts had been built by the British to accommodate bombed out families. The huts had earth floors and a central aisle with two tiers of sleeping platforms on either side. A small wooden ladder connected lower to higher platform at intervals along the hut.

Our hut was L6, the L standing for labour . Other huts had an MT designation and were for drivers and mechanics. We had half a metre of bed space allotted to each man. This meant that each was crushed against his neighbour and, as is usual in such circumstances a joke was made of it. Seven wags lay side by side on the planking. One at the end would shout, "Turn," and all would turn over in unison — causing great amusement.

Naturally, ingenuity came to the fore and in no time at all modifications were being made to afford more living space. The camp guards never interfered with such arrangements.

Being among the first to enter the hut, I joined up with three others and we set about scrounging odd bits of timber from around the area and using it to build four bunk beds, crude but effective, which reached up to under the roof from the lower shelf level. We had "bagged" the end of the hut adjacent to the entrance and it made for a light and convenient position. The pooling of four bed spaces left us with enough floor for a living area, and for this we made a small table.

As part of our settling in, and because no outside working party had as yet been called for, our officers decided we should be kept fully occupied and in addition to work about the camp one thought we should do P.T.

There followed a session under a young lieutenant during which a burly and truculent cockney expressed his displeasure to the officer, who had upbraided him for slacking, in no uncertain terms. Such a thing had never happened to him before and the lieutenant, crimson-faced, did not know what to do about it. The squad was hurriedly dismissed and no further sessions ensued!

A shout of "Fight! Fight!" would fly around the camp with the speed of a bush fire and men would stampede from all corners to watch the "entertainment".

This sort of spectacle soon disappeared as the first symptoms of malnutrition made their appearance among us.

A very painful and unpleasant condition became prevalent . It affected the scrotum, which became inflamed and as fiery red as a baboon's buttocks. Treatment was given after work each day in front of a small hut which served as a medical centre. The afflicted would form a long queue between the huts, moving forwards slowly towards the medical orderly, where shorts were dropped and a liquid from a bottle was applied by paint brush to the afflicted area. The result was astonishing. With "ooh — aah — ooh — aah — aah!" The patient would dash away with a strange bandy, leaping gait, to the great amusement of the queue.

When my turn came I quickly learned what made the men's eyes water and why they rushed off to a quiet corner to fan themselves.

The pain was excruciating, an unbearable stinging sensation. But the treatment worked — eventually!

One member of our little group was Sergeant Frankie Bowler. He was called Frankie by all, and was a regular soldier whose family had been living in married quarters and who had been evacuated quite late in the day. Frankie did not know whether they had reached safety or not. But I found out after the war that they had.

Frank stood about six feet tall and was a big man who possessed a great sense of humour. He was quite irrepressible and it seemed that nothing could get him down, but it did, eventually, as I shall relate later. Coming from the same home town we shared a lot in common.

"*Otaki and Co*" came into our lives at this time.

Sojiro Otaki, private first class with three little yellow stars on a red collar tab, was in charge of us and a squad of four, two-star privates.

The myth of all orientals looking alike could not stand up when compared with this group of individuals;

IVKA   HARADA   OTAKI   YAMADA   KAWASAKI

Otaki: was (he told me) an ex boy-scout, and proud of it. Short in stature (as were
the rest) he was neat and intelligent, and knew a little English.
Harada: fastidiously neat (among the neatest men I ever knew), he was quietly spoken, and of a gentle, kindly disposition, in short a complete contrast to the usual Japanese male.
Ivka: a little less neat, almost an individual (a rare trait among his race), he had a bit of a "bolshy" streak and a quirky sense of humour. It was possible to quite like him!

Kawasaki: couldn't look neat if he tried. The most taciturn of the squad, squat, burly, scowling, completely without a sense of humour, with a heavy blue-black shadow on his jowls. He seemed isolated from the world around him.

Yamada: a shapeless shrimp, a small heap of a being, he resembled Dopey of the Seven Dwarfs. Harmless, seeming to be without intellect, the other Japs treated him almost like a buffoon. So did we — when we got to know him. As we soon did!

It was *Otaki's* task to teach us basic footdrill in Japanese, and we were paraded outside the hut for instruction.

Our tutors were as uncertain of us as we were of them, and the relationship between us was very different to the one that was to develop between PoW and guard during our imprisonment later on.

We were given demonstrations and practice in the commands for all movements such as Attention ! Stand at ease ! Quick march ! and so on, and were taught the numbers from one upwards. "*Bangol*" was the order to number.

The number for seventeen is, in Japanese, "*ju sijit*". This sounds, quite like a crude
expression widely in use among troops and proved irresistible to Frankie Bowler. He
made sure that he occupied the position of number seventeen in the front rank. The order, "*Bangol!*" was given and the parade numbered off from the right. *Otaki* moved along the rank, prompting a response where necessary. There was no need to prompt Frankie. When his turn came he flung back his head, and with all the power of his lungs, shouted, "**Joo sheet**?" The parade erupted in laughter, in which the Japs joined — but not for the same reason!

We marched out to work daily to an area of filled ground about three miles away. *Otaki's* squad escorted us with fixed bayonets; and we whistled stirring military airs as we swung along. "Colonel Bogey" was a regular favourite. There is a very vulgar verse to it, as every soldier knows, and it served as a gesture of defiance. It became famous after the war in the film "The Bridge on the River Kwai", a film that ex-PoW survivors found insulting.

The work was manual, digging drains, mixing concrete and labour of various kinds connected with the erection of a number of large brick buildings. We were kept at it all day except for a half-hour break (*yasume*) at noon. The working "week" was of ten days. The eleventh day was spent in camp, when any necessary work was done. One very unpleasant camp chore was the removal of latrine buckets. Like most of Singapore the sanitary arrangements were very primitive: the use and collection of ordure containers. These revolting, full-to-the-brim oval buckets were carried, with their liquid filth slopping over the sides, to the camp gate where Chinese coolies took it away for use on farms and smallholdings. Untreated sewage was a valuable fertiliser! I am eternally grateful that I never had to perform this odious task.

It was in Havelock Road camp that we were given the small piece of paper to write our twenty words home on. The ones that never got away! At about the same time, all personnel were assembled for an address by a British colonel. He stood on a small dais and told us of an infamous event that had recently taken place in Changi, and is known as the *Selarang* Barracks Atrocity. All PoWs had been ordered to sign a parole in which a promise was made not to attempt to escape. This is, of course, contrary to International Rules of War, but these meant nothing to the Japanese, anyway. The order was refused, and in order to enforce it all prisoners were made to assemble on the barracks square. They were surrounded by machine guns and armed guards and were kept out in the sun all day without food or drink. Latrines were dug in the square itself. The seriously sick, many with dysentery and other infectious diseases, were crushed in among the 14,000 men sweltering there. Hour after hour elapsed with the risk of an epidemic growing greater all the time. In the end, in the name of humanity, the senior British officer ordered all ranks to sign, while making it clear to the Japanese that it was being done under duress.

The Colonel explained all this to us and finished by saying, "I therefore order you all to sign". We queued up to sign the worthless scrap of paper.

While work was going on one day, an unusual sight arrived among us in the form of a skinny Chinese man on an old-fashioned ice cream tricycle with its box-like container at the front. He was so slightly built, and the machine so heavy, that he was having to stand on the pedals to ride it. A guard signalled for him to stop, which he did and was immediately surrounded by a number of Japanese soldiers, all of whom demanded ice cream. The little man, pleased at such a crowd of customers, served as quickly as he could, beaming as he did so. As soon as the last man was served the whole lot turned away at once and left, laughing, without paying. The vendor's smile dissolved into misery. I felt very sorry for him, and angry but, as usual helpless. There was nothing I could do about it. Or was there? Yes, there was!

From then on each time I passed *Otaki* I pretended to hold a conversation with my companion.

Speaking slowly and loudly so that *Otaki* must hear, I said, "No good! No good! Japan soldier take ice cream. No pay."

On the next pass I continued, "Chinese man go home . Wife say, where money? Chinese man say, No money! Wife, baby no food, very hungry!"

I went on in that vein. At first *Otaki* gave a weak, embarrassed grin, but suddenly my barbs must have struck home. He stopped abruptly in front of me, halting me in my tracks. Arms akimbo, feet astride. Suddenly, without warning he landed a stinging blow to my face, to be immediately followed by another to the other side.

Rage flooded me. An instant, and furious storm. How I managed to stop myself hitting back I shall never know. My fists clenched convulsively at my sides and I fought to keep them there. The penalty for striking a Japanese soldier was death. *Otaki* was not worth it!

I could not disguise my rage though. I felt my eyes narrow to slits of hate. Something in my expression must have affected my assailant for he did not hit me again.

Instead he snarled angrily, "You — see — me — take — ice cream?"

"No," I replied, " but you number one soldier here. You no stop Japan soldier take ice cream. No make pay. You boy scout. This bad! This very bad!"

Otaki seethed and was embarrassed but made no more attempts to hit me. We were never on good terms again.

Ivka had seen what had happened. He had not been among those who stole the ice creams. He had admired my stand against *Otaki* and urged me to report him to a Japanese officer. I don't think *Ivka* liked *Otaki*!

Such a report would have been a waste of time and could have earned me a far more severe beating.

The area in which we worked was large and close supervision of so many men was difficult. It was relatively easy for me to slip away now and again to a nearby cluster of neat wooden bungalows which had been provided for families of Harbour Board employees.

It was there I met *'Kak Yam,* a pleasant Malay woman in her mid-thirties who lived in one of the bungalows. She asked me if I spoke Malay. I did.

"Do you know Tuan Fitton? Is he in your camp?"

I did not know, but it was possible that he could be.

"Will you try to find him, and give him this?" She showed me a screw-top jar which contained curried chicken. I agreed to try and smuggle the food back into camp later that day.

There was a difficult moment during the afternoon when I had to pass a small group of Japanese soldiers on a narrow wooden bridge. I had tucked the jar into my armpit but it was spotted.

"*Sore wa nan desu ka?*" (What is that?) one demanded.

I held it out boldly for inspection, and shrugged as if I really didn't know.

One peered at the jar then, contemptuously, he said, "*Sukanar China!*" (Chinese fish) and I was allowed to pass on.

I asked around the camp for someone called Fitton and found out that he was a Private Fitton of the local volunteer forces and was held in the nearby camp of River Valley Road. It was very close to our camp but was better situated. One side of it bordered the road, and locals traded fairly freely through the fence, keeping a lookout for guards, of course, as they did so.

I therefore had to eat the chicken curry myself.

It was delicious!

More and more time was spent at *'Kak Yam's* house. One morning I met her mother who looked to be very old and shrunken but who was probably only in her fifties.

When *'Kak Yam* introduced us to each other the old lady tried some English.

"This morning, John," she said as we shook hands. She meant of course "Good morning," and had probably used up her entire vocabulary.

'Kak Yam seemed embarrassed by the slip and hastily said, "He speaks good Malay,

'Mak."

Her mother handled the situation gracefully and with unruffled aplomb said, "Ah, well in that case it makes it easier for us all!"

Another day I met *'Kak's* daughter, a laughing slender girl, already some years married. We chatted amiably for a while, then with conspiratorial giggles the two women produced a white canvas kit bag and began packing it with articles of clothing. When it was filled to bursting point I helped tie the neck, which they seemed unable to do.

" It's for you," they chorused, bursting into another fit of chuckles at my surprised expression.

They saw me out of the front door hardly able to contain their mirth. I was able to rejoin the working party undetected and hid the bag in a corner until the time came to leave.

As we marched past the bungalows on the way back to camp *'Kak Yam* and daughter, who had obviously been waiting for this moment and were standing in front of the house, spotted me striding boldly along with bulging kit bag on my shoulder.

'Kak gave a vigorous wave and the girl gave a shriek of laughter and jumped up and down like a child, clapping her hands in joy.

At the camp gate, instead of being allowed straight through as we usually were, the Taiwanese guard halted the column and moved down checking each four men as he passed. As he came closer I eased the kit bag off my shoulder and set it down by my left foot, inching it round to hide it better as he approached. The suspense was almost unbearable. He was practically breathing in my right ear. I looked him right in the eye. He didn't look down and passed on. I breathed again. The column was allowed to march off.

During my visits to the bungalow I had many interesting conversations with *'Kak*. She did not approve of my relationship with *Sumini* and said that it was wicked of *Sumini's* mother to allow it. *'Kak* of course was well provided for with a husband and family and could not really appreciate *Sumini's* situation. But we agreed to differ and remained good friends. *'Kak* had worked for a European family who had treated her well and more as a friend than a servant. It was how she had come to know Tuan Fitton, and was perhaps the reason she was so kind to me.

Came the day, the inevitable day when my frequent absences from the working party became noticed. I was hurrying back from the bungalow when I met the little sergeant-major with his waxed Kaiser

Bill moustache. He was the senior rank in L6 hut, and had been attached to a local volunteer company as a permanent staff instructor. No taller than a Japanese he had sandy colouring, generous pink ears and prominent very pale blue eyes. Of a nervous disposition he bent over backwards to keep *Otaki* amused, and he did this by twirling the waxed spikes of his moustache (a feature the Japs found fascinating) and rolling his watery blue eyes. One day *Otaki* tired of him and pushed him contemptuously to one side. The "twiddle" had lost its magic.

He regarded me worriedly, "Where've you bin?" he queried. "*Otaki's* bin looking for you."

I had to think quickly. I did not want to give *Otaki* an excuse for another bashing. I had a brainwave! Unlike most men on these details I always wore a shirt and slacks. This was because I was aware of the offence that the unclothed body in public gives to Muslim people, and I was therefore always decently dressed when I visited. '*Kak Yam.*

This then was my idea; I took off my shirt and borrowed a bush hat from a friend. I had no hat of my own at the time. Dressed this way I put a heavy sack of rice on my shoulder and attached myself to the end of a line of men humping the sacks up a pile that reached up to just below the roof. Near the top of the heap *Otaki* stood, directing the stacking. I passed very close to him, almost brushing him as I went by. I looked into his face. He took no notice other than an expression of annoyance at my clumsiness. I dumped my load and climbed down the heap to rejoin the queue, hoisting another sack onto my shoulder.

This time I actually knocked against him. He snarled and peered under the broad brim of the bush hat.

I smiled cheekily at him. The effect was comical. He recognised me and in that instant his snarl changed to a groan of frustration. He now had no idea how long I had been working there. For all he knew I could have been there all the time. He was frustrated, and I was pleased; pleased at the success of my simple ruse and the feeling that I had won a little victory.

Sergeant Frankie Bowler was being his irrepressible self. Put to work with a handcart to pull around he reduced Japanese and PoWs alike to near hysterics by opening the fly of his trousers and parading proudly along, with everything on display.

"They've got me working like a horse," he shouted, "so I might as well look like one!"

Another time he had poor simple *Yamada* in tears of frustration. This occurred during a march back to camp after work one day. For a while there had been a full escort at these times, but eventually when they realised that the PoWs were well disciplined and not out to make trouble one guard was deemed sufficient for this duty, and the rest of them went off to their billets a little earlier.

PRIVATE YAMADA

This day it was *Yamada's* turn to escort us, which he did, marching beside Frankie at the head of the column. Suddenly the devil got into Frank and he began to quicken the pace and lengthen his stride. We immediately caught on to what he was doing, and followed suit.

Little *Yamada* tried to keep up on his short legs. It was impossible. He began to shout at Frankie, whose response was to march even quicker. By now *Yamada* was running and began jumping up, trying to land a blow on Frankie's face as they went along. No heed was paid to *Yamada's* frantic shouts and finally he gave up and settled for running along at the side with a comical half hopping, half waddling, gait.

Pte. YAMADA TRYING TO JUMP UP AND HIT FRANKIE BOWLER ON THE WAY BACK TO CAMP AT HAVELOCK ROAD

I have mentioned the gentle *Harada* . One day I was digging a drain channel and conversing with *Harada* at the same time. He was explaining the different ways that a Japanese bows.
The deep bow to a much superior person, and the shallow bow to a less superior person. "*Hi Kiri*" and "*Lo Kiri*" he called them.
To get his point across he demonstrated each method, and fellow prisoners were astonished to see a Japanese guard bowing to me in what looked like a very obsequious manner!

The time came when a change of guard personnel took place. Fresh Japanese troops began to occupy some of the completed buildings on which we had been working. PoWs never missed a chance of revenge however small and began bringing match boxes containing bed bugs from the hoards that were plaguing us in our camp. These little, evil smelling blood suckers were furtively tipped into their new Jap quarters. Whether the bugs appreciated this change of diet or not we shall never know, but the new hosts did not like it for we heard many complaints in no time at all and a new word entered our vocabulary. It was the Japanese for bed bug; *dani*, and lots of bed bugs were "*taksan dani*". So the insects appeared to have settled in quite happily!

During a break one day *Ivka* sat looking pensively at his boots, then looking around to see if anyone were listening he said to me, "*Me, Otaki, Harada, Yamada, Kawasaki* — Burma go!"
I shook my head in mock sympathy and said, "Burma no good, *Ivka*. Burma plenty boom boom!"
He gave a nod of understanding and a small, regretful grin. The flood tide of easy Japanese conquests had already passed its peak. *Otaki* and Co left shortly after.

We were set to work in a different part of the area, quite a long way away from the bungalows and it was not possible to see '*Kak Yam* any more.

However, at the new work place I was to meet some trouble; and be "adopted" by a new family.

The trouble came one broiling afternoon. The pick and shovel work had been hard and tiring. The guards had been in a foul temper all day, screaming at the PoWs and handing out beatings indiscriminately. We were already missing the relatively benign supervision of *Otaki* and squad.

I was hacking away at a particularly hard piece of ground when I became aware that a guard was watching me intently. He was an ugly, scowling brute who made *Kawazaki's* blue-jowled visage seem handsome by comparison. He came to me and pointed at the ring on my little finger.
"*Presento!*" — (give it to me) he said.
I shook my head, "*Presento nai!*".
"*Presento!*" this time louder and more forcibly.
"*Presento nai!*" again I refused.

He offered a packet of cigarettes.

"*Kokang — kokang!*" — (exchange). Again I refused.

"*Watakushi cigareto nai!*" (I don't smoke) I told him.

He began muttering angrily to himself, then decided on one last effort.

"One dolla!" again I refused.

He got nastier and made tugging gestures at his own finger as if pulling a ring off forcibly, implying that I had got it that way from some victim.

I tried an explanation of why I could not give up the ring. "*Watakushi no oksan presento,*" (my wife gave it to me) I said, bending the truth a little.

He was now quite enraged, shouting "*Bakar! Bakar!*" (fool! fool!) He picked up a nearby pick handle menacingly. I was expecting to be beaten up at any moment when a Japanese officer appeared nearby. My ugly pest dropped the pick handle and slunk off, leaving me in peace, and very much relieved.

My new "family" was an elderly Malay couple who were living in a palm thatched house close by the area in which we were now working. The construction area had been built up to a level several feet above the ground on which the Malay house stood with its screen of palm trees and banana plants. It was easy for me to slip away to it unobserved, which I often did, the first time being during a midday break. The guards were relaxing in the shade somewhere and were not at all vigilant.

We made friends quickly and I was soon addressing them as *Ma'* and *Bapa*. They in turn called me *Anak* (son). They were distressingly poor and made a few cents by selling little banana cakes made with coconut oil and rice flour. They asked if I could perhaps help by selling some to the British soldiers. I said I would try.

The next day when I called they had prepared fifty cakes in a small canvas bag. The price was one cent each. I had no money to pay for them but they were quite happy for me to bring the takings next time I came.

Smuggling the goods into camp presented no difficulty and selling them that evening was easy. Many vendors went round the huts selling or trading items obtained while out on working parties during the day. Cigarettes could be bought singly, so could pilchards in tomato sauce. A diminutive Ulsterman sold these, doubling his money on a tin.

His cry was, "Hoo says a fush?" (who says a fish?); and a Gordon Highlander named Snuffy Craig had a regular supply of duck eggs. He bought them at night, leaving the camp by way of the perimeter creek, wading knee deep through stinking mud. A resourceful man! One I saw a lot more of later on.

Visits to the Malay house continued without incident. The elderly Malays were delighted with their new income and I was doing well for myself as the cakes sold readily at two cents each.

One day I was sitting on the veranda waiting for the cakes to be produced when I saw a Japanese soldier ducking under the banana plants and coming straight towards me. It was too late to escape so I just sat tight. In fact, I froze. He came and sat beside me, taking out a packet of cigarettes. Without a word he offered me one.

I said, "*Origato,*" but explained that I did not smoke. Just then the elderly Malay appeared with his bag of cakes. I took the bag from him. The Jap looked into the bag.

"*Ah so ka! Tempera ka?*"

"*Hai, tempera,*" I said. I offered him one but he declined. I left him enjoying his cigarette while I departed to rejoin the working party.

I can only imagine that, like myself, he had slipped away to enjoy a quiet moment and had no intention of causing trouble or drawing unwelcome attention to his absence. The incident was yet another example of the unpredictability of the Japanese.

Days passed in an unchanging routine: marching out from camp; toiling throughout the hot day: marching back in the late afternoon. In the evenings there would sometimes be an impromptu show on a small, temporary stage made by laying boards across the aisle between the upper sleeping platforms in one of the huts. Simple shows of stand up comics telling blue jokes, and solo singers with a repertoire of ballads and popular songs. Around the camp prisoners would gather in small groups swapping jokes or talking of home. Eventually all would drift back into their huts and quiet would descend over all.

High up under the attap roof of L6 hut I would lie on my bunk, bathed in perspiration from the sweltering heat rising from the packed bodies below. Fortunately for my sanity I had an escape. I could leave my physical body to the discomfort and bed bugs and find solace with *Sumini*.

I saw her before me. I heard her voice. She was tangible, *Bayang bayang* — shadows — or the meeting of minds? Was it possible that we travelled on the astral plane of the mystics? Did our minds meet? Was I too before her eyes? Was my "shadow" with her? Whatever the explanation it seemed real to me, it was an escape from squalor and despair to a world of sunshine and happiness.

We talked together of little things, events of no importance, but quite unforgettable. Like the *tingkap*.

A *tingkap* is a small window found in a Malay house, usually it has a pair of wooden shutters.

Sumini and I had spent the whole day together, some of it in the garden, filling gaps in the hedge with cuttings of hibiscus and frangipani. I learned that these could be planted either way up. In that hot, moist and fecund climate the shoots would turn upwards in the right direction.

Sumini crept up behind me and put a large stick insect on my neck, causing me to jump in surprise.

She laughed heartily and mocked me, "Jek was not afraid of the bombs but he is afraid of a harmless insect!" I assured her that it was only the unexpectedness of the scaly feet that had startled me.

It was one of those totally happy days that deserved to be called perfect, but then it wasn't really perfect because it had to come, like all others, to an end.

We had said our reluctant goodnights and I had gone outside to my bicycle. Above my head I could see small shafts of golden light spilling through the louvres at the bedroom window. On impulse I propped the cycle against one of the stout pillars supporting the house, climbed up to stand on the saddle and, opening the shutters, I looked into the room, folding the shutters together behind my head to make a screen.

Sumini was lying on the bed just inside. She was alarmed at the opening of the shutters, then, with a happy smile she jumped up to kneel before me with her face on a level with mine. She chuckled. I took her face between my hands and drew her closer and kissed her.

"*Selamat tidur, sayang*" (sleep well, my love) I said.

"*Selamat jalan, sayang*" (go in safety, my love) she whispered in reply.

Sumini told me sometime later that she dreamed of me at the *tingkap*.
For me it remains an indelible memory.

However dull the days may be, however unvarying the routine, an event may come along that will imprint itself upon the memory. The unexpected happened in L6 hut on a *Yasume* day, during which we stayed in camp.
It came in the form of a large brown snake, a cobra of all things! It appeared suddenly from the attap thatch at the rear of the sleeping platform directly opposite to where I stood speaking to a Private Rogers. Rogers had just turned away and was about to step up onto the platform when the cobra reared up, its hood dilated, its head swaying from side to side. The jaws gaped wide, exposing two large, wickedly curved fangs. Two thick jets of venom streaked across the intervening space to strike Rogers in the centre of the forehead just above the eyes. The reptile turned away and swiftly made its escape, weaving in and out of the thatch, and was gone. It could have hidden anywhere under the lower platforms. We searched for it but were unable to find it. Rogers' eyes were terribly red and sore for some time afterwards, but he had had a lucky escape and could perhaps have been blinded.
Everyone walked cautiously for a long while afterwards.

One morning we paraded for work as usual but instead of marching out to the site we were detailed off for work around the camp and told we would not be going out again.

That evening a Japanese officer came into the camp, presumably to practice his English, which was excellent. The subject of course, was the war, and the usual sort of badinage was taking place, in which we insisted that the British would return and that we were certain that the Allies would win the war. Surprisingly he agreed.
"Yes," he said. "You will win the war, but it will not be with brave soldiers. It will be with money."

Then he told us why we would not be working in this area anymore.
"You are all going to Siam," he informed us.
There was an excited buzz from the small crowd that had gathered about him, and questions were fired at him from all sides.

"Will it be a better camp than this?"

"Yes, much better."
"Will there be electricity? Running water?"
"Yes, there will be all those things."
"What work will we be doing?"
"You will be doing construction work."
"How will we travel to where we are going?"
"You will all travel by train."

Visions of comfortable railway coaches with proper seats filled our heads.

The conversation continued in the same way until the smart young officer left.

Then I became worried. I had sold all my cakes the previous evening and had the cash for them. *Ma'* and *Bapa* — how could I get it to them? What would they think had happened? They would notice the absence of British PoWs from the building site and would surely understand. There was no way I could contact them. I hoped they would find another outlet for their produce and was sorry that I had not had the chance to bid them goodbye.

The prospect of a move to Siam caused great excitement. Mr.Churchill had decided that the name Siam would be used because the modern title was *Muang Thai* meaning The Land of the Free, and was no longer true now that Japan occupied it. Even more excitement came with the arrival of a shipment of Red Cross goods, a generous gift from South Africa in the form of excellent felt hats, boots, articles of clothing and food stuffs. Our hopes for the future brightened. Regular supplies such as these would keep us fit and healthy. But there were to be no regular supplies. Japanese propaganda was painting a dismal picture of the dire state of Great Britain and its empire and here was a tangible example that the opposite was true. No more Red Cross parcels reached us. They were sent, we found out later, but were not distributed. For whatever reason they were withheld, the hardship and deaths resulting from the lack of them was the same.

MYANMA
(BURMA)
LAOS
VIENTIANE
RANGOON
THAILAND
(SIAM)
BANGKOK
CAMBODIA
ANDAMAN SEA
PHNOM PEN
GULF OF
THAILAND
KUALA
LUMPUR
SINGAPORE

MILES
60
0
KILOMETRES
100
CAMP
BURMA SIAM RAILWAY
EXISTING RAILWAY 1941
THANBUZAYAT
YO
THREE PAGODAS
PASS
THAILAND (SIAM)
WAMPO
R. KWAI
BURMA
BANGKOK
ANDAMAN SEA
GULF OF SIAM
TO SINGAPORE

CHAPTER 8   Thailand Hell Camps

On a fine morning with hopes high we marched between armed guards through the handsome building that was Singapore railway station. Bright colour surrounded us; the artistic detail of the station interior; the throng of travellers in bright sarongs, saris and *cheongsams*. Amid the bustle and stir of humanity on the move, the shuffle of slippered feet, and the clack of wooden clogs, covert glances were cast in our direction as we made our way out of the main building to a siding where transport awaited us. Not the anticipated railway coaches with cushioned seats but a line of grey steel box cars. Into these grim containers we were packed about forty men to each. Forty men plus baggage.

There was not sufficient room to lie down. With our backs against the sides of the car our outstretched legs formed a pile in the centre. Screaming guards stupidly closed the doors upon us . It was pitch dark within and there was no ventilation. A great chorus of shouted protests arose from the line of wagons. Doors were forced open, and heated arguments took place between PoWs and guards, but at last common sense prevailed and the doors were left open. This made it possible for men to take turns at sitting in the openings with legs dangling outside.

In these cramped and uncomfortable conditions we travelled the length of the Malay Peninsular. Exhaustion would eventually bring some sleep, but only in short periods, for the hillock of legs in the centre of the carriage was like the children's game in which hands are piled one on the other and the hand at the bottom of the pile is pulled out and placed on the top once more. Once a pair of legs reached the bottom of the heap the weight of the other limbs would press them hard against the metal floor and sometimes the head of a rivet or two. This was painful enough to waken a man and make him drag his legs out from under the pile and transfer them to the top. The process would be repeated over and over. At times like this good companionship is invaluable and men were able to joke and make light of the hardships of the crowded conditions and the fierce heat from the sun that turned our container into an oven.

The Red Cross provisions proved to be a life saver. We were not working, and the Japanese were not in the business of feeding idle mouths, and hardly any sustenance was provided throughout the long trek.

There were no latrine facilities. Calls of nature were answered perilously at the open doors while the train was moving, or at the track-side during halts.

At Kuala Lumpur station prisoners taken short had perforce to squat between the rails, with members of the public looking down at them from the platforms. The more sensitive or sympathetic would look away .

It was the undoubted intention of the Japanese to humiliate us in the eyes of the Asiatics, and to destroy all vestiges of British prestige. Despite our dolorous condition they did not always succeed in this, and when indigenous peoples were themselves subjected to the same callous treatment, they tended to remember the civilised conditions they had enjoyed under the British, and despised the Japanese accordingly.

The journey was long, drawn out and slow, day after day the painful hours crawled by. Many bridges had been destroyed during the war and subsequently hurriedly repaired. Our train crept over them at snail's pace. But eventually we arrived at the border of Siam. A few miles beyond *Padang Besar* there was a halt. A small Thai peasant approached and stood fascinated, looking up at us and listening to our speech. Perhaps we were the first Europeans he had seen in a crowd. After a while he gave a pantomime of the impressions we had made on him. With thumb and finger he pinched his nose to indicate that we had long, thin noses. Then he made a hissing sound, "ssss-ssss-ssss," to let us know how sibilant our speech sounded to him. I don't suppose he ever forgot that brief encounter. After all, I haven't!

For six long days and six dreary nights our metal caterpillar had dragged its way up to Siam. Our destination was the small station of *Ban Pong* and by the time we reached it one wit had already summarised our uncomfortable journey with an improvised parody of the popular George Formby song: "Mother What'll I Do Now?" This is how it went:

"We came up from Singapore,
Forty in a truck, they couldn't get more,

And it didn't half make my arse-hole sore
  Mother, what'll I do now?"
The next verse to the Formby song needed no alteration:
  "First I stand and then I sit,
  Then I sit and stand a bit
  But I can't stand much more of it,
  Mother, what'll I do now?"
That describes, perfectly, our six hellish days in a steel inferno, but now, thankfully, we were out in the fresh air with just a short march down a dirt road to a camp
  —— straight out of hell!

Our new quarters were attap huts which were built without walls. The roofs rested on the ground, making tent-like shelters. Recent rains had flooded much of the small camp and we had to wade through water over our ankles, ducking under a low doorway to reach the split bamboo sleeping platforms in the gloomy interior. The area was enclosed by a flimsy bamboo fence and the latrine was an open trench, the contents of which had overflowed and were floating about the camp and into the huts, bobbing about the supports of the sleeping platforms.

It was a filthy, disgusting and squalid place. Pigs would have despised it and no peasant would have allowed his pigs to use it.

The tiny graveyard within its own bamboo fence enclosure already contained some graves. Each pitiful grave had a wooden cross at the head. Not one of them showed an age of more than 22 years. The despair of the place was heightened by the presence of large vultures which waited hunch-backed in the branches of trees close by.

VULTURES AT BAN PONG, SIAM

    Our time in that dismal place was mercifully brief. We now knew that we were to build a railroad from *Ban Pong* to Burma. What we did not know at that time, of course, was that it would become infamous as the Railroad of Death. So it was in happy ignorance that we assembled on the dirt road before sunrise one day, ready to move upcountry.

    We had been ordered to leave all heavy baggage behind, to be sent on, and to take with us a haversack containing bare necessities. This seemed a good arrangement at the time but we were to live to regret it.

    Awaiting the order to move off, we stood in the pre-dawn darkness, the silhouettes of my companions barely discernible about me. A fulminous glow reddened the eastern horizon below a louring sky. It brought to mind Kipling's words about the dawn coming up like thunder, and I thought, with a feeling of excitement, "I'm on the road to Mandalay!" I was pleased to be leaving the squalor of the camp behind, and excited by the adventure of venturing into the unknown. The others would have thought me mad, but I was still very much an optimist!

A short march brought us to a river-side where we scrambled down a steep clay bank to cross a rickety plank and embark onto a Thai barge. There were eyes painted, Chinese fashion, on the sharp bows; a small altar with joss sticks at the foremost part of the deck (the boatman explained later that this spot was sacred to the spirits of the river and forest and must not be touched. Obviously they were animists as well as Buddhists!) A split cane canopy covered a capacious hold and there was a small canopied area at the stern.

We were packed into the hold almost as tightly as in the box cars, but with room to stretch legs out.

There was a dumpy little towing launch on which the guards travelled. None fancied sharing the prisoners' quarters!

An elderly man and his son crewed the barge and lived on the stern deck under the canopy. A small charcoal stove made from a clay-lined, galvanised pail cooked their simple rice meals, and a large earthenware *tong* contained water. The latrine was a cane screen suspended over the side of the vessel towards the bows.

Being near the Thais' quarters we soon engaged them in conversation. I had learned a few Thai phrases from *Sumini*, these and gestures were sufficient, and soon Frank Bowler, a Liverpool lad and I were invited to climb up and join them.

The pop-pop-popping of the launch sounded across the water. The tow rope tightened and we moved slowly out against the current. We were heading upstream and our voyage along the River Kwai had begun. Progress was slow. We had no idea of where we were going but it was pleasantly cool under the canopy and we had a fine view of the river. We passed *Kan Chan Buri* where a paper mill covered the river in a kind of thick white foam for a while, and floated past banks where tall, tassel-headed reeds grew and on the opposite bank kapok trees stretched gaunt arms straight out at right angles from their trunks and bore large brown pods and no discernible leaves.

Frankie kept our hosts happy with presents of cigarettes from the ample supply he had in his haversack. He supplied the Liverpudlian too, but later when the stock ran out (after our journey ended) the lad, who had attached himself to us like a limpet, went off to seek new companions.

Signs of civilisation were left behind and we progressed along an empty river where dense, green tropical forest grew in lush profusion right to the very riverbank.

The river wound a sinuous course and sandbanks made it sometimes necessary for the launch to steer close into a bank. At one place where the barge brushed against overhanging foliage a thin, bright green tree snake fell onto the mat at the elderly Thai's feet. In a flash a *parang* appeared in his hand and in one deft swipe he sliced the head off the snake. He dipped two crooked fingers to his forearm, then drooped his head telling us that a bite would be lethal.

We were warned not to dangle our legs over the side of the barge, and this was accompanied by a mime that clearly indicated the danger of crocodiles. Not having seen any so far we laughed, but he assured us that it was true. Many months later I was to see for myself a very large crocodile, swimming effortlessly against a strong current in mid-stream, by merely flicking its tail!

Occasionally a long raft of bamboo would float past on its way downstream. The bamboos were cut in the jungle and floated down on the current; there would be a small shelter at the rear, a crew of two, and a large sweep to steer the course .The forest provided the bamboo, the river provided the transportation. The men's expenses, it seems, would have been small.

Days passed as we chugged upstream. One night we were all allowed ashore to sleep in a fenced area on the river bank. The luxury of all that space was rather spoiled by a herd of water buffaloes that shared the enclosure with us, and were milling clumsily about during the night, probably disturbed by the jungle noises, and putting the sleeping men in danger of being trampled.

The next day our pleasant stay in the boatmen's quarters was ended when a guard ordered us down into the hold before returning to his own comfortable billet on the towing launch.

After about 6 days on the river we made landfall where a number of huts stood close by. We shouted across to some PoWs on the bank; they told us the name of the camp was *Tarsoa*, and we wondered if it was to be our destination. It was not. Instead, after an hour or so, while the guards conferred ashore, we turned around and went back down-river, travelled a mile or so then disembarked at a small gap in the dense greenery. Our voyage up the River Kwai (for now, at least) had ended.

As if to make us welcome, feel at home and wanted, the following explicit announcement was posted prominently in our new camp:

NOTICE

The name of this camp is *Wampo*.

Camp Rules

Man who escapes or attempts to escape will be put to death by shooting.

Man who refuses order of Japanese soldier will be put to death by shooting.

Man who resists or hurts Japanese soldier will be put to death by shooting.

Man who commits sabotage will receive 20 years solitary confinement with hard
    labour.

The first night after disembarkation had been spent in the open. Some yards back from the river a small area had been cleared around which piles of attap and bamboos were dumped. Helping ourselves to these materials, we made simple shelters for the night and soon the flickering light of camp fires danced across the surrounding walls of foliage. Men fortunate enough to have food, cooked it as best they could. I had only four very small very hard, green bananas. I roasted them in their skins and fooled myself they had the (almost forgotten) taste of roast potatoes.

The next day we began building huts of a superior design to those at *Ban Pong*. They had side walls with space along the top for ventilation, were equipped with a split-bamboo sleeping platform each side of a central aisle and there was the usual ½ metre of space allowed per prisoner. Covered latrines were dug and had oriental squat-type facilities . Latrine paper was plentiful in the form of leaves from surrounding trees. In later camps this was not so and prisoners had to be sure to bring a sufficient supply into camp daily!

Finally the building of the camp was completed and the real work — construction of the railway began.

Camps like *Wampo* were being started at intervals all along the River Kwai and we were to see many of them during the coming years.

More men joined us, having trekked all the way up from *Ban Pong*. Sleeping in the open, carrying all the necessary gear with them, cooking en route and being beaten along by sadistic guards using, boots, bamboo rods and rifle butts; they were in a sorry condition.

Our days began at five o'clock. In darkness we drew a breakfast of boiled rice at the cookhouse, and filled our water bottles from a 40 gallon oil drum kept constantly boiling outside. Then came a roll call (*tenko*) and our engineer supervisor took us along a path to where jungle clearing went on. Here we felled great old teak trees; massive thickets of bamboo, 40 feet tall, some as thick as buckets at the base and all banded together by an interwoven network of long, slender side shoots with spikes like the spurs on a prize fighting cock, hard and springy as steel; dense thorny undergrowth; termite mounds, tall as a man and as hard as concrete; all were hacked, chopped, sawn or torn away with the simple tools provided: axes, *parang*s, Dutch hoes, picks, shovels and cross-cut saws. The small calluses on our hands grew into big ones, new ones developed on shoulders from the rough bark of heavy logs and the pressure of carrying-poles.

CLEARING BAMBOO THICKETS, WAMPO 1942

    We had come up from Singapore in October 1942. It was the dry season and the naked sun poured merciless heat down on a scene reminiscent of Dante's Inferno. Evenings felt cool at 60°F (16° C) after years of Singapore's constant 90° F (33° C).

Clearing was proceeding in two directions; north and south. Debris was burnt at the sides of the track. A wide swathe was being cut through the dense forest. Embankments were built and cuttings dug out. Soil was moved about in small baskets or on *Tonkas*, (stretchers of rice straw matting and bamboo poles) by lines of men passing up and down for all the world like columns of ants. Salt bees settled on us to suck our sweating bodies. Luckily they were small insects and would only sting when trapped by a fold of flesh. The stings, like the bees were insignificant. Other bites were far more serious, such as those of the blue-black scorpions, the size of small lobsters, which were dug out of cavities below ground level. A smaller variety, even more venomous could be unsuspectedly picked up on a piece of wood — or worse still — sat on! Centipedes 8 inches (20cm) to 10 inches (25 cm) long were common; these ferocious beasts possessed a fearsome pair of pincers, as well as sharp claws along their length. Snakes abounded and once one slithered between my ankles from behind as I was hacking down at a log. I froze, with the axe poised above my head and the black reptile had slithered away before I recovered.

There was a type of caterpillar, a beautiful specimen about 4 inches (10cm) long. It was vividly coloured in green and yellow with pale grey panels like windows along its sides. It reminded me of a Southdown bus. It too had a nasty sting which was delivered by a ridge of spines along the top of each flank. I brushed against one of these insects when passing a bush. There was an instant, searing pain across one thigh and an angry red rash appeared. It was several days before pain and rash faded away.

There was a break at midday when a meal of boiled rice and watery pumpkin stew was brought out from camp. Sometimes in addition, a short break, known as a *"Smoke-O"* would be allowed. Otherwise work went on non-stop all day long, driven relentlessly on by the hoarse shouting and screaming of the guards:
"Bakar!" (Fool!) ; *"Konero!"* (Idiot!) ; *"Kura!"* (You! — to an inferior) ; *"Dame-dame!"* (No good-no good!) ; *"Speedo!"* (Hurry up!).
The epithets were hurled at the PoWs in ceaseless repetition until we dragged ourselves exhausted back to camp at the day's end, many bruised from undeserved beatings, or beatings given for the slightest

offence, real or imagined, delivered by whatever was to hand, bamboo stick, pick handle or shovel; all served.

The beatings came often from the Korean guards, and perhaps compensated for their lowly status, for they, as opposed to the engineers, were used only as guards, lower than the lowest Japanese private; only we, the PoWs were lower than they were. We had only now begun to learn the difference.

At night we slept crushed together without mosquito nets. Clouds of female anopheles whined about us, singing and dancing the night away; sucking, gorging themselves on our blood, the strange new taste that sent them off with distended, crimson bellies; in exchange for which they infected us with the deadly parasite that was to exact a heavy toll.

The dark rain forest was alive with sound; the shrill chirring of insects; The " kodok, katak" call of frogs; the "tok-ay; tok-aay; tok-aaaay!" of geckos. The noise would stop abruptly, as if a switch had been thrown: a palpable silence would blanket the night. Then — a solitary call would start the din off again.

The Japanese soldier in charge of our work party was a two-star private of the engineers, named *Honjo*. In his thirties, he was a reservist who had served in Manchuria during the annexation of that country.

He was mature and reserved in character, and we were lucky to have him. He was neither abusive or violent, and treated us as well as conditions allowed.

Of an evening he would join the group which formed to chat outside our hut. It was a chance to use the small amount of English he had, and I my smaller knowledge of Japanese. *Honjo* had a wife in *Kobe* and two young children. He had been a car salesman. Enthralled by a visit to the famous all-girl revue in Tokyo, he had particularly enjoyed one of the songs, and wanted to learn the words. I did not know them, but Sergeant Tommy George of our Battery did.

The song was "Get out and get under the moon."

Tommy taught us the words. We sang the song several times, much to *Honjo's* delight. I remember the words to this day. They always recall the event to me, and I only wish I knew what became of friendly Tommy. Our ways parted after we moved on from *Wampo* camp and I heard no more of him.

One evening *Honjo* arrived upset. He had lost face because one of our party had taken to begging outside the Japanese quarters after the evening meal, asking for the leavings that the soldiers were emptying into the swill bin. The offender was Ikey Glickman of London, who was already unpopular with us. He had offended *Honjo* on a previous occasion by rudely demanding a light for a cigarette.

Honjo had noticed the omission of a polite word, and asked me, "*O kudasahi — prease-ka?*" (Is "please" the English for *o kudasahi*?) *O kudasahi* is literally "Honourably condescend." He would not give Glickman a light until Glickman said "Please."

Honjo made plain his feelings about the begging practice, and Glickman was given a direct order by Tommy George to stop it. We were all very hungry, but still had some pride left.

Hunger had left its mark on us. We thought constantly about food, and looked like skeletons. The ravages of malnutrition and tropical diseases were widespread among us; beri-beri, malaria, dysentery and ulcers, were taking their toll. The rice diet was sufficient to keep men alive, but not to nourish and keep them healthy.

We had a marvellous protagonist in the battle against these scourges, in the form of a remarkable medical officer. It is said that the hour produces the man. For us the hour did produce the man, a truly exceptional man: Dr. S. S. Pavillard of the local volunteer forces of Singapore.

A hut in the camp was given over for treatment of the sick. To use the word "hospital" will give the wrong impression, but I shall use it for the sake of simplicity.

This was Dr. Pavillard's domain in which he coped with every condition that came along. He was a marvel, working with very few medical supplies and improvising implements from whatever materials he could find.

In appearance he resembled a character in a Velacquez painting: a Canary Islander of English/Spanish parentage, he had a small Van Dyke beard, a slightly swarthy complexion, and the merest trace of an accent. Kindly and approachable, with a good sense of humour, he was held in high regard by all.

After work one day a call came for men of blood group OU to donate blood. With three other men I went to the hospital. Dr. Pavillard came outside, looked us up and down and asked each of us questions. He chose me and dismissed the others.

In a small cubicle near the hut entrance were two single beds of bamboo. On one lay an emaciated private of the volunteer forces. He was critically ill and looked near death.

I lay upon the other bed while Dr. Pavillard and Pinkie, his medical orderly (so named because of his near-albino colouring) took blood from my left arm, using a hollow needle, a short piece of rubber tubing, and a small rod with which Pinkie stirred the blood continuously as it flowed into a glass container.

An attempt was made to transfer the blood into the patient's arm, but an accident occurred and it was spilled. They came back to me for more.

The patient did not survive.

After the war I found out that my blood group is O rhesus negative, and was tormented by the thought that this may have caused the man's death. The doctor whom I questioned said that he thought it would not.

DOCTOR S.S. PAVILLARD

The next time I went to the cookhouse to draw my rice I was called to the head of the queue. A burly cook gave the stew a vigorous stirring and pulled up a full ladle that held more than the usual amount of solid matter. With a loud shout he announced to the hungry queue, "You won't all be getting this . This poor little bugger needs it!"

One night, a day or so later, two figures approached me in the dark, in what seemed a furtive manner. I need not have been apprehensive.
One said, "Are you Bombardier King?"
I said I was.
"We want to thank you for what you did." He named the patient who had died.
"He was our brother-in-law. If ever you want a job in Malaya after the war, we'll see there's one for you.
Both then solemnly shook my hand and departed. A blood transfusion given under the existing conditions was obviously regarded as something special.

Days passed. Work went on in the usual way. But I felt a change come over me. It became more and more tiring to do anything, and harder and harder to keep up with the gang.

I reported sick and explained my symptoms. Dr. Pavillard was surprised to see me.

"A few days ago you were the fittest man in camp; now here you are, complaining of debility. Oh, well, I'll have you in for observation," and I was admitted to hospital.
There I was given a dose of magnesium sulphate, which turned me out very quickly (and needlessly!), and was given a place on a sleeping platform. That same night the rigors struck. My first bout of malaria had begun.

Days later, when I was strong enough to sit up *Honjo* came to visit. He pointed at me, put his elbows together and shook violently, miming malaria. I confirmed it by nodding. Quietly he produced a gift, a very small chicken leg, golden, delicately fried.
I thanked him, *"Origato, Honjo-san"*, and hungrily ate the tasty morsel.

Back in the hut there was great excitement. Our baggage was to be collected from somewhere up river and a small party was to be sent to get it. Frankie Bowler was on the detail and was away from camp for several days. He arrived back with two kitbags. Mine was not one of them; which was a disappointment. The baggage had been looted, where, when, or by whom, Thai, Japanese or PoW, it was impossible to tell. So, once again I and many others had no more than we had left *Ban Pong* with months before, and sweat, hard wear-and-tear had already destroyed much of that. Frankie had been resourceful, however, and had filled the two bags with tinned foodstuffs and toilet soap, among other valuable items. These he shared with me and another lad who had little to his name . We had invaluable extra nourishment at a critical time, plus the luxury of toilet soap, while it lasted, when we took our daily baths in the river.

The southbound stretch of clearing eventually came out above the bend of the river where a range of low hills ended in a steep cliff. A ledge was to be blasted around the face of the cliff which, together with a timber gantry would form a bridge for the rail track.

Behind us the results of our clearing work stretched away into the distance; down below, the river flowed, shallow and quiet. On the opposite bank there was an area of sand and shingle, exposed by the falling river; it was to be the site of a new camp, the work base for the gantry bridge, and it was to be named *Wampo* South.

During the months that had been spent in cutting our way through the forest, I had been helpful to *Honjo* in getting his instructions understood by our group. At one point I had been sent on ahead to cut a narrow trail back for use as a directional guide. I pushed my way through the undergrowth until the noises of the work party were quite faint. It was pleasant to be completely alone for once, and in a small clearing I sat down on a fallen tree trunk to steal a short rest.

At my feet there was a patch of soft mud. I looked down and, to my horror saw the deep, fresh imprint of a tiger's paw. I was entirely on my own, and felt very vulnerable. The hairs on my neck stood on end. I terminated my rest immediately and hacked my way back to the main party with indecent haste .

In the rocky hillside above the river was a large, but shallow cave. It offered welcome shade for the midday break, and I decided to explore it . At the back was a low cavity into which I crept on hands and knees. The roof sloped down and soon I had to wriggle forward on my stomach. With just enough light to see, I suddenly realised there were porcupine quills about me on the floor. Was the animal still there? Would I at any moment receive a shower of poisonous spines in my face? I did not wait to find out but backed off every bit as hastily as I had moved after seeing the tiger's paw print!

Although the clearing work in our area was completed work still went on in the building of embankments and the levelling of the track. It was at this time that Ikey Clickman was the victim of an accident so strange as to be almost weird. A skinny, gangling man, he walked with a distinctive gait, swinging his arms freely to waist height back and front, with his thumbs sticking upwards.

Glickman was walking past, about six yards away from a man who was hacking vigorously at a tough clump of roots, when the head flew off the axe, spinning as it flashed through the air. It clipped Glickman's raised thumb as it passed, cleanly removing the upper part at the knuckle. He stopped in his tracks and looked at the stump of his thumb.

"Cor!" he said, in surprise. "I should get a pension for that!"
Who else in the world would have made a remark like that? Obviously there was no pain at that moment.

Men were being detailed for removal to *Wampo* South. *Honjo* told me that he was to take charge of the Japanese cookhouse; and asked me if I wanted to go. I said I was no cook; but on thinking it over I could see that there might be advantages to be gained.

By this time I was very underweight after several bouts of malaria and dysentery, had scabies and the first signs of wet beri-beri; a thumb pressed into my shin would leave a dent that took time to fill out again. The chance of more , or at least better food, was too good to be missed. I said I would go. (PoWs were not normally asked to do anything!). Others, claiming to be cooks clamoured to be accepted. Two more were chosen besides me.

The new camp was built on the dry sandbank exposed by the falling river. Our new quarters were in a store hut away from the main buildings. We had a sleeping platform at the rear end of the store which held rice and other items for the Japanese kitchen. The work was not as hard as the track clearing had been, but there was plenty to do.

Water had to be carried up from the river, and there never seemed to be enough of it; rice for every meal for the Japanese detachment had to be washed and re-washed several times, vegetables prepared, firewood collected, fires attended and cooking pots (large *kualis*) scrubbed out, among many other tasks.

Honjo soon found out that there was not one genuine cook among us, but managed to cope, assisted by *Shimonosaki*, a small, nervous soul who knitted cummerbunds (a garment favoured by other soldiers as a precaution against stomach ailments) and spent a lot of his time buying any available woollen items from the PoWs. In many ways he resembled our Private *Yamada* in Singapore.

The food was no more plentiful than we had been having; but the rice was better quality and it was clean! PoW rice was not washed. The British authorities had forbidden it in the belief that to do so would cause the loss of any goodness it might have. As a result it contained weevils; white maggots about ¾ inch (2cm) long and rat droppings. It was best eaten in the dark. In the light I always picked out and discarded what I could!

Deficiencies in the Japanese diet, chiefly vitamin B, were compensated for by the addition of a small amount of a substance called "*Mitzui*", the invention of a Japanese admiral to combat scurvy in the Japanese fleet. It was brown in colour, and in texture it was a thick, sticky, paste of unpleasant taste. I think the main ingredient was soya bean. I stole some whenever I could and put it on my morning rice. I got rid of the yellow scurvy pustules between my fingers by scrubbing them hard with a kitchen brush and soap.

The spelling bee came as an unexpected diversion one evening. A group of men had gathered around a camp fire in the open space between the huts, and were exchanging the usual banter and jokes, when *Honjo* appeared on the scene. Perhaps wanting to try out new words, he began asking the men names of the schools they had attended. The first question was directed at a young officer who said that he had been to Cambridge. The next to be asked was one of the volunteer "cooks", Smith, a short cockney who answered, in a flash of his native wit, "Oxford". Working round the circle the answers came uniformly: "Cambridge — Oxford — Queen's College," and so on. I claimed Oxford, because as a boy it had been my boat race favourite.

Honjo quickly realised that his leg was being pulled. He beckoned a number of us to follow him and sat us down on the ground by the Japanese kitchen. He left us for a few moments, entered his quarters, then reappeared carrying a heavy bamboo cane, a thick book and tin of rice biscuits.

The book, I saw later, was a vocabulary which gave the Japanese word as an ideograph, then the English equivalent in *Katakana* (the script used for foreign words; phonetically) followed by the English word in Roman letters.

Honjo sat down with the stick at one side, the tin of biscuits at the other, and the book open across his knees.

He pointed to the first of the small circle of "scholars" and slowly read out "Rhododendron". Smith, it was, who had claimed Oxford as his alma mater. He was obviously being asked to spell the word. He gave a groan of protest. *Honjo* repeated the word slowly and clearly.

Smith made an attempt, "R — o — d —." He got no further. The stick descended upon his head with a lusty crack. *Honjo's* lips curled, "Smith speak cook — no cook! Smith speak Oxford — no Oxford!"

The word was directed at the next man, and the next and moved around the circle accompanied by a series of thwacks. Then *Honjo* decided to change the question, his next victim being the young officer. The book was consulted and the "quizmaster" looked up. "Cystophyllum fusiform," he announced to gasps of surprise and protests that it was not English. *Honjo* insisted.

The officer made an attempt,"C — y — s — t — o" . *Honjo* nodded and grunted at each correct letter, "f —— y." Crack! The stick flashed down with considerable force.

Honjo was enjoying our discomfort. After another man had tried and failed, It was my turn. The book was again scrutinised. My scalp was already crawling in anticipation! Slowly, what seemed one long word to *Honjo,* was read out. I could hardly believe my luck. Protests broke out all round, about it not being fair. *Honjo* was unmoved and read it out again.
It was; "Return home with honour." I spelt it out slowly to a series of approving nods. A hand flashed out and I was given a handful of biscuits as a reward. (Obviously, there must be one word for the phrase in Japanese)

When I had access to the book later I memorised the spelling of cystophyllum fusiform. It is a type of seaweed. The Japanese name for it is *hijiki*. Easy enough — if you've been to Cambridge!

One day our captors decided they would like some fish. A number of us swam across the river to the other side and climbed the steep path up the cliff. The Japanese crossed in a shallow-draft landing craft, and we were marched some distance along the cleared track, turning off down a path to the river bank a few miles upstream from the camp.

Here a barge waited, and some guards boarded it carrying sticks of gelignite with detonators and fuses attached. The barge moved out to midstream while PoWs and remaining guards remained on the bank.

Fuses were lit and the gelignite dropped into the water. The resulting explosions brought to the surface a great number of fish of all sizes. The prisoners were ordered into the river to collect the harvest.

I was a strong swimmer and headed for the far bank where a large fish was surfacing. Beside me another swimmer began to race me towards it. More and more of the fish appeared. It was a great catfish, the size of a man! It looked very fierce and only partly stunned. My rival and I exchanged startled glances, and with one accord turned away to collect smaller victims.

On the river bank men were busily collecting fish and hiding the odd one or two away among the reeds. Guards were patrolling up and down and just as busily retrieving them, and handing out cuffs round the ear to culprits.

When the time came to return to camp I did not fancy the long, hot march back. I decided it would be far more pleasant to swim downriver on the current. I made my intention known to *Honjo*, who, as my immediate boss, gave his permission, and off I went.

Soon the sounds of the fishing party were fading away behind me as I swam easily, effortlessly along in mid-stream. All was calm and peaceful, I felt alone in a tranquil world of primeval beauty.

The river began to swing round a great bend. A gorgeous peacock with two dowdy hens flew across overhead. I became aware of a sound, barely audible at first, because I had swum in silence except for the quiet chuckling sounds my arm movements made in the quiet water. A low murmuring was growing louder as I neared the end of the bend. Suddenly, as I rounded the bend, the noise grew really loud and before me I saw a stretch of white water which seethed and foamed. My speed increased and under me I could see the bed of the river only inches below; a bed of rocks and large pebbles. I cursed myself for a fool but could do nothing to escape the pull of the current and then I was right in the middle of the mill race. I let myself go with the flow, ceasing all movement of my arms and legs, making myself as flat as possible. There was the fearful thought that I could be ripped open at any moment by a jagged rock, but there was also a certain thrill of sheer excitement, and a fatalistic acceptance that there was nothing whatsoever I could do about it.

I emerged from the rapids unscathed, and into calm, flat water again, not far up-river from the camp, and arrived back long before, and much fresher than the fishing party!

Excitement was crackling through the camp like the discharge of static electricity. Someone had shouted the magic word —— WOMEN!
A noise like the buzz of a disturbed hornets' nest arose as the incredible news flew from lip to lip.

A floating brothel had arrived! Not for the PoWs, of course, but for the Japs. There was a stampede to the river bank, but there was not much to see; the girls remained under cover. Nevertheless, the barge was the focus of all eyes, as if the very intensity of the scrutiny to which it was subjected could render its canopy transparent, and expose the exotic occupants to the ravenous gaze of the sex-starved spectators.

Honjo visited the barge, out of curiosity, he said, but was unimpressed by the colour and quality of the harlots.

Other guards were not so fastidious and queued to take advantage of their services.

The prisoners saw nothing of the women, other than early morning swimmers who happened to look up when swimming round the barge and caught sight of unconcerned female users, answering the call of nature in the latrine which hung over the side.

Excitement in the camp died with the departure of the love boat.

CHAPTER 9   PoW Life and Liberation

It was now over a year since we had become prisoners of war. Dubious scraps of news about the progress of the war circulated from time to time, but there was never a hint of how much longer it would continue. There were no letters, no word from or about loved ones at home. There were no signs of Allied activity in this sphere of operations, nothing at all to indicate that the outside world knew of our existence.

Bad as conditions were for us, they were soon to become infinitely worse, and any one who possessed a crystal ball would have been well advised to smash it!

For me luck ran out on March 13th, 1943.
My recent change of work and diet during my short time in the kitchen had resulted in an improvement in my physical condition. This came to an abrupt end one afternoon towards the end of a day's work on the ledge for the gantry bridge opposite the campsite.

Men had laboured all day at the hard rock face. Holes had been drilled with steel rods and sledge hammers, using the "tap and turn" method. Gelignite had been rammed down the drill holes and fuses lit.

PREPARING THE LEDGE FOR GANTRY BRIDGE WAMPO SOUTH

The first explosions boomed across the river, causing me to turn and look. Too late I saw a lump of rock hurtling towards me.

Instinctively my hands flew up, but too late! I heard a loud, hollow crack, and I was knocked flat on my back. I came to to find a ring of concerned faces looking down at me. There was shouting, and I was carried to the store hut and placed on the sleeping platform.

"Pinkie" the medical orderly was at my side.
"His skull is fractured," he announced, and I panicked.
Pinkie leaned closer. "Now — you're worrying," he said soothingly. "Don't worry. It will be all right. Take some deep breaths."
I did so, and began to calm down.

Dr. Pavillard arrived soon after from the main camp, and I was taken across the river and stretchered up the steep cliff path to where a small truck was waiting. (Help had been summoned from the main camp by a wiry little R.S.M. who had swum across the river and had run non-stop all the way from the scene of my accident, apparently in record time. I did not get the chance to thank him for I never saw him again.)

As we jolted along in the back of the truck, Dr. Pavillard asked Pinkie if he had given me morphine. He had not, so the doctor gave me an injection, despite the erratic lurching motion of the vehicle.

At *Wampo* camp I was taken to the small cubicle in which I had given blood only weeks before. There was a cavity in my forehead which the doctor very gently washed out with boiled water. He crushed up a precious May and Baker sulphanilamide tablet (of which he had very few), sprinkled the exposed tissue within the fracture with the powder, and gave me the second tablet to swallow.

He said, "You have a hole in your forehead that has penetrated the left frontal sinus. You may lose the sight of your left eye." (After the war Dr. Pavillard published a book of his experiences. It was called, Bamboo Doctor. In it he describes how he had actually washed bone fragments off the exposed brain, and gives the size of the hole made by the rock as being approximately the diameter of an old penny, one inch).

I was given the rock, a piece of quartzite of irregular shape, roughly like an axe head, 3 ½ ins. (8.5cm) long by 2 ½ ins. (6.5cm) wide at the broadest part. The doctor pointed out a small, pyramid shaped protuberance that had made the hole, it had a flat step at its base, which, he said had probably prevented further penetration. Had the wedge-shaped other end of the missile hit me, he said, it would probably have split my skull. I had also been fortunate in that the

rock had struck where the bone of the skull is thickest. Had I not been facing the front the rock would have hit the side or the back of my head, in which case I would certainly have been killed.
In a way, I had been both unlucky and lucky!

The next day our M.O. appeared with the camp commandant, Lieutenant *Ibuka* at his side. They came to where I lay. I attempted to rise to a sitting position.
"Lie down!" Dr. Pavillard snapped. "And don't look so bloody cheerful. You're supposed to be dying!"
I instantly did as I was told!

After the visitors had left, another medical officer explained why I should not sit up.
"You have a hole in your head," he said "and the fluid is coming out from around the brain. You must lie down." He paused. "And d'you know," he added, referring to Dr. Pavillard's remark, "the camp commandant speaks good English!"

Although fluid and swelling closed my left eye for a time, I did not lose the sight of it. Nor was I dying — I was making a good recovery. But in the opposite bed an infantry private was in a very bad way. Suffering from stomach ulcers, he was raving, constantly shouting for a friend, calling his name time and again. About two days later a man visited him. It was the friend for whom he had been calling. The strange thing was that the patient could not have known: his friend had arrived that day from another camp.

From that time on we two patients made progress together, and knew that we were officially out of the woods when we heard an announcement to that effect made in the hospital one evening later, when the padre came to hold a service. Dr. Pavillard had performed two more miracles on the River Kwai.

I was relieved to find that the symptoms of beri-beri that I had noticed, were arrested by the better diet and stolen vitamin supplement obtained during the time spent in *Wampo* South camp. There was a frightful example of the effects of this deficiency disease in the hospital. On one of the bed spaces lay a patient with his legs spread wide.
They had swelled to enormous size, and between them was the grotesque sight of a scrotum the size of a football

In time the wound in my forehead closed up and I returned to my old, crowded hut in *Wampo* Central.

Work on the track was continuing in a northern direction. The food was as poor as it had always been, and the cemetery out beside the track held many more graves.

The first PoW funeral in the camp had been attended by the camp commandant, smartly dressed in his best uniform with a large samurai sword at his side; and a simple wooden coffin had been provided. The next funeral was not attended, nor was there a coffin. Instead a strange covering of attap had been contrived. After this bodies were buried in blankets, until it was realised that it was a waste of valuable, in fact irreplaceable material; after which rice sacking was used to cover the face.

The scourge of tropical diseases, malnutrition and exhaustion was taking a heavy toll. A man who lost hope was a dead man. Someone I had known in England, and who had sailed east on the same draft, fell ill. I saw him looking despondent.

"Here's another one for the end of the track!" he said miserably. Within two weeks we had buried him.

A short time was allowed for me to convalesce in camp, then I rejoined the work parties, cutting our way to Burma.

A number of us moved up to the next camp on the line: *Wampo North*, a smaller, grimmer version of the one we had left. It was situated in jungle away from the river and we lost the advantage of a swim at the end of a day of hard, sweating labour.

The huts were infested with bed bugs and lice (grey racers the men called them). The lice, pale grey in colour and wafer thin would get into the seams of a pair of shorts and set up an irritation with their bites. They were hard to dislodge but one effective method was to hang the infected garment in hot sunshine, then the lice would drop out and track back to the shelter of the hut.

On a *yasume* day it was possible to see lines of these pests making their way across ground to safety.

Bed bugs were easily killed by squashing them between thumb and finger, but they gave off a sickly smell which was most unpleasant.

To escape the unwelcome attention of these irritating insects some of us took to sleeping outside on the ground, accepting the risk of whatever else might be crawling about in the darkness, and for a while the only thing that disturbed us was rain. Light showers we ignored. Only heavy rain would send us back into those pestiferous huts.

However, one night something other than rain did disturb us; it was the loud scream of man bitten by a large centipede which had crawled over his arm, and had sunk its formidable pincers in when he had tried to brush it off. This made us more wary when sleeping in the open and we kept the fire going all night.

Some nights after this episode I was awoken by something scaly creeping down my chest. I steeled myself to remain perfectly still, determined to make no movement that would provoke what ever it was, and to wait until it crawled off of its own accord.

I could feel the pricking of claws as it slowly, deliberately crept down over my abdomen, lower and lower. Then, all at once my nerve cracked — I brushed at it, merely succeeding in pushing it further down. Certain now, that I was going to feel the fiery pain of its bite at any moment, I brushed wildly, frantically, and an involuntary shout of, "Aaaargh!" burst from my lungs.

The man beside me sat up, laughing heartily. He knew what it was. It had landed on him, and the firelight had shown it to be a harmless, if big, stick insect. He had curled his fingers under it and flicked it high into the air from whence, of course, it had landed on me. It was a long time before I enjoyed the joke as much as he did!

Not everything in the rain forest is harmful or poisonous, although there is much that is. To learn the difference can mean life or death. A useful commodity grew around us in the form of wild spinach, and I took to gathering it at every opportunity. The leaves were small, and sufficient to fill a 4 gallon kerosene can would boil down to a layer only ½ inch deep. It was a rich source of iron and vitamin C and, as such, a valuable addition to my diet. With a lizard or two and a snake I could make an acceptable soup. Snakes became prey to be chased and caught whenever possible, and later on I learned a method of trapping large ground lizards that was a great improvement on chasing them with a stick. Pigweed, also rich in vitamin C could be grown quickly and easily on a piece of wet sacking, as could a small bean which would produce nutritious shoots almost overnight. To be jungle-wise was the key to survival, and I was learning all the time. Another key to survival was a sense of humour. Jokes were very popular and a fresh crop of them was collected at every opportunity. A different camp always provided a fresh supply, and there seemed to be an inexhaustible reserve of them.

Entertainment of any kind was always welcome, and always therapeutic. Some camps were fortunate in having performers and a prisoner-built theatre of sorts. Some camps had nothing at all; in which case an open space and a camp fire would do.

Some camps had an orchestra (of sorts!), some had nothing more than an accordion, but it all, whatever it was, provided an escape from grim reality for a while, and music of any kind provided a balm.

Wampo North had no theatre. There was no time to spare to build one; but it had Pte. "Snuffy" Craig of the Gordon Highlanders, a man of unquenchable spirit, one I came to know well and one who had found his own key to survival: entertaining others. This he did at the drop of a hat, at every opportunity!

I remember seeing him after an exhausting day on the railroad, performing beside a camp fire outside one of the huts, telling jokes and trying to get members of a small audience to sing along with him, without much success .It began to rain and the audience moved away to watch from the shelter of the hut. Snuffy threw more wood on the fire and continued with his performance. The rain fell with increasing intensity. Snuffy carried on until the downpour doused the fire and forced him to retreat. In later camps Snuffy was instrumental in organising concert parties, building stages, providing scripts and performing . His humour was of the old red-nosed comic variety, but always very popular.

At this point it seems apposite to include in this narrative Taffy Long and his accordion. The two were inseparable and whatever things men discarded during the rigours of long gruelling marches, Taffy would never part with the instrument; it was his alter ego.

Wherever we went, while Taffy was with us we had music. He seemed able to play anything and everything. An accomplished accompanist to any singer, he would also play solo pieces at any performances. His rendition of "Granada!", "The Holy City" and such popular works never failed to evoke an ovation.

In appearance Taffy gave the impression of being short and tubby (not easy when you are half-starved!) with a cheerful expression on his chubby cheeks. He enjoyed a good sense of humour, was fair in colouring, with blue eyes; in short, he looked and was thoroughly Welsh.

To him the accordion was like a baby, and like a child it would receive the occasional buffet when it misbehaved; as it did when monsoon damp would cause a reed to stick in mid-performance. Taffy would swear under his breath, swiftly give the instrument an almighty thump with the heel of his hand, and play on regardless.

His contribution to our morale was immense. Like that of the Minstrel Boy to the Men of Harlech.

I am happy to say that he survived and was on the same ship home with me, and among my souvenirs is the tattered copy of a programme for the ship's concert. Among the items is listed : Taffy Long and His Accordion.

When Taffy arrives at the Pearly Gates it will be with his accordion slung on his back. They will never get him to play a harp!

None of us was sorry when weeks later we left the dreary camp behind and trekked farther north through the jungle to our next stop.

The saying: it is better to travel hopefully than to arrive, proved true in this case. Our destination was *Tarsoa* Camp.
No longer a few huts on the river bank it had grown in size and now sprawled over a large area.

The camp into which we marched was encircled by a tall bamboo fence (there had been none at *Wampo*), and there was a wide gateway with a sentry post at one side, built on bamboo stilts with a small attap shelter at the top.

A guard hut stood beside a dirt road across the way, and the road ran between clusters of huts down to the river.

The river! A treat! We would be able to bathe again; it was a happy thought.

Our huts, however, were bad; of the same type as those at *Ban Pong*, eaves that rested on the ground, no side walls, dark and gloomy within; and with the same degree of overcrowding.

The latrine, too, was no more than an open trench with bamboo poles across it to squat on.

Numbers of prisoners and guards alike were greater here. Some of the better-quality huts over the way were occupied by Japanese, others by Koreans. They always had separate quarters.

At first I had been unable to distinguish the difference between the two races. *Honjo* explained it one day. The Koreans were held in contempt by the Japanese, and were not used as fighting soldiers, but were given other duties,. They wore similar uniforms but held no rank, whereas the Japanese soldier wore yellow stars on a red tab to denote his status, the Korean had no red tabs but wore one large star on his tunic pocket.

As *Honjo* had grinned, sneeringly, "No star, but one <u>BIG</u> star!" making his contempt obvious.

The Korean was subordinate to the lowest Japanese private, and we, officers included were subordinate to the Koreans.

Our officers were made to remove all badges of rank from their shoulders and to wear instead one "pip" on a small square of linen on the chest.

We were ordered to salute or bow to all Japanese and Korean soldiers, something we had not had to do at *Wampo*.

Not being aware of the order when we first arrived, I received a heavy bang on the top of my head, from a guard known as Donald Duck, because of his cleft palate. (A sadistic individual he was hanged as a war criminal after the war). I had walked past without saluting and, without altering his stride, he had dealt me a cracking blow from a thick piece of bamboo about 3 feet long. This was repeated on several heads along the way, so it was obviously a well practised manoeuvre, dealt out to all and sundry, something he enjoyed; and the fact that prisoners were unable to understand his orders gave Donald Duck plenty of chances to indulge in his favourite hobby.

Old hands, rubber planters, tin miners and such, who were members of the volunteer forces, told us that we would soon be moved south out of this area altogether, because the monsoon would come, conditions would become impossible, and no one could work in the monsoon rains. How wrong they were! How very wrong!

Heavy rain was no stranger to us. In Singapore there was a shower, sometimes
more daily; and it could rain very heavily, more heavily than I had known before.
But there it stopped as suddenly as it began, and within minutes the sun would draw it all back up again, in streams of vapour from every surface. There were storms when the tail end of the monsoon came across the Straits, known locally as *sumatras*.

Tom Williams and I were once caught in one when we were out in our small boat. We made for the island, aided by the strong wind but the downpour was so torrential that the boat was filling more rapidly than we could bail it out, and it sank beneath us just as we reached the safety of the shore.

But these were pygmies and the monsoon was a giant; a tireless giant of primeval fury and power, who would attack the jungle in insensate rage; who could fell giant trees and fill the sky from horizon to horizon with a dense mass of black clouds, and then, as if displeased with his handiwork, would rip it apart with great bolts of lightning and deafening thunder claps. He could rain for weeks on end in a drenching deluge of stinging shafts, thick as stair rods. The ceaseless onslaught turned ground into swamps and tracks into quagmires; everything, everywhere dripping. Damp and dismal. But this was yet to come, and we had a new camp, new companions and new guards to become accustomed to.

The temper of our new oppressors was made clear quite early on . The evening *tenko* (roll call) took the form of a parade on the large square of beaten earth within our camp. We formed up in units, of four ranks in each. Our own NCO's would count the men present and report to the RSM, who in turn reported to the senior British Officer, a Lieutenant Colonel. The parade would then wait at attention for the Camp Commandant to appear accompanied by a Korean interpreter.

At our first parade the Colonel marched smartly up to the Japanese officer and began to make his report. There was a sharp crack that echoed across the parade ground as the Korean slapped him hard across the face.

"You — wait — till — officer come down hand!" he snarled.
The Colonel had finished his salute (British fashion) before the Commandant had lowered his hand. Apparently this was considered rude!

The role calls, morning and evening were always long drawn out affairs, with the Japs counting and recounting, never accepting the numbers quoted by our own people.

The regime here was oppressive. There was a "no whistling" order and I received a quick bashing for forgetting this one day when crossing the square.

There was also another strange ban. A request was made to hold a concert in camp. Permission was asked of the Camp Commandant.

"Yes," he replied, "You may have a concert, but there must be no singing and no talking."

No doubt he thought this was very funny, and an effective way of ensuring that there would be no concert. But he had reckoned without PoW ingenuity, and without Joe Spielman. But I must tell of this later for now I have something else to relate.

It was in a small hut at the riverside where I met Sammy Fuller, a fellow junior NCO, recently arrived after a gruelling march up from base. He was doing duty as a medical orderly and had apparently done fine work, as such, in helping the sick, and had been congratulated by our hard-of-hearing Major, who was now, also, somewhere in the camp.

Sammy looked startled when he saw me and looked at me with a strange expression.

"You look terrible!" he said.

I'm sure I did, but the thought had not struck me until then. At that time, with so many bouts of malaria and dysentery behind me, I was reduced in weight to 7 stone, and the dent and scar on my forehead were still lurid.

Sammy did not look too good himself; he was hollow-eyed and much gaunter than the last time I had seen him at Changi.

I was totally unprepared for his next remark and it left me speechless for a moment or two.

"I saw your pusher (girlfriend)" he said.

"What! — where? — when?" My words came in a rush.

He then described how, after leaving Changi he had been in a working camp (the name of which I have forgotten) where a strange event occurred. One morning the prisoners awoke to find the guards had gone. Apparently, the new detachment had failed to arrive. The PoW's waited for some hours but no one appeared, and there was no food in the camp. Hunger eventually got the better of discretion and groups of men drifted out into the surrounding area to find what they could.

It was with one of these parties that Sammy was approached by a young lady asking if anyone knew Bombardier King. Sammy said that he did, and the party was invited to go home with her.

It was a kind of torture for me to hear this.

Sammy went on, "She took us to her house and gave us something to eat. She showed me a store of tinned food and said, 'Tell Jack to come.'"

I agonised over how things might have been had I been there. How could I not have stayed with *Sumini?* I knew that I would not have been able to leave her again, and it would have inevitably have ended in tragedy for us both.

Someone in the *kampong;* in the hope of reward, or out of fear for his own safety would have betrayed us to the Japanese. But, even so, knowing this, I was still young enough, and foolish enough, and so deeply in love with that sweet and lovely young girl, that I would have risked it. I would have risked it all. But I was not in that place at that time, and it was not to be.

The mere thought that *Sumini* was still alive, and I was in her thoughts, was sufficient to fan the fire of longing in me, and to bring closer and clearer her image, her *bayang*, in reverie and dreams. Like the fever, *Sumini* was in my very blood. Sammy Fuller's words had rekindled hope in me, and made me determined more than ever to survive — as Sammy did.

He remained at the camp for a while after we moved on and later had a miraculous escape while on a packed transport to Japan. His ship was torpedoed by an American submarine. Sammy had just gone up on deck with Sergeant George Pritchard, (our unit's pay sergeant) to answer a call of nature, when the ship was hit. Both jumped into the water, but George never surfaced again. Sammy was picked up by the submarine and eventually arrived safely in England, where he gave my name to the authorities as having been seen alive in the jungle six months previously. My parents were notified. It was the first they had heard of me for two years.

The news spread around the camp that there was to be a concert that night. A stage already existed in one corner and the ground in front of it was occupied by an expectant crowd well before the time for curtain up. All knew of the Commandant's ban on singing and talking, and wondered what was going to happen.
The exciting sounds of instruments tuning up came from behind the curtain. The concert was about to begin!

To loud applause the curtains parted to reveal a stage on which sat an orchestra; musicians with proper instruments; violin, woodwind, brass, drum and a jungle bass fiddle of a tea chest, pole and Signal Corps wire.

The applause died away and an expectant hush settled on the audience. Then from back stage there entered a dapper figure in evening dress. He walked sedately to the proscenium and bowed from the waist to the audience, left, right and centre then to the orchestra. The applause broke out again and continued as he turned to face the musicians, taking some thin batons from under his arm and placing them on a small table at his side.

This was the maestro, Joe Spielman, a White Russian, lately of the Raffles Hotel Singapore; a cultured gentleman of great charm, a neat figure with a trim moustache and small, pointed beard. Music was his life.

He raised his baton for silence, and then down it came and we were enraptured by the first real music we had heard in a long, long time. The piece was listened to intently, with keen appreciation that would have done credit to a aficionados at the first performance of a great new work. The ovation it received was deafening and continued for several minutes, until silenced by a wave of the bowing maestro's wand.

The second number began in respectful silence; then slowly, and subtly a series of "accidents" began to happen as the maestro eased into a Chaplinesque routine.

A baton snapped in two as it struck the small table in an excess of exuberance during a lively passage.

The audience, politely silent at first, except for the odd, embarrassed snigger, began to realise it was a spoof and the laughter came in great gusts.

The violin stood to play a moving piece with great feeling. The maestro turned his face to the auditorium, wearing an expression of the deepest rapture; then went to the violinist, cupped his chin in one hand and stroked his head with the other, as if overcome with emotion. The audience screamed with laughter.

The trumpeter, a chubby Australian, could not keep his face straight and joined in the hilarity. This enraged the maestro who snapped a baton over his head, followed by another when it failed to get the trumpeter to compose himself.

The concert lasted a full hour, with Joe brilliantly improvising comic touches approaching genius. There was so much laughter and noise that some Japanese who had come to investigate stayed to watch, and thereafter the front rows at any concert were occupied by Japanese and Koreans. It was, after all, the only entertainment available; the foolish ban was lifted and proper performances allowed.

A talented concert party was formed, and all stage properties were made from materials available about the camp. With ingenuity, rice sacking and bamboo matting could be made into practically anything. Dyes were improvised from clays, soot and charcoal; make-up from crushed red crayon pencils, coconut oil and rice flower; wigs from coconut fibre, old rope, or cattle tails.

Two talented Dutchmen tailored suits and dresses of hessian, to Saville Row standards. The only draw back being that they refused their services unless given parts in a production. Sadly, they had no talent at all in that direction, so that any parts allotted them were always as small as could diplomatically be managed!

I had many conversations with Joe Spielman. He was a man of even temper and sunny temperament, but was moved to anger when ignorant but well-meaning men speaking of Joseph Stalin said to him "Good old Joe!" (Russia, of course, being an ally at the time).

"He's not good old Joe!" our Joe would retort angrily. "He's a murderer; a bloddy robber! He's a thief!"

There was another Russian in the camp, as unlike Joe as could be imagined. He was squat, with Slav features, broad cheekbones and narrow eyes. He was taciturn and did not mix, probably because his English was poor. He would often sit with Joe and converse in Russian, but I believe that Joe really preferred our company.

In *Wampo* camp Joe had formed a choir to sing The Volga Boatmen's Song in three part harmony. He had written out parts for it and gave each of us a copy. None of us could read the notation, and although it was never performed in public, we enjoyed singing it for our own enjoyment; and quite unphased by our inability to read, Joe sang each of the parts for us until we grasped what was wanted.

Despite the gap in our ages, Joe and I enjoyed a close rapport. He expressed surprise at my inability to read music, and said, "Your father was a Captain, and he did not have you taught music?"

It was hard for him to understand. He shook his head in disapproval.

"Such a waste! Such an ear for music!"

Knowing my feel for languages, Joe decided to teach me the Russian words to *Ochi Chornya*. He was pedantic, insisting that I got the pronunciation absolutely right. It was all good fun and eventually we would sing it together.

The orchestra may have been excellent, but conditions in the camp were very bad. Heavy showers were now frequent. While sleeping in the open one night, I woke to find myself lying at the centre of a shallow lake. Picking up my sodden blanket and the bundle of rags I used for a pillow, I made my way back to the hut but was unable to find a place between the packed bodies. I lay on the ground in the aisle, tucking myself in tightly against the base of a sleeping platform to be out of the way of the constant passage of feet going to and from the latrine. Dysentery was rife; visits were many. Going to the latrine at night in the pouring rain was an ordeal. Rain had filled the trench to the very brim, the squatting-poles were slimy with filth, and there was great danger of falling in. Thousands of fat maggots writhed around in a wriggling carpet; they covered the squat-poles and the ground about, they crawled over feet and legs in a loathsome mass. No matter how you tried to brush them off many were carried back to the hut, where wet feet had turned the aisle into slippery mud.

It was a nightmare night that would leave an ineradicable memory for all time.

Malaria attacks came so often that men lost count of them. I did not: during the years in the jungle I had over 75 bouts, two of which were cerebral malaria, generally fatal. I was lucky to survive. Raw quinine powder was the only treatment available. It had a horridly bitter taste, and I discovered that the best way to take it was to wrap it in a pellet of cement bag paper and swallow it quickly.

It was a basic medicine, but it saved many lives.

After days of violent shivers, burning fevers and psychedelic hallucinations, a sufferer could fall into a sleep of sheer exhaustion, and awake feeling marvellously refreshed but ravenously hungry. For this reason it was a good thing to have as a partner someone whose bouts did not coincide with your own. Such an arrangement allowed him to eat your rations while you were unable to, and vice versa.

Malaria cases generally remained in their own huts. The hospital huts were full of contagious, or more serious cases.

It was in this gloomy camp that I saw the change in the previously irrepressible Frankie Bowler. He had a place at the far end of the hut I had moved into, next to the doorway. He looked a figure of despondency, very sick with fever but he gave a wan smile as I passed, and called "Hello, Badgie!"

I did not see much of him in *Tarsoa*, and our ways parted later on. He was a changed man to the one I had known as the life and soul of the party at Havelock Road Camp in Singapore, and I heard no further news of him until after the end of the war. And it was sad news.

Entertainment could take many forms, and was not only confined to the stage. Despite the miserable conditions in which we lived, humour was almost always present. An irrepressible spirit existed which, given the chance, would, like a mushroom under an asphalt path, burst through and provide a lighter moment amid the gloom.

There was, for instance, Gunner "Slasher" Harris. In appearance he rather resembled an oriental, because of his cropped head, high cheek bones, yellow colouring and slanted, light green eyes. In fact he resembled Van Gogh's self portrait "As a Japanese".

Slasher had a peculiar accomplishment, which he demonstrated one night by a camp fire. He claimed to be able to draw air in through the anus and release it at will.

Of course no-one believed him, and the air was thick with ribald comment. He insisted that what he said was true, and invited us to listen closely.

He bent forward with hands on knees. We placed our ears in a suitable if hazardous position and listened with rapt attention.

There was, distinctly, an audible hiss from the appropriate organ; then, the performance began. Slasher lifted one knee and produced the promised noise. This was repeated several more times by request, and evoked hearty laughter each time, followed by enthusiastic applause; but there was more to follow.

He acknowledged the applause, and like Al Jolson he said, "You ain't heard nuthin' yet!"

Leaning forward again, he drew in a prodigious current of air; then flapping his arms and skipping daintily around the fire in a fairy dance, he let forth a whole series of synchronised farts.

By now his audience was in hysterics, and in one gigantic bound he leapt right over the fire, expelling at the apex of his jump, one great, cracking trump.

This was his finale, and like a true artiste who leaves the audience wanting more he rushed off into the darkness without a word. We were holding our sides, helpless with laughter.

In time we had the job of building new huts to replace the ones we were occupying. The construction was supervised by a Korean whose keenness exceeded his intelligence by a wide margin. The bamboo skeleton of a new hut, lashed together with ties cut from the bark of a tree, was in position and ready to be thatched. Strips of prepared thatch were hoisted at the end of long canes by men on the ground to those on the framework of the roof, who tied each piece in place.

The Korean guard decided that this work was not proceeding fast enough and began driving more and more men up onto the roof. He speeded up those reluctant to climb by lashing about him enthusiastically with a thick length of bamboo.

Soon there were very few men on the ground, and a great number on the roof.

As we worked, I complained to a man at my side, "I don't like heights at all!"

He laughed and replied, "It's a good job we're not building an attap skyscraper, Badgie!"

No sooner had he said this than there came a groaning, creaking sound and the whole flimsy structure began to move; It was collapsing under the weight of the men on the roof, gathering momentum very quickly. I had the presence of mind to pull my legs and feet up, clear of the lattice work and cross-members on which we were perched, to prevent them being crushed; then, with a loud thump, structure and men hit the ground.

With many others, I was flung clear on impact, twisting my back painfully in the process. The ground was littered with groaning men, many unable to rise. The Korean, beside himself with rage, lined us all up and carried out an impromptu medical examination. A few were allowed to return to their huts and limped, or were helped away. I was unable to straighten my back and was in considerable pain but was made to stay. However, when the framework of the hut was re-erected, the guard had learnt his lesson and fewer men were forced back to the roof.

The new buildings were an improvement on the old, having side walls and better ventilation. It made our long stay in that camp more tolerable.

There was quite a long walk down to the river, and to get there we had to pass the Japanese guard hut at the side of the dirt road. The sentry, representing the Emperor, had to be saluted or bowed to on passing. I had long been without the felt hat that I had received in Singapore, it had disappeared, probably stolen and sold in trade, during one of my bouts of malaria. Without a hat, I would have to bow, and I disliked that very much, so I made myself a hat from the leg of a pair of shorts. Crudely sewn across the top, it vaguely resembled a forage cap, and could be worn at a jaunty angle on the side of the head. To go with it I devised a salute that gave me amusement and offered the Japanese an (unrecognised!) insult at the same time.

My salute was made with fingers and thumb spread out in the manner of a naughty child making a rude gesture; that is, with thumb to nose. I called it my Rising Sun Salute; and had I ever been pulled up for it, I would have explained that it was a respectful representation of the Japanese flag. But I was never called to account.

Further down the track on the way to the river Major Dunlop was doing wonderful work in awful conditions.
I will never be able to forget the sight and sound of him sawing off limbs, using a butcher's saw. He worked in unsterile conditions in an ordinary hut and it was possible to see the top part of him, over the side thatch, as we passed along the road. He was an Australian medical officer.

His patients were often victims of the terrible jungle ulcers. An ulcer on the shin could eat away most of the flesh, exposing the tibia and fibula, with no hope of cure. Gangrene would set in and amputation was inevitable. Such patients, who survived would have a bamboo prosthesis made for them, and many took the souvenirs home after the war.

Treatment for an ulcer was incredibly painful and required scraping away putrefying matter with an ordinary spoon, followed by washing out with a carbolic solution.

Later on an old treatment was re-discovered which was less painful and more effective: a blowfly would be allowed to settle on the ulcer and lay its eggs, which in a very short time became maggots. The maggots would consume all the decaying matter and then drop off, leaving clean pink flesh.

I dreaded the ulcers, and when I had one start just above one of my heels, I tried a treatment of my own. The ulcer was still quite small when I devised a poultice from soft brown cane-sugar and soap. After a few applications, to my great relief, the ulcer healed.

Examples of Japanese cruelty were around us daily. Outside the guard hut a prisoner was made to stand all day in the sun, hatless and wearing only a loin cloth.

Day by day his legs swelled, until he resembled an advanced case of elephantiasis. Bad-tempered sentries would sometimes vent their spleen by knocking him about. It was pitiful to see his condition.

His crime was that he had slipped out to a nearby Thai village and had contracted syphylis. Our doctors, having no drug to treat the condition, had no choice but to notify the Japanese authorities.

By this time work on the railway had progressed to the point that rails had been laid up to a place about two miles inland from *Tarsoa* camp and the track was in use by lorries fitted with flanged wheels, enabling them to act as locomotives, pulling wagons bearing rails and sleepers.

Somehow the prisoner escaped one night and hid in the jungle beside the track. When the next train came along he laid his head on a rail and ended his suffering.

This incident typifies the brutality and insensitivity of the Japanese to their prisoners of war.

I had not seen our Major since leaving Changi barracks about two years previously.
"I was sorry to hear that Bombardier Phillips had died," he said, leaning forward and cupping one ear, in the same old way. I noticed that he still had his pipe.
His news was quite a shock to me.
"I didn't know," I answered, "I'm very sorry. He was a friend."

I was truly sorry, poor old Lofty, gone for good.
What a tragedy for his family! It felt a personal loss, never to see his lanky frame, or toothy grin again. One by one I was losing my friends.

Soon more men were needed for work farther up the river, and once again I found myself one of a party trekking along a narrow jungle path in blistering heat.

Ahead of the column marched Piper Wully Broon, leading us with the skirl and drone of his bagpipes.
It made the carrying of a heavy *kuali* seem lighter! The combination of ragged, scarecrow men stumbling along through the rain forest, and a cocky wee highlander piping away bravely before, made a memorable impression, and one that had an unusual sequel many years later.

After the war, when I was a Battery Sergeant Major in the British Army of the Rhine (BAOR) there was, among my troops, a difficult National Serviceman, a young Scot who gave my NCOs a lot of trouble.

One day when on a train in Germany I entered a carriage and found the only occupant to be the Scots lad.

Perhaps being closeted in a carriage with his Sergeant Major was a bit too much for him; he began an over-polite conversation, liberally besprinkled with, "Sirs".
To put him at his ease, I told him that I had been with the Gordon Highlanders during the war, and how the piper had piped us through the jungle.
He became very excited and his eyes lit up.
"That was ma uncle, Sir . Wully Broon was ma uncle!"
I was pleased to learn that Wully Broon had survived to return home safely.
"Ah've been a fool, Sir. Ah'm goin' to change from noo on!"
He did; there was no more trouble from him.

Wully Broon had stopped piping long before we reached our destination. He had run out of puff, and we were short of water. The only rations we had were dried, salted fish. It was yellow in colour and was shaped like a harp. It made us very thirsty and once water bottles were emptied there was no more water to be had. This experience put me off smoked haddock for life.

Our destination was a small camp named *Tonchan South*. It was also known as Tiger Camp, after the commandant, a man feared by his own men as much as by the prisoners.

The attap huts were already full, so we were put into leaky tents, about 10 men to a tent. A small stream ran through the camp, with a pretty waterfall just outside.

The Japanese had their compound on the opposite bank to the tents, and there was a camp containing Tamils a short way upstream. This was a very unhealthy arrangement as most of the Tamils were sick, and used the little stream for all purposes. Conditions which proved to be disastrous in a very short time.

The work on this stretch of railway was extremely hard and demanding. Solid rock all the way had to be drilled and blasted, pick-axed, shovelled and cleared by hand.

A drill required two men to operate it, one to hold and turn the metal rod, the other to swing a 14lb sledge hammer and strike the rod a heavy blow. For every blow, the rod was turned a quarter turn; one "tap", one turn. And every so often a small amount of water had to be poured into the boring to turn the rock dust into a paste that could be scooped out with a wire hoop. The holes had to be bored to the depth of one metre, and a Japanese with a marked probe stick would come to check that this was done correctly. It was exhausting work and it was necessary for tapper and turner to take turn about at it.

Bombardier Maurice Cerexhe had the appearance of a Saxon. He was very blond, with blue eyes, and had grown a moustache and beard. In manner he was pleasant and unassuming. I had seen him gradually go down hill, getting gaunter and weaker, and now he was almost blind from malnutrition.

Taking pity on him, and because no-one else would do so, I partnered him on this particular day. It meant I would have to swing the hammer all day long, but I was determined to do it.

To start drilling it was necessary to begin a boring by means of a short drill, about 18 inches long. With two men it is not difficult; with one man it is.

Cerexhe could not help. I sat on a low rock ledge, held the short rod in my left hand and the sledge hammer in my right. As I made to strike the drill the shaft of the hammer was jerked forward as it caught my thigh. The nail of my right index finger was crushed against the top of the drill causing excruciating pain.

In no time at all blood swelled up beneath the finger nail, and I was in great pain all day. By evening the nail had turned blue-green, and it kept me awake all night.

Later some-one told me I should have drilled the nail to relieve the pressure. On other occasions I followed this advice, using a needle to do so, and always got immediate relief.

The nail never really got back to normal and to this day it reminds me of poor Maurice Cerexhe. I call it my Cerexhe nail.

Maurice died in another camp at another time. He was then in the dysentery hut, where I went with a friend to see him. He was a bag of bones on the sleeping platform, but he managed a welcoming smile, and said,

"You're as welcome as the flowers in May — you boys coming up here to see me!"

It was the last time we saw him. He died after we left.

Among the many afflictions visited upon us was the non-fatal, but nevertheless pestilential tropical ringworm, which usually affected the crotch; but not always, for an outstanding example of this scourge was an unfortunate sufferer, "Ringworm" Smith, named for the great, weeping ringworm which, starting on the top of his cropped head, had spread over and down his face, neck and shoulders to the chest and upper arms, where it ended in a red-edged ring, giving him the appearance of wearing a strange mantilla. But irritating as this infection was there was soon a far more deadly epidemic to appear among us; and its name was cholera!

"RINGWORM SMITH"

It was during rock drilling in the South *Tonchan* area, when fuses had been lit and the workers took cover while blasting took place. I took up position behind, and as close as I could get to the trunk of a tree, and looking to my right I was surprised to see none other than Harry Brush, my double-jointed friend who had danced in the Great World cabaret; he looked even thinner now and very despondent.

"We're not safe, even behind a tree," he moaned.
"I was behind a tree the other day when a great big lump of rock came straight down, right close against the next tree. So it can still get you!"
With my own experience of what a rock can do to the head, Harry's remarks did little to cheer me up!

Some days later, back in camp, Harry came to see me. He was chewing charcoal and his lips were black; he explained that it was good for the stomach.

Cholera had broken out in the Tamil camp. The Japanese had taken to walking through trays of disinfectant at the gate to their own enclosure, and were less keen to walk among us.

Harry had been put to work collecting the dead Tamils and piling the corpses for burning. With utter despair in his kind brown eyes he told me this and added,
"We're bound to get it."

His words were prophetic, for when my party moved on later a friend and I called to see him in his hut. He was lying apathetically in the gloom of his bedspace and was too sick and too steeped in misery to even speak to us.
We called out, "Goodbye, Harry," and departed.
A few days later we heard that he was dead.

Harry, my good friend from Brighton. What happy times we had shared, at one time owning between us an ancient dickie-seated Fiat car, which only he could drive.

Far from beautiful Sussex, Harry had breathed his last in this remote, pestilence-ridden hell-hole.

The cholera spread rapidly to our part of the camp. It was a particularly virulent strain and its rapid course could carry off a victim within hours.
A prime example of this was Captain "Andy" Abrams a ranker officer who came out to the workings daily with the party bringing midday rice. Puffing away on his pipe he would sit with us and relate the most optimistic "news". (He was ever cheerful).

One day the midday rice appeared, but Andy did not.
When we asked where he was, we were told he had cholera.
Back in camp that evening the first question we asked was, "How is Andy?"
The answer was that Andy had been taken to the isolation tent that morning and was already dead and buried.

Another good man lost. A popular officer wasted.

Doctor Pavillard had obtained, from goodness knows where, some anti-cholera vaccine.

As we lined up for the inoculation he stood at the head of the queue, syringe in hand and joked, "Roll up roll up. Come and see the fat lady!"

We presented our arms to the needle far more keenly than any fairground customers ever produced their pennies at a side show booth.

Doctor Pavillard's great gift of humour brought a welcome touch of lightness to a grim situation.

One person who derived some benefit from the circumstances was Padre Harry Thorpe of the Australian Armed Forces. He had fenced off a small space by the stream for a church and had erected a large wooden cross. He made a wry comment on the increased size of his congregation.

"It takes cholera to get you to come to my services," he complained.

"Oh well, I suppose it's better than nothing!"

Then this dedicated man, who looked rather like a caricature of a chinless vicar, carried on his ministration.

Hygiene precautions in all British camps were always strictly observed, although there was little we could do other than try to keep flies off our food, and never fail to sterilize mess tins and mugs in the boiling water provided in 40 gallon drums outside every cookhouse.

The mixture of Asian races that worked on the railroad did not practise the same precautions, and also, of course, did not have the same discipline. The great number of their fatalities will never be known.

Among the various Asiatics was a number of Annamites, from French Indo China, very friendly little men, who for a while worked beside us on the *Wampo* portion of the railway.

One day one of them drew my attention to his friend who was squatting with hands on knees, looking up into the sky. I could not understand what he was doing and, seeing my puzzlement he pointed to his eyes. To my amazement I saw the sun reflected in the pupils. He was staring, unblinking at the sun. He was not blind, and it was a phenomenon that I cannot explain. Had I not seen it myself I would have been unable to believe it. Eventually this "party trick" must have ended in blindness.

This unusual contingent actually shared *Wampo* camp with us for some weeks, giving us the opportunity to practise some schoolboy French. This was the first and only time we shared a camp with natives; then they left to be swallowed up by the jungle with countless other unfortunates.

It was in *Tonchan* South camp that I had my second brush with a tiger. There was to be another in the future, but this one was with Tiger, the camp commandant!

With three other PoWs I was talking with some Malays beside a path at the edge of the camp. They were complaining about the bad conditions they were living in and how nothing had been prepared for them, no huts built nor any facilities. All agreed that things were much better under the British, how everything would have been prepared before they were called in.

One gave me a small book of Malay *Pantuns* (four-line verses) and at that moment I saw a Korean guard making his way furtively towards us.

The Malays vanished into the jungle, and I just had time to hide the little book away in my pocket.

Pleased with himself at his "capture", the guard levelled his rifle and bayonet at us and escorted us to the Tiger's office, where we waited outside, standing at attention.

We waited, and waited, and waited. It grew dark and a pressure lamp was lit inside the hut. We pondered our fate.

After what seemed an eternity, a Dutch Eurasian interpreter emerged from the office and ordered us inside.

We marched smartly in and saluted, facing the Tiger, a brooding menace at a large desk.

The Korean guard was present, looking smug and frightened at the same time.

A low, mumbling growl erupted from the Tiger's chest, "*Nan desu— ka?*" (What is it?)

Twitching nervously, the Korean gave his account. We, of course not understanding a word of what was said.

The tiger slowly raised his head, and his basilisk stare moved slowly over us. He began to question us through the interpreter, who seemed to be more on the Tiger's side than ours.

"Why did you go to talk to the Malays?"

"We were sitting talking to each other when the Malays came up to us," the first man answered.

I was glad that I stood on the right, the last man in the row; I would never have been quick-witted enough to think up such a good reply.

"What did the Malays say to you?"

The second man: "I don't know. I couldn't understand them." It was another good reply.

"What were you talking to each other about?"

There was a pregnant pause, then,

"We were talking about the day's work." A brilliant reply. It could not have been better. The Tiger grunted, then actually smiled, and tension left the air. He was either very pleased to have such conscientious workers, or simply amused at the cheek. It did not matter which. The atmosphere had changed.

"Do you speak Malay?"

The question was asked of each of us in turn. Each said no. When it came to my turn I lied, "No", mentally crossing my fingers, hoping against hope that I would not be searched.

The tiny book in my pocket now felt like a volume of the Encyclopaedia Britannica — but we were not searched. We were ordered not to speak to natives, and then given the command to dismiss. In true British Army fashion we turned to the right and saluted smartly, to be instantly stopped short by the Eurasian interpreter.

"As you were!" he snarled. "You do not salute into thin air in the stupid British manner. Face the commandant and salute, then turn and march out."

We did as we were told, even more smartly than before, and marched off, conscious that we had had a lucky escape.

The evening rice was finished, so we went hungry, but even so we were grateful that we had found the capricious Tiger in a good mood.

A short while after this incident some of us were detailed to report to the stores where we were each given two of the steel drill rods to carry. We were led off along a track leading northward. Recent heavy rain had made the ground slippery and the going was difficult.

By now I had been barefooted for sometime and was very weak from malaria and diarrhoea. The hilly terrain soon found me flagging badly, and I fell behind the column.

The two drills became an insupportable weight, and the straggling line of stumbling figures soon disappeared round a bend in the trail ahead.

The rain teemed down, making a soft roaring sound as it beat upon the leaves of the forest around me. I made a supreme effort to keep going, but as I rounded the corner I was dismayed to see an empty track before me. Not a man was in sight; the column had disappeared.

I struggled on, then the worst possible thing befell me — I came upon a fork in the road, and there was no way of telling which way the gang had taken.

Stumbling along, growing more desperate with every step, I felt the drills pressing more and more heavily on my shoulders The rain beat steadily down without let up. I was shivering uncontrollably, and my morale sank lower and lower.

I was about to sink down onto the mud in despair when, through the grey miasma ahead I saw an attap roof. My spirits lifted as hope was re-kindled that I had caught up with the party.

As swiftly as a small fire doused by a pail of water, my optimism was extinguished — the place was deserted.

There was not a soul to be seen. Under the attap roof were rows and rows of neatly stacked drills, shovels and pick-axes. I had stumbled upon a cache of tools for the next stage of construction.

If my morale had been low before, it now sank completely. I was shattered, desperate. Found alone in the jungle so far from camp — there was no doubt as to what my fate would be!

In my awful, weakened state, I am ashamed to admit that there, alone in the dripping forest, for the first and only time during the years of my captivity, I wept helpless, desperate tears.

To retrace my steps and take the right fork in an attempt to catch up with the group again, was physically beyond me. There was nothing to do but return to the camp.

I placed my two drills on top of the nearest pile in the open-sided building and forced my sore feet and tired legs back the way I had come.

Eventually I reached the camp and was able to enter it unseen in the downpour, and when the party returned later, I was relieved to find that my absence had not been noticed. Whether the two rods were missed or not I shall never know. It was fortunate that the guards always seemed to have trouble counting!

Each day now we walked further to work as the construction went on. To add to our woes — we had become pariahs! One morning as we passed *Tonchan* Central some men outside a tent shouted, "Keep away! Don't come near us. You've got cholera in your camp!"

Such is the fear that the dreaded disease can arouse.

What became known as the infamous "Speedo" had begun. Increasing pressure to complete the railroad had apparently come down from above, and it had driven the Japanese engineers into a frenzy.

Work went on all day under a barrage of shouts and blows. *Yasume* (rest) periods were disregarded and the terrible day seemed never to end. Nor did it. The usual time for returning to camp came and went — we were kept working.

The brief tropical twilight was upon us. Lamps arrived and fires were lit. In a state of desperate tiredness we were driven on by kicks and blows.

Men found patches of darkness in which to steal a few minutes of rest. When discovered they were beaten up mercilessly with whatever came to hand. Standing on a low bridge an engineer, screaming with rage hurled a heavy iron bar down at a group of prisoners who were toiling below.

On and on throughout the night the hideous slavery continued. The dawn came. Captors and captives alike were exhausted. Eventually even the demented yellow demons who drove us on could see there was no more to be gained from men barely able to lift a pick-axe, and we were released to return to camp as the next shift arrived.

There a shock awaited us. Our tents were gone. Folded and gone ahead to the next destination.

We lay on the ground among our few possessions and fell instantly asleep.

The heat of the sun blazing down awoke us. It was over 24 hours since we had last eaten, and, after a meal of rice and boiled water, we set off on a march to the north.

There now followed a series of moves from camp to camp, each seeming worse than the previous one. Throughout the monsoon we worked under appalling difficulties and were engaged in a wide variety of tasks.

It would be tiresome to relate in sequence the events that occurred; the whole tragic litany of hardships and deaths would inevitably depress the reader, who is probably reading this in comfort in a cosy atmosphere; and who may never have experienced deprivation and constant hunger, and may perhaps be unable to imagine it.

I feel, therefore, it better to relate a series of cameos as they come to mind, with no attempt made, in these cameos, at chronological exactitude.

All of these things I saw with my own eyes.

Up a steep and slippery river bank, about 30 feet high, toiled a gang of Australians, misery etched on their faces, shoulders bowed under the weight of lengths of railway line. A pile of these attested to the awful burden of work that would be needed to bear them up from where they lay beside the water's edge. The Australians were so deep in despair that they did not return our greetings.

During a march to another camp we were resting beside a narrow trail. Behind us was a company of Australian troops. An Australian officer moved along the line of his men calling for volunteers to carry a stretcher case who was at the rear of the column.

"We're not carrying him. He's got cholera," I heard a surly voice saying.

The officer had similar replies from the other men, and was looking desperate, yet he never remonstrated with them.
Disgusted by such insubordination, I got to my feet and said , "Come on lads. Let's give a hand."
Three lads got up without hesitation and came with me.
"It's all right," said the officer, "These British boys are going to help us." He sounded relieved and grateful.

I hoped his men felt suitably ashamed. We lifted the stretcher between us and carried it to the next camp, which turned out to be about 3 miles farther on.

We had been in camp only a short time when the man who had been on the stretcher came looking for us. He shook hands, explained that he had been exhausted, thanked us and left. A short time later another Australian came to me and said,

"That man's a bludger. He's always doing that!"
Was it true? Or was it an attempt to excuse a blatant disregard of another's need of help?

This is something else that I shall never know!

At a small camp near the border with Burma a man-eating tiger prowled the vicinity. On two recent occasions, from a nearby hut it had taken and eaten Indian labourers. Our camp was on tenterhooks, and at night we kept a fire burning at the door of the hut and another in front of the latrine, which was about twenty paces away at the edge of the forest.

Crossing this space in the dark was nerve racking, and one felt particularly vulnerable in the latrine, separated from thick jungle by no more than a thin attap wall. A generous pile of dry bamboo was kept at hand for feeding the flames on these occasions!

Even during daylight there was tension when working out of the camp, and once when a small party was outside repairing a rutted track, under a Korean guard, we heard a noise among nearby trees, and our first thought was, "Tiger!"

Then we saw a tawny form, apparently making its way towards us. "Tiger!" the shout went up, "Tiger!"

An incredible thing happened — the Korean handed his rifle to one of the PoWs, indicating that he should shoot the tiger, then went and placed himself in the middle of the gang.

The tawny form suddenly burst out from the undergrowth a few yards in front of us, and with one look at us it turned and ran off. It was a large wild dog.

Shamefacedly, and to the mocking laughter of the prisoners the Korean took his rifle back. It was as well that none of his own comrades had witnessed this loss of face!

POW QUARTERS, THAILAND

In one of the camps up-river we were fortunate enough to find a small stage, an establishment set up by previous occupants who had now moved on. I had found an escape from harsh reality by taking an enthusiastic interest in concert party work, writing my own material and taking part in sketches, singing and sometimes dancing (not, I hasten to add, of the ballroom variety.)

Behind the stage was a dressing room-cum-props store. Another member of the concert party and myself slept there to guard the props against theft, and enjoyed the luxury of having so much space to ourselves.

I wrote, produced and took part in some shows,(all preparations for which were done outside working hours) and one of them included a skit called; The Private Life of Cleopatra.

The camp commandant had attended the show, and after it sent me a bouquet and a brickbat.
He said that he had enjoyed the show, but he also disapproved.
"You should not," he said, "make fun of your ancestors".

He sent round a roast duck, small but beautifully cooked. There were thirteen concert party members. We shared that tasty little fowl. It was delicious! We ate bones and all. Not a scrap was wasted.

As with skinning a cat, there are many more ways than one of catching a fish. I learnt a new one by watching a Thai on the river bank. The river was low and slow moving, and the man was tossing small rice balls out into the stream; in what appeared to be an act of madness. He then moved a few yards down river to where the current swung in close to the bank. Within a few minutes three or four fish came to the surface, floating on their sides.

The fisherman waded in and retrieved his catch; threaded a cord through their gills, and moved off through the forest.
The method in his madness was a pellet of tobacco rolled up inside the rice ball. Fish swallowed the bait which broke open in the stomach, and — presto! instant knockout.

The tobacco, grown locally, was known to the PoWs as Sikh's beard, because it was sold in cushions, like large hanks of shredded wheat. It was dark brown in colour and was so strong that smokers always rinsed it several times to make it mild enough for use. This action resulted in any number (when carried out in the river) of small fry in the vicinity, floating to the surface, dead. It made a cheap substitute for the manufactured brands of Thai cigarettes such as the popular brands of Red Bull and Battle Gong.

The river became a very different creature according to the season. In the dry months it could be a gentle, placid thing, flowing at a leisurely pace, very low, between high banks; so shallow in places that Thai barges, which carried goods up and down it, were unable to pass.

In the monsoon season it was a fat, angry yellow monster, a ferocious dragon, swollen by the myriad of streams come down from the mountains, each a torrent in its own right, roaring through deep rock gorges carved out through aeons of time. It rose high up its banks, its current now a snarling demon bearing on its back all manner of debris, sticks, clumps of bamboo, massive tree trunks, and carrying such a burden of yellow mud that it took on the consistency of runny honey.

Across the gorges of the mountain streams that fed the Kwai, the PoWs built bridges, as will be shown in the next cameo.

The bridges we built were of the trestle type, some of them 60 to 70 feet high; a wooden lattice work constructed with the green teak hewn from the surrounding forest by cross-cut saws and axes, and borne on the bony shoulders of emaciated prisoners. The first timbers were hammered into place by a crude pile driver; a gang of twenty men pulling on a rope to hoist the heavy hammer to the top of a gantry to let it drop, all done to a chant of, *"Ichi, ni, a — sayo— a — sayo!"* — Thud! Crude — but it worked; even if it took all day to drive a difficult pile in.

In pouring rain, with sharp limestone rock just below the surface of liquid, slippery mud, teams of men almost at the limit of endurance staggered along under the great weight of the massive trunks, stumbling over the uneven terrain, moaning as the rough bark bit into almost fleshless shoulders.

Bull elephants working nearby, for all their mighty strength, were barely able to lift these monsters, and would only apply their great curving tusks when driven to it by their mahouts, who brought the blunt end of a small axe down upon the great dome of an animal's forehead with a resounding crack. The huge beasts would respond with a scream of rage and pain that echoed through the tall timber.

The rain hissed ceaselessly down in a steady roar, and the spirits of we tormented, badly used, half-dead specimens of humanity were hovering close to absolute zero. Of dark hours, this was among the darkest. We were all near despair.

That we were less than animals to the Japanese was exemplified by their dictum:
Ten Ingrish sojah — one erephunt — same! (Ten English soldier — one elephant — same!)

Crossing a trestle bridge on foot was an ordeal. There were no handrails and it was necessary to step across from sleeper to sleeper, always very aware of the great drop down to the floor of the gorge below; a slip would inevitably mean death.

One man in front of me trod on a hot cinder which had fallen from a locomotive; he gave a shout, jumped and fell between two sleepers; by a fluke he managed to grab the one in front of him and save himself.

To cross a bridge in one of the open rail trucks was just as bad, perhaps worse. The tall wooden structures were very shaky, so much so that on some stretches of the railroad the Japanese would risk using locomotives on them as little as possible. Instead, wagons would be shunted across from a locomotive on one side to another on the other.

To sit helpless in an open wagon, while this procedure was being carried out, was hair-raising. A mighty thump would send you rolling out to the centre of the bridge, with the whole structure trembling beneath you. There you would wait in great trepidation for the next series of thumps to send you to the other side. It was nerve racking, but the relief felt, on arriving safely on firm ground again was a wonderful feeling indeed.

In one camp a monkey came to us from the Korean quarters. It was a pathetic sight, its hands were tied behind its back and the end of its tail had been held in a fire. It had been punished for "stealing".

A sympathetic PoW freed its hands and bandaged its tail, and the distressed little creature remained among us from then on. None of us, after our own experiences, felt we would ever again want to keep anything captive, and the monkey was perfectly free to go wherever it wished. It was fed on scraps and given water, and it took up residence in the rafters of a hut, always hiding whenever a guard appeared.

Although free to do so it never made any attempt at escaping into the jungle and seemed to look upon itself as a member of our group.

It could be a nuisance but no-one ever made a move to punish it, even when provoked. For instance: at one camp where a well had to be dug for our water supply, it would wait while a prisoner filled a four gallon kerosene can at the well, then screaming menace and baring its teeth, it would grab the can forcing the owner to relinquish it until it had thoroughly enjoyed playing with the water and finally bathing in it. It was in no hurry to end this performance but eventually it would take itself off, bedraggled but happy.

Later in the war when Allied warplanes flew overhead the frightened little simian would crouch terror stricken in the rafters with its tiny hands clasped over its ears.

There was a huge billy goat which one day wandered into our camp. It seemed very friendly and came up to me and stood quietly, but I soon found out that it was a mistake to pat its head, which is what I did.

It liked the gesture and seemed to be wanting more for when I patted it again it pushed its big head against my hand.

This was a fine game! It backed off a little and gave my hand a gentle butt. Then, as if seized by an impish impulse, it leant back on its haunches and lunged forward with more force.

When it backed off a full three paces and compressed its muscular hind quarters like powerful springs ready to hurl itself forward like a battering ram, I decided that discretion was the better part of valour and turned and fled.

I could see that there was fun to be had here and I watched from a safe vantage point as it selected other victims around the camp.

It was having a marvellous time. At one stage I witnessed a scene that was straight out of a comic, silent movie.

Looking down the lane between two huts I saw a PoW tear across the gap at the far end; seconds later the big animal came hurtling after him.

Seemingly the billy goat possessed a human sense of humour, and it was some time before he tired of his practical jokes and trotted out of the camp to return from whence he came.

Pets were, of course, rare in the prison camps but what there were are worthy of mention. There was a little brown hen, perhaps not really a pet for it must surely have been destined for the pot, but in the meantime it was so small and scrawny that it was no more than feathers and skin draped over a bony carcass. Everyone knew to whom it belonged, and even as there is honour among thieves, so there is much the same among hungry PoWs, and nobody had stolen it — so far!

However, it was known that a chicken could be mesmerised if it was held to the ground while a circle was drawn in the dirt by its head; and quite often the poor fowl would be seen motionless on its side on the floor of a hut with its eye fixed on a circle.

It would remain thus until some sympathetic rescuer picked it up and set it on its feet, breaking the spell.

Sadly the Good Samaritan often succumbed to the temptation of trying the same experiment a few yards further on.

I am ashamed to say that I was one of these!

The true story of the white duck really belongs during the time that we spent in our last camp towards the end of the war. I relate it here for convenience. The story that appeared on the front page of a national daily news-paper after our release was a bit like the curate's egg, but in this case — true in parts.

There was, in this particular camp, a young Scottish soldier. He had obtained a fertile duck egg which he carried around on his person until it was hatched by the warmth of his body. The duckling thrived on a diet of maggots from the ample supply to be found in the latrine, and it followed its "mother" everywhere. When the soldier worked in the moat surrounding this camp his duck swam about close to him.

Soldier and duck survived and in some way the pair reached England together (the duck must, obviously, have been smuggled in).

The item of news, when it appeared on the front page, was presented in its own box, captioned "Saint Donald" and had a cartoon of Donald Duck with a halo above his head.

The article related the story and said that the soldier had explained to the Japanese authorities that he belonged to a remote Scottish clan that worshipped ducks; and he was allowed to keep it.

This is the only part of the story I cannot vouch for; the rest I saw with my own eyes.

Besides pets, there were other bizarre things that I encountered during the years spent in the various camps.

One occurred during an evening roll call. The parade was lined up facing west; the weather was fine and everything was quiet; across the river, far away above the tree tops, just above the horizon hung a fat moon; the most beautiful pale blue disc, on a field of saffron yellow.

The next evening for a while it took on the same exquisite colour, so, in my life I have seen not just one — but two blue moons.

Perhaps even stranger still, in another camp at another time, a most extraordinary phenomenon happened: although, I have since learned that it is not so very uncommon.

During a sudden, heavy downpour a man came running into the hut, greatly excited and looking for a container.

"Fish!" he shouted, "it's raining fish!"

Of course no-one believed him and he was subjected to loud derision, in the choicest barrack room language.

Along with a few others I went to see for myself, and sure enough, little silver fish were flapping about on the parade ground and in puddles and runnels around its edges.

The downpour ceased as quickly as it had begun, and by the time I had rushed back into the hut and returned again with my mess tin most of the fish had been collected.

Apparently the fish are sucked up in storm conditions over the Gulf of Siam and are sometimes carried many miles inland before falling to earth again. Perhaps this would have been described as a miracle, in an earlier age.

What seemed a miracle at the time, happened to me. A sort of Lazarus miracle.

After many months up country, moving from camp to camp. I found myself back in *Tarsoa* having been evacuated down river by barge with a number of other sick men.

We disembarked at the foot of a high, ochre-coloured bank and were met at the top by a Korean guard who made us walk through a tray of disinfectant before spraying us from something that looked like an old-fashioned Flit pump.

We were then left to our own devices and I was looking about me when I was startled, and annoyed, by a sharp, painful slap on the back.

I swung round and looked into the grinning face of Lofty Phillips. I felt a physical shock.

"You —— you're dead!" I gasped. "Major Jackson told me you were dead!"

"No, I'm not", he grinned even more widely. "That was another Bombardier Phillips!"

For months I had believed him dead, now he burst upon me like a bombshell — no warning whatsoever.

It took me a moment or two to recover my wits, then we went together to the main camp where I was to meet a number of old friends. I am happy to say that Lofty and his false teeth survived to get home to his wife and family

Surprises seldom come singly and I had another one some weeks later when I met another old friend, Joe Lowe, the pal I had shared many happy hours with in Singapore and had not seen since the day he left Changi for a working party in the city.

He had an unusual tale to relate. Hearing I was at *Tarsoa* he had come to my hut to find me, and had laughed at the expression of amazement and delight he saw on my face when he appeared so completely unexpectedly.

He was not housed in *Tarsoa* camp but was instead in a small place about two miles away down the path, where there was a Railway Engineers Regiment depot. Together with a few other British PoWs he had an easy number, supervising native labour gangs. Joe had been sent up to *Tarsoa* with a message. On being challenged by a sentry he had only to mention the name of the Japanese commandant of the depot, and he was immediately allowed to pass unmolested.

We had the most enjoyable chat about old times, and must have reminisced for almost two hours. Joe seemed in no hurry to leave, but eventually had to go, having explained to me exactly where the depot was situated.

The life there sounded paradisical compared to life in *Tarsoa*. Joe's gang were all Malays. What would I not have given to have been in his place?

That same evening, after roll call, on a mad impulse I walked out of the camp gate. It was no more than a wide gap in the fence and was constantly busy with PoWs coming and going from the river.

The path to the depot crossed the concourse at right angles by the gate. Keeping close in against the fence I walked off down the path, which was also busy with a stream of Asiatics coming along it from the other direction. Malays and Chinese with their belongings on their backs and families following, were quarrelling among themselves as I passed. No-one gave me a second glance.

It was getting dark by the time I reached Joe's hut.

He was amazed to see me, but made me welcome, and soon had a meal ready for me. He had not exaggerated, it was far better than *Tarsoa* fare.

After talking for a while we went into the next hut to meet Joe's gang. The Malays were delighted to have an *orang puteh* (white man) converse with them in their own language, and soon we were singing songs together and putting *pantuns* in between choruses of the popular tune: *Rasa Sayang-i.*

It was with a sense of shock that I saw a Japanese guard enter the hut. I held my breath for fear that he would notice that I was not one of the attached personnel. If he did, I should be in deep trouble. I need not have worried; after a glance at Joe and me, he spoke to someone farther down the hut, then left. I was greatly relieved to see him go.

There was plenty of room in Joe's hut. I slept there that night and left before dawn next morning. Daylight came as I made my way along the now empty path. I had to get back into camp without being observed.

The bamboo fence came into sight ahead. Then I froze! A guard was patrolling <u>outside</u> the camp with his rifle and bayonet at the ready.

As he paced slowly along I kept a tree trunk between us, keeping as still as possible, knowing that any movement instantly attracts the eye. I watched intently as he made his way along the fence, then, as soon as he turned the corner, I moved across swiftly and flattened myself against the fence. I crept along and got through the gate without being seen.

The relief I felt was indescribable. At the same time I realised the full extent of the foolish risk I had taken. A snap roll call could have disclosed my absence. A second or two earlier on the path and the sentry would have seen me. It was by the greatest stroke of luck that I had seen him first! I was not likely to take the same stupid risk again.

If it was so easy to walk out of a camp, why did no-one escape? A moment's thought will answer this question.

The sick and debilitated condition of the PoWs precluded their getting far; the jungle itself was a formidable barrier, and there was the threat of reprisals against comrades left behind. These were reasons enough; then again this was not Europe, and we were not Asiatics. At another camp two young officers who attempted escape were brought back, desperately sick, not even having reached the Burma border. They were bruised and bloodied from beatings; were taken away by the *Kempei Tai* (the dreaded military police) and were not seen again.

India held the nearest Allied bases and India was hundreds of miles away through hostile country.

When I arrived back in *Tarsoa* my physical condition was very low. Constant sickness and heavy labour had taken its toll, and my worldly possessions at this time amounted to the following items: one half of a thin red blanket; a piece of canvas the size and shape of that on a deck chair; a small bundle of rags that I used as a pillow; a little red enamelled bowl with a hole plugged by a piece of bamboo, and with a lid to keep out the flies; my Army haversack and water bottle; one dessert spoon, half its original size, and one side worn down flat, with a piece of cane in place of its missing handle; and one ragged pair of shorts plus a "forage cap" (made from the leg of an old pair of shorts).

One day a friendly Eurasian lad, who could never resist making a pun of my name and called me Rajah,(there were several Eurasian boys among us and they had the old fashioned custom of addressing each other by surnames), told me that I would be better off working in camp. At first I rejected the idea because it meant working for the officers. Officers were not made to work, although one always went out with the working parties. They had their own hut within our camp and, of course, attended all roll call parades.

"Rajah, the work is very easy. You just do a bit of washing — and get a swim while the rest are out working hard; and you take a turn at the serving point when the officers collect their meals. You'll be much better off!"

I had to admit that it sounded very attractive. Really this was no time or place for false pride, so I applied for and was accepted in the role of batman to three delightful officers: Major "Tosh" Rowson R.A., Lieutenant Hayles-Finch a real gentleman of the old school who wore a monocle and had served in W.W.1., and a Straits volunteer Forces lieutenant who spoke fluent Malay but made no attempt at correct pronunciation.

These gentlemen were very kind and undemanding, and, being relieved of the heavy outside labour, my condition began to improve.

Major Rowson was of slight build with sandy hair and a neat moustache. He had a calm manner and never raised his voice. We shared an interest in Malay, and he advised me to leave the Army after the war and to take up work in the Malayan Customs Service, as this would offer a better future. He always conversed with me as if we were on equal terms.

On my first morning in the new job, I went to wake him up and was given my first taste of his good humour.

Standing at the door of the cubicle that he shared with the two other officers I called out.

"Awake for Morning in the Bowl of Night
  Has flung the Stone that puts the Stars to Flight:"

The major opened one eye and fixed it on me. For a moment I wondered if I had over-stepped the mark. But I need not have worried, for he replied,

"And Lo! The Hunter of the East has caught
  The Sultan's Turret in a Noose of Light."

The rapport that developed was as close as it could be between two such disparate ranks.

Often we would converse together in Malay, and sometimes compete, to test our vocabularies. One would give a Malay word beginning with the letter A. The other would reply with another, and so on until no more could be found. The winner, of course, being the one who found the last word. We worked through the alphabet this way, and it was good fun as an aid to increasing our vocabularies.

I hope the reader will not think me immodest when I claim to have won most of these friendly contests!

Major Rowson was not averse to laughing at himself, and told me the following anecdote:

He once had a Malay *munshi* (language teacher) who seemed keener to learn English than to teach him Malay.

One day the Major made an error, and being anxious to air new words, and intending to say. "I am very ashamed," said, *"Kemaluan saya besar!"*

The *munshi* rocked with laughter. (*Kemaluan* does mean shame, but is a euphemism for something else).

When he had regained his composure he told the major that what he actually said was:

"I have big female parts!"

Which exemplifies the value of a guide through the subtleties of a new language!

During the dry season ground lizards emerged from their burrows and were active about the camp.
Although easily seen as they scuttled over the bare brown earth, they were not easily caught. Possessed of an amazing turn of speed, when chased their legs whizzed round, taking on the appearance of small wheels.

The only effective way of catching them was by using a trap, and for this I was prepared.

One day at the edge of the jungle beside the railway I had seen a Thai who was carrying a large bundle of lizards and had some sort of gadget on his shoulder. Pleased by my interest, he had shown me the device and explained by gestures how it worked. It was ingenious in its simplicity and was a trap made entirely from bamboo and a piece of string.

It consisted of three pieces; a thin, flexible cane about 15 inches (46 cm) long, sharpened at one end; a cylinder 2 inches (5 cm) high by 1 ½ inches (3.5 cm) in diameter, with two small holes drilled near the base, which allowed a noose of the string to be positioned within; a "trigger" fashioned into a small, flat spade-shape with a ridge on the underside to hook onto the rim of the cylinder and hold the string in tension. The cylinder was tied about two inches up from the base of the cane.

The working of the trap is better explained in the diagram which accompanies this narrative.

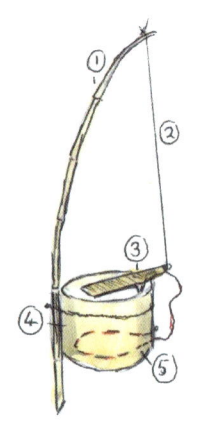

① SPRINGY BAMBOO
② "BOW STRING"
③ LIGHT (NOTCHED) BAMBOO TRIGGER
④ BAMBOO CYLINDER
⑤ NOOSE WITHIN CYLINDER

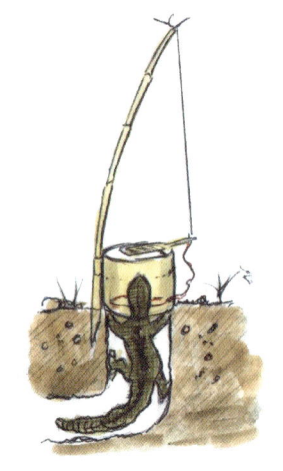

TRAP IN POSITION OVER HOLE.
LIZARD PASSES HEAD THROUGH NOOSE TO KNOCK TRIGGER OUT OF WAY.
THIS RELEASES TENSION ON BOW STRING.
BOW STRING ALLOWS SPRINGY BAMBOO TO STRAIGHTEN UP.
NOOSE IS PULLED TIGHT AROUND NECK.
LIZARD IS TRAPPED.

THAI LIZARD TRAP

After a few failed attempts I succeeded in making a trap for myself and used it to catch lizards whenever I wanted.

Being about 12 inches (30 cm) long and much plumper than when they first emerged from hibernation at the beginning of the season, they made a welcome and nourishing addition to my rations.

As a welcome change to stew, whenever I could get some rice flour and coconut oil, I would make tasty lizard pasties.

These must have gained some notoriety in the camp, for one day a captain came to me and said,

"I hear you make good lizard pasties, Bombardier!"

I admitted that I did.

"If I give you some rice flour and coconut oil will you make two for me?"

I agreed that I would.

The captain departed and returned shortly with the promised items. These were very welcome for I had had none for a week or two. I said I would let him have two pasties as soon as they were ready, and we went our separate ways; he back to his billet and I to set off with my trap on a lizard hunt.

It was nearing the end of the dry season, this and my depredations had caused a drop in the number of lizards to be found, and it took longer than usual to secure two victims. Trapped lizards were humanely despatched with a quick blow to the head from a stout stick. The fact that I carried one as well as the trap was to prove an advantage before very much longer.

I took my catch back to the hut and cooked them over a small fire in a tin on the earth at the foot of my sleeping platform. When the flesh had boiled off the bones I used the flour and oil and fried two small pasties. They looked delicious, and I was hungry. I ate the two of them.

Now I must trap two more lizards for the captain's share. As I tramped around the camp in a search for more, I began to regret having given way to my hunger, for I found no more victims. The ground was as empty as Mother Hubbard's cupboard. There was not a solitary ground lizard to be seen and my desperation grew as I imagined facing the captain with no pasties, and half his stock of flour and rice gone.

I was about to give up the hunt, when I caught a movement out of the corner of my eye. Just above my head, clinging to the rough bark of a tree was a lizard. It was very different to the ground lizards, being slightly smaller, very dark in colour and covered in spikes. It was extremely ugly and looked like a miniature dinosaur.

Quick as a flash. I hit it with my stick, killing it instantly. I was not sure it was edible, but it seemed worth the risk, under the circumstances, and was better than nothing.

I returned to my hut and began to cook it. As I squatted watching the pot, the soil moved near my feet.

At first I thought I had imagined it, but after a moment or two it moved again. There was a definite humping of the earth.

I reached for my stick and waited. Again the earth heaved up and a small snout appeared. Down flashed the stick as a black head emerged from the soil, and I had slain another victim.

Pulling the body from the loose dirt, I saw it was a small mammal, not unlike a mole. Whatever it was, I skinned it and cooked it after the lizard was done.

Now I had the two required pasties. I noticed that the water in which I had boiled the little animal was a pretty blue colour. At that moment the men were coming into the hut from work. Purely as a joke I called out,

"Anyone fancy some mole soup?"

I gave the pot to the first eager claimant, who drank it, and to my relief pronounced it very tasty.

When I took the two pasties to the captain he thanked me profusely. I left, and over the next day or two watched him surreptitiously from cover and saw no ill effects.

Finally I plucked up courage to approach him.

"How were the pasties, sir?"

"Very good thank you, Bombardier. They were delicious. Will you be making any more soon?"

"I'm afraid not, sir. The season's almost over and there are very few lizards about now."

"Oh, what a shame!" he said.

For my part I was quite relieved. The strain of the last two pasties had proved a little too much!

As for lizards, the dry season was a time for dust devils. These capricious winds would appear without any warning, and could vary in size and strength from an insignificant, whirling cylinder of dust and dry leaves, to a miniature tornado, a fury the size and strength of which could lift heavy objects, and be as tall as a factory chimney in a Lowry painting.

The baked and dusty earth of a parade square made a playground for them and they would pick up debris and fashion a whirligig which would veer in eccentric orbits around the area like a demented dervish, speeding up and slowing down, dying and being born again, lifting strips of attap up and tossing them down as suddenly, like a child in a tantrum, hurling them to one side then sucking them up again into its vortex.

One might make a single walker jump out of it's path. Another could scatter a crowd of men like skittles.

At a later time on the Isthmus of *Kra*, I saw a prisoner who was thatching the apex of a roof, lifted bodily by one of these winds and set down standing upright a foot or so in front of me.

He seemed dazed, "I don't know what happened, Badgie," he said.

"One minute I was up there, and the next I was down here!" He was completely unharmed, and the whirlwind had already disappeared.

Such unpredictable visitors could be a nuisance, but they were not the only ones. There was another menace — in the river; it was fish!

We swam naked and had quickly been made aware of a certain danger that lurked there.

Small fish would dart in and take a quick bite at, what must have appeared to be a tasty morsel.

A sharp nip and tug at a very tender part of the anatomy soon taught us to cup our hands over our manhood on entering the water, but by the time this lesson had been learned some victims had already suffered the attentions of larger, stronger fish (with, presumably, sharper teeth) and had left the river lesser men than when they had entered it, having lost a piece of valuable flesh!

In some cases sympathetic medical officers issued certificates attesting the cause of the bite-size disfigurements, to be taken home to suspicious spouses as proof of innocence.

Nor were small fish the only pests we encountered. Leeches, for instance would attach themselves to a limb and, as with river fish, we had learned how to deal with them.

It was a grave mistake to pull them off, for this would leave a small, circular wound which would not heal easily and could become a sore, or even an ulcer. One way to make them drop off was to touch them with a lighted cigarette.

An equally effective way was to soak a pinch of Sikh's beard tobacco in water and squeeze it just above the leech's head. The juice would run down the leg onto the blood-sucker, causing it to fall off instantly.

In the event of neither of these two remedies being available, the only recourse was to allow the leech to gorge itself, changing during this action from a thin boot lace into a thick black pencil, but no harm was done to the skin.

Nasty as they were, the type of leech that pestered us was a mere baby compared to the ones that infected the water buffaloes in the rice paddies.

These monsters, when gorged, hung from the flanks of the animals like obscene, thick black cylinders, longer than a man's forearm.

Tinier by far than the leeches but pestiferous enough to drive a man mad, were the sand flies. This pest descended on us during a rainy season, at a place where we were labouring at the almost impossible task of digging in clinging red clay.

This difficult, glutinous substance stuck tenaciously to our spades, and gurgled and sucked about our feet as the rain beat down in a steady roar, hiding the surrounding jungle in a grey miasma, and, despite the labour of digging, chilling us to the bone, making us long for a let-up in the continuous, cold drenching.

There was a great feeling of relief when the fat, grey clouds parted and the sun broke through, giving a marvellous sensation of warmth, but it was short-lived, for in an instant our near-naked bodies were enveloped in a cloud of voracious, biting sand flies; insects so tiny that they were no bigger than the point of a pin, yet so numerous that they cloaked a man from head to foot in a curtain of irritation.

Nothing could keep them from our flesh, flailing arms, prancing about, slapping; there was no escaping their attention, no respite from their relentless assault.

What blessed relief when the rain hissed down once more and the pests vanished as quickly as they had appeared. But soon we were chilled again, and the day wore on in an endless misery.

There was an experience awaiting me in the future with something bigger than a leech and more painful than a sand fly.

It happened on a jungle path. A friend was in the sick hut at some distance away from the living quarters and I was walking between undergrowth and tall trees to visit him.

About twenty yards in front of me were two prisoners, going in the same direction. Suddenly they broke into a strange, energetic dance, high stepping with arms waving overhead, as if rehearsing for some pantomime. Then, like the White Rabbit they dashed off as if late for an appointment.

Their behaviour seemed strange, but not strange enough to cause comment in a PoW camp, and I continued placidly on my way.

Suddenly, as I was passing a tall tree, I heard a loud noise, like a buzz saw, and in the same instant felt a fiery pain on the top of my head. I gave a scream, and looked up in time to see a large hornet, at least 2 inches (5 cm) long pulling out of its dive like a Stuka bomber, and above it a small crowd of these insects was hovering about in front of a hole, high up in the trunk, which had a horn-like shape of yellowish rubbery substance at the entrance.

THE HORNET DANCE

I sped off like a greyhound out of a trap with never a glance backward. The pain in my cranium was unbearable. I did a 100 yard dash to the hospital and found my friend.

"Sorry" I explained . "I came to see you but I can't keep still!" It was true, the intensity of the agony was so great that I could hardly endure it.

The thin flesh on the top of my head had instantly swollen into a tight-fitting helmet that rose in a ridge on my forehead and over the ears, and down to the nape of my neck.

The intense pain raged unabated for 24 hours, and the swelling remained for several days longer. Oh! but what blessed relief when that terrible agony subsided! Three or four stings from those monstrous hornets would surely kill a man. I had been lucky enough to escape with only one. I learned later that some Japanese had disturbed the nest by throwing things at it. No wonder the hornets were angry!

The next monsoon found me up-country once again, in the same dreadful conditions, among men who looked and moved like Zombies; men drained of hope, men in the last stages of sickness, men who died and were buried naked in pathetic graveyards beside the railroad.

Such places when passed only months later would already have been swallowed by fecund greenery; marked only by a toppling wooden cross visible above the vigorous young growth.

In one such camp I met *Honjo* again. He was a different man to the confident one I had known in *Wampo* South. His demeanour was almost as dejected as that of the prisoners. Was he perhaps ashamed of what his countrymen were doing to their hapless captives? Where now was the chivalry of the code of *Bushido*?

Honjo had once told me that he had formerly believed all English soldiers to be gentlemen. Ikey Glickman's begging had caused him to modify that opinion.
Did he wonder now what <u>we</u> must think of his own kind?

He looked subdued and melancholy, greeted me quietly and gave me a small piece of peanut toffee. We passed a few words then he pointed, first to my right hip and then to the small dent in my forehead and said,

"Next time — finish Badgie!" Meaning that I had run out of good luck and the next accident to befall me would be my last!

Well, he was nearly right, as we shall see later, but for now, against all odds I continued to exist.

I did not see *Honjo* again, and often wondered if he survived the war, or did this quite decent man return from Burma in one of the little white boxes that filled the railway box cars carrying the ashes of soldiers on their way home to Japan.

These shipments were portents that said the tide of war had turned in our favour, and raised the hope that this long drawn-out conflict might be drawing to a close.

I had never doubted that we would win. In the darkest times I never lost the conviction that we would end up victorious. But for us there was still a long way to go!

For those who have never seen a monsoon it will be difficult to even imagine the sheer volume of the rainfall, the persistence of it, the ferocity of the storms that accompany it, and the terrifying effect of lightning ripping across the sky at tree top height, with deafening, shattering crash of thunder close at hand; the darkness of the days and the all pervading wetness in the air; all things dripping, all tracks quagmires and water, water everywhere.

During one of these violent storms we lost a popular Troop Sergeant Major; a good soldier, so keen that he would scale the "unclimbable" fence around the gun emplacement at night in Singapore to test the alertness of sentries. His name was "Slasher" Harris (not the human gasometer of our camp fire entertainment, all Harrises were nicknamed Slasher in the Army).

A tree fell on the tent in which he was sleeping, killing him instantly. Another mother's son who would never return.

We had nothing other than our skins to protect us from the rain; but Chinese coolies who, as in so many other things, were very practical in matters of clothing, had the widest brimmed hats I ever saw. They were being worn by a group I found sheltering at the track-side during a heavy downpour. The conical hats had brims as big as cartwheels. Squatting on their haunches beneath them, each coolie was completely protected, as if he had his own individual hut. I quite envied them (their hats, at least!)

CHINESE COOLIES IN MONSOON HATS

    Time passed and once again I was sent down-river and found myself back in *Tarsoa* camp. But things were different and the PoW compound had been re-built nearer the river, and was more securely fenced in.

    The work was different, too. With three other men I was put to work at charcoal burning. This entailed digging out circular pits about 3 metres in diameter and 1½ metres deep. Cut timber was stacked in neat layers from sides to centre until all space was utilised and packed tight. A roof of bamboo matting was placed over it, and a layer of wet clay was packed down onto the roof. A cylinder of the same bamboo matting was used to form a chimney at one end. A small fire of kindling was lit at the bottom of a narrow ramp that sloped down from ground level at the opposite end to the chimney.

   The pit was left to burn until all smoke had ceased to issue from the chimney. Several pits were kept on the go, under the charge of a bad tempered, scowling and impatient Japanese, squat and bow-legged, who looked as if he had spent his life in the depths of some dismal, primeval forest with only the lowest animals for company. The big stick he used, and which he applied enthusiastically, ensured that we worked with at least the same, apparent, diligence.

 His impatience would have us emptying pits before the charcoal had completely cooled down. This was hot, dirty work that required a man to go right inside the pit as soon as enough charcoal had been removed to make sufficient space.

   I was almost grateful for the next attack of malaria that kept me unfit for work for a while. When I recovered I found that I had been replaced on that unpleasant detail.

   It was while digging out one of the pits I had found a small brass Buddha figure. It had been repaired at some time because there was a small section, a carefully inserted patch on its fat belly. I wondered at the cause of the damage; a bullet perhaps in one of the old Siam-Burma wars?

   It will remain a mystery, for the little idol was stolen some months later by a Thai thief who prowled about the camp at night, naked and oiled from head to foot. Armed with a vicious-looking *parang* he moved fearlessly among our sleeping figures. When seen, no-one challenged him.

   I would have liked to have kept that little brass souvenir.

    My next job was short-lived. I was put to work in a forge and had to sit behind a thin bamboo screen and turn the handle of a rotary blower.

   The screen was the only thing that separated me from the furnace, and the heat was unbearable.

   From time to time I was ordered to swing a heavy hammer while the blacksmith worked the white-hot iron with a smaller one.

Because I had no idea of what I was about, and because I was unable to understand the ill-tempered monosyllabic grunts that were snarled at me by the way of orders, I was soon kicked out in disgrace as useless.

That was "another fine mess" I was glad to get out of!

The next type of work was better. The weather was fine and we were out in the nearby jungle felling small trees. These were sawn into one metre lengths which were taken away to be split into firewood for the wood-burning locomotives which were currently using the railway.

In no time at all we became expert at judging the weight of a tree and, of course, always selected the lightest.

One type was similar to balsa wood. There was always a rush to these. It was good fun to spend as long as possible in felling them and cutting them to length; and to stagger past an unsuspecting guard, groaning under imaginary weight.

One day while at this not unpleasant task, I was approached by a Major of the R.A.M.C. He came from a camp not far off which was being used as a hospital for Asian workers.

It was rumoured that only extreme cases went there and that the medical staff were being forced to despatch them by means of an air bubble injected by hypodermic syringe.

I do not know the truth of this allegation, but it was widely believed in our camp.

The major asked if I would help him. He wanted to obtain some coconut oil and gave me a bottle and a small sum of money for the purpose.

I agreed to buy the oil in camp. He then produced from his pocket a brass finger ring and a coin from French Indo-China and asked if I would sell them for him. I said that I would try.

That evening I bought a small measure of coconut oil at the camp canteen. This was a small establishment where it was possible to buy a few items such as duck eggs, coconut oil and bananas; it was authorised by the Japanese and run by the PoWs.

The next day I met the major again and gave him the oil, explaining at the same time that I had not yet been able to sell the other items. He thanked me and left.

After work that day we were kept longer than usual at the evening *tenko*. A buzz of conjecture sped along the ranks as the men sensed that something was amiss.

Then we saw that our colonel and a party, which included some Japanese who did not belong in our camp, were moving along the parade scrutinising every figure.

The inspection arrived at our group and moved slowly along until it stopped in front of me.

The R.A.M.C. major, a dejected figure between two guards, pointed me out. He indicated me by tapping me on the chest; at the same time he whispered from the corner of his mouth, "They found the oil. Don't say anything about the other things. You can keep them."

Then he was hustled out of the camp and I was marched to the commandant's office.

After a nerve-racking wait I was marched inside by a British captain who was accompanied by our colonel. I was warned to bow to the commandant. Hatless, I obeyed.

The commandant here was a *gunso* (sergeant), a figure squatting hunched and frog-like at a scrubbed table. Before him stood the incriminating little bottle of coconut oil.

The colonel, the captain and I waited at attention. A fly buzzed past the Frog's head. I half expected him to snap at it.

A low croak emerged from the humourless mouth. The Captain interpreted.

"Where did you steal this oil?"

"I did not steal it. I bought it at the camp canteen."

"How much did you pay for it?"

"Twenty cents." I felt a nerve in my left leg beginning to twitch. I tensed my buttocks in an attempt to control it.

Hard brown eyes moved over me in close scrutiny. What they saw was an emaciated yellow being resembling a cadaver. If I was a thief I was not a very successful one.

The Frog croaked again. The interpreter saluted smartly, turned about and left the office.

The colonel and I stood at attention in the thick silence that engulfed the room.

The Frog sat motionless. I fixed my eyes on the attap wall above his head as the minutes ticked by.

After what seemed an age the Captain returned with a PoW who took up position on my left. He was the man who had served me with the oil.

The Frog moved his hand for the first time and indicated me.

The man looked at me. I was hoping he would help my case.

"Do you recognise this man?" the Frog asked.

"No sir." (I was lost!) "I see so many at the canteen."

(Perhaps I was not.) The Frog seemed satisfied at this reasonable reply. The canteen man was dismissed.

The next question was more loaded.

"Why did you buy the oil?"

Obviously he already new the answer to that and was perhaps expecting me to lie.

I bought it for a major of the R.A.M.C.," I replied.

"Why were you sneaking around the jungle when you should have been working?"

"I was not sneaking around the jungle. The major came to me where I was working and asked me to buy it for him."

The Frog remained silent while this reply was being considered. His next remark came as a pleasant surprise.

"You appear to be an honest man, but you seem to have more oil here than you should have."

This seemed a puzzle that required more time to think about.

Then came the verdict.

"The next time an officer asks you ——"; the interpreter corrected himself to give a more literal version of the commandant's words, "— <u>orders</u> you to buy something for him you must tell the Japanese guard!"

It was obviously impossible for the *gunso* to imagine an officer <u>asking</u> a soldier to do anything. As a result he believed I had been given an order and could therefore be only partly at fault. I was dismissed without punishment — yet another lucky escape!

Outside the office the colonel spoke kindly to me.

"Didn't the Captain make a good job of pretending to be angry with you, Bombardier?"

I agreed that he did, for in fact he really had.

I returned, thankfully to my hut where surprised friends had not expected to see me again for some time.

There is no way of knowing what happened to the R.A.M.C. major after he was taken away, but it is certain that he would be badly beaten, and it is sad to think that a doctor with many years of expertise and dedication behind him should be at the mercy of ignorant brutes; and all for the petty crime of obtaining a small amount of coconut oil. Such was the perverse world of the prisoners of war camps along the Kwai.

In so much as many of us owed our lives to the skills and care of such medical officers, so, I believe, I owed my sanity to my sweetheart, *Sumini*, who was never far from my thoughts.

The grim surroundings of my prison would dissolve around me as, in my mind I pictured an *ashram*, a quiet retreat to which I could constantly escape.

It took the form of a high white wall. Set in the thickness of the wall was a little lattice gate of wrought ironwork, to which only I had a key.

Within the wall was a wonderful garden; no Sultan ever had finer; no desert traveller ever chanced upon a more beautiful or welcoming oasis.

A sinuous path wound through a luminous world of rich, glowing colour, where hibiscus, oleander, frangipani, and a myriad unnamed flowers breathed a heavenly fragrance into the air; and flame of the forest and jacaranda trees flaunted their gorgeous hues against a sky of cerulean blue. Through this paradise I would seek *Sumini* and, at last, in a far corner I would find her in a little arbour, quietly waiting, looking exactly as she had at our first meeting.

She would be seated on a sleeping mat of pure gold, with a pillow of the same red gold as that of the little ring she had given me, and which I prized so much.

A happy smile would light her sweet face as she rose and ran to greet me with hands outstretched.

After a warm embrace and a tender kiss, I would hold her at arms length for a while, and feast love-starved eyes on the creamy, flawless perfection of her lovely skin; and feel myself drowning in the unfathomable darkness of her radiant eyes.

Seated upon the mat, we would talk earnestly together, excited as children, happy in each other's company; my ears intoxicated by the cadences of her gentle voice; my hand stroking the luxuriant midnight blackness of her hair.

Time and the outside world ceased to exist. There seemed no beginning and no end. We were alone in a magic world of contentment.

But for every Alpha there must be an Omega, and our tryst would end as my love, with a sad countenance, waved farewell, and the garden and its splendour faded into nothingness, and my *Ashram* disappeared.

A feeling of emptiness followed every visit to that enchanted place, but my soul had been refreshed, and the hope and resolution that one day I would return to find *Sumini* was reborn, with new strength.

There was consolation in the thought that, until that happy day, I could enter that *ashram* at will, and my beautiful *Sumini* would always be there waiting, tender and smiling.
The years can never dim such a vision; and they never have.

There was a problem in our camp, which in some respects might be said to have resembled Hamelin Town in Brunswick. True we had no Pied Piper, but there was a river deep and wide and there were rats.

The rats were here, the rats were there. In fact the rats were everywhere! The camp was infested. They had gnawed through the sections in the bamboos that supported the sleeping platforms and had made a tube system that ran from one end of a hut to the other, with exit holes along the way. They grew bolder in their desperate scavenging for food and scampered about fearlessly among us.

One night as one of these repulsive creatures ran over my face, its foot slipped between my lips and went into my mouth. I sat up and spat vigorously into the darkness, feeling revolted.

The rats had to go. They overran PoW huts and Japanese quarters alike. They had to go!

A *yasume* day was set aside for a great rat hunt. Our belongings were removed from the huts and placed on the ground outside. We armed ourselves with stout cudgels and positioned ourselves around the huts.

With a shout of *"Hajume!"* (start work) a deafening racket arose; a fusillade of cracks, bangs, crashes and wallops, as we began beating the sleeping platforms and their supports; the uprights of the huts; the longitudinal and cross members, and the rafters.

We bashed away at the attap walls; we smashed happily at everything and anything. It was wonderful; it was therapeutic; it was a marvellous release of pent-up frustration and tension. It was all very enjoyable!

Rats of all shapes and sizes, and of all ages were bursting out from every nook and cranny, making a dash for open ground.

The clubs were kept busy despatching them as quickly as they appeared, and very few escaped to the sanctuary of the jungle. The hundreds which did not were incinerated on a bonfire.

Even without a Pied Piper we had rid the camp of rats! With them died their fleas and the threat of typhus.

Later on a similar war, on flies, was declared. The Japanese offered a small bounty for a stated number of dead flies. It was quite easy, at first, for the fly hunters to produce the required quota, and a guard would laboriously count the number of bodies in a jar. Inevitably this tedious task soon palled, the amount in a jar would be assessed at a glance, and the counting was allowed to lapse.

Thus an irresistible opportunity for fraud presented itself and was soon taken advantage of.

Frauds on the Japanese constituted legitimate sport, and it was not long before the jars contained dry tea leaves with a layer of dead flies on top.

Inevitably this ruse was eventually discovered, and the "nice little earner" was abolished. The exposed culprit, of course, earned himself a good, traditional bashing.

No chance to exploit or fool our opponents was ever neglected, and every now and again a chance would present itself, as happened during an enforced singing lesson in one of the camps up-river.

In some of these camps a ceremony was carried out whereby the Japanese and Koreans were paraded and the flag was raised and saluted as the rising sun cleared the eastern horizon.

After the parade was dismissed the Japanese personnel returned to their huts while the Koreans remained and were formed into a circle around an instructor who stood in the centre with feet placed wide apart and arms akimbo.

THE SINGING MASTER

With head thrown back and a bull-frog voice the instructor would roar out the chorus of a song then stand in silence while the circle repeated it, some voices cracking under the strain of trying to reach the higher notes, as they marched around.
It looked and sounded rather comic and caused some amusement among the PoWs.
It did not, at first at least, seem so funny when what later became known as the Singing Master Incident occurred.
The prisoners would be made to learn these patriotic songs.
As we had been made to pierce the yolk when frying eggs so as to be thus unable to eat a replica of the national emblem; now we would be made to sing the praises of the Japanese empire.

With the prisoners paraded, the Singing Master took up his usual stance. Back went the head, and from the cavernous mouth, out roared the first verse.

He waited for the response. There was silence, broken only by a feeble, tentative attempt from one or two voices which quickly tailed off. The majority of the assembly remained quiet and completely at a loss.

The instructor flushed angrily at the lack of response. He repeated the verse; even louder this time. Again there was practically no reaction.

A scream of rage left him and he rushed among the ranks dealing out blows left, right and centre before resuming his position out in front.

Scarlet faced, once again he bellowed out the harsh words.
This time someone in the rear rank had an inspiration and as the instructor reached the end of the verse a voice sang out in a ludicrous parody of the tune:
"*Tojo* is a bastardo, a bastardo is he!"
At once the air filled with a deafening caterwauling as everyone joined in with his own extemporised version of words and tune.

The sudden explosion of sound delighted the Singing Master whose expression changed to one of surprised pleasure, and every following chorus was bawled out in the same wild enthusiasm.

The sheer exuberance of the responses had saved the face of our tutor, as, to any listener it must have seemed that his instruction was achieving great success.

The fact that he might have suspected that the words were a compromise, could perhaps explain why no more attempts were made to teach the prisoners patriotic songs.

More prisoners had arrived in camp, from the hell camps up-river, and among them was my old mentor, Sam Mayo.
I had not seen him since leaving Changi, and had had no news of him at all in the time between .

I went to the sick hut to see him; Sam Mayo the ultra-smart sergeant who had met my draft on the troopship H.T.Dilwara in Singapore docks, and escorted us to our new regiment on *Pulau Belakang Mati*; who had taken me under his wing; shepherded me on my first outings to the city, and had written letters to my parents about my progress.

He had been promoted, had met an Eurasian nurse, married her and had one child during the time we had been posted to different war stations.

When Sam saw me he sat up in surprise and recognised me immediately. Amazingly, he stood out among the wasted company that lay around him by virtue of the fact that he still presented a smart appearance. He wore a clean shirt and slacks and his hair was neatly parted.

Sam's face lit up and he became animated as he reminisced about old times, especially boat trips from *Belakang Mati* island, and insisted that we must do it again some day.

After a while his manner changed and he dropped his voice to a conspiratorial whisper.

"Since I've been here, I've had all my kit stolen. Will you go and report it to the orderly?"

I went off to find the medical orderly in charge of the hut, and told him of the accusation.

The harassed orderly's face registered annoyance, and I was quite taken aback by what he said.

"Nobody has been stealing from sergeant major Mayo." He paused, "He has done nothing but complain and has been a nuisance ever since he got here. He had no kit other than what he's got now, and that is all he arrived with!"

I did not know what to say when I went back to Sam and, strangely, he made no mention of it again.

After a while I left, saying that I would call again tomorrow.

The next day a friend came to me and asked, "Have you heard the news?"

"News? What news?"

"Sammy. Sammy Mayo died last night."

It was hard to believe. "What! I only saw him yesterday!"

"I know, Badgie, but your old mate, Sammy has gone."

I was unable to understand it and could only surmise that he had been far weaker than I had realised when I visited him and that his aberrant behaviour had been a result of his condition.

As a friend he left an impression on me which endures, and gave me a standard to live up to, or at least to be striven for.

After the war, Sam's family contacted me through the Royal Artillery Records office, and I went to see them.

It was an eerie feeling, almost a shock when we met, because his mother and sister both bore a striking resemblance to him facially, in the colour of fair hair and grey-blue eyes, and each had Sammy's archetypal Irish nose; snub and tip-turned. There was also a stepfather whom Sam had never mentioned.

Mrs. Mayo showed me a photograph of Sam's Eurasian nurse and the little boy. I dutifully admired it but was taken aback by the reaction.

"He's not Sam's child! He's a little Jap! Isn't he? He's a little Jap!" And she wept.

I left as soon as decency allowed.

The news swept round the camp. Another move was in the offing. If it meant another move up-river, that would be bad because it had always resulted in worse conditions. If it were to be down-river, that could be good; so it was with relief that we learned that that would be the case.

It would still be a move into the unknown, but it was viewed with optimism; and we were to have the luxury of going by rail.

For our luxury ride we were standing up, crowded together in open wagons, continuously rained on by a shower of red-hot wood ash from the locomotive's thick, belching smoke.

However, the old soldier's maxim that a third class ride is better than a first class walk, was something to bear in mind, and it was interesting to see the change that had taken place during the time that we had been up-country.

The raw red scar that we had hacked through the dense jungle was now overgrown with thick greenery that pressed right up against the railway itself.

The area around our first jungle camp, *Wampo*, was unrecognisable until we came out in the open where the track ran on to the gantry bridge around the rocky cliff face opposite to where *Wampo* South Camp had been.

Memories were reawakened there but of the camp there was no sign. The river covered the sandbank on which it had once stood, and two monsoons had washed over it since that piece of rock had flown across the river to fracture my skull.

The camp, the spelling bee, and *Honjo* — all gone, as if they had never been, and all existing now only in memory.

Our train eventually passed over the only steel and concrete bridge that had been built with PoW labour. It was the one now made world famous by a work of fiction, which was made into a film, "The Bridge on the River Kwai", and by hordes of tourists that now have easy and comfortable access to it. Our destination was *Tamarkan.*

Our new camp was situated close by the bridge, an anti-aircraft battery, and the river. It was quite a pleasant surprise. After the jungle camps it looked clean and tidy, with the usual attap huts and a large beaten earth parade square.

At one end of the square a large theatre stage of bamboo and attap had been erected. This played an important part in the lives of the prisoners, and especially for me. The Japanese compound was kept separate, to one side, between us and the river.

It was pleasing to find that there was more space per man in the huts. Work was carried out in and around the camp and was of a lighter nature than had been the case during the actual clearing and construction of the railway.

Before coming to the camp I had written the script for a simple pantomime. I offered it to the concert party. They kept my work and invited me to join the group, which I was happy to do. My script was not used but the idea was, and later on an ambitious production of Aladdin was made.

It was a lavish show that displayed to the full the many talents of a group of gifted men.

The concert party was originally founded by Australians, some of whom were professionals in civilian life. The artist who designed the sets and painted the scenery was Frank Bridges, formerly an artist on a prominent Sydney newspaper.

His work was excellent, and a good example can be cited in a papier maché dummy he had made for a production of Pinocchio. It was made to the exact size and appearance of a diminutive Australian comedian who was playing the name part.

The problem of bringing the puppet to life was solved by having the old wood carver place it in a drawer made for the purpose. The drawer when closed was pulled through the back of the set, and the live Pinocchio exchanged for the dummy.

When the drawer was opened out jumped the live Pinocchio. The only thing papier maché about him was his long nose. It was very effective and is only one of the ingenious effects that were seen on that stage.

At one performance the curtains parted to reveal a stunning tableau. Centre stage on a pedestal a beautiful nude young woman posed, one hand reaching above her head, golden hair cascading over her shoulders, a wisp of chiffon in a strategic position, two proud little breasts pointing heavenward.

An audible gasp arose from the amazed audience, to be replaced by a tumult of whistles and catcalls of disappointment as the curtains closed all too soon on this vision of delight.

The "lovely young" woman was an Australian captain. The golden hair was made of cows tails, and the pert breasts were two cones of flesh-coloured papier maché held in place by a length of cotton, that was, of course, invisible to the audience.

Among a variety of roles, I played a silly-ass Englishman in a show put on by Dutch prisoners who shared our camp.

I had been invited to take part by a Dutch officer, a polite Afrikaner who insisted on addressing me as Mister King; something I was not at all accustomed to!

The cast contained a large proportion of Dutch Eurasian boys and one scene was set in an Indonesian restaurant. One of the songs was about one of the spicy dishes on offer and was titled *Sambal Goreng*. It was first sung in Dutch and then in English, after which I was to speak my line.

During rehearsal I waited patiently for my cue. The Afrikaner producer looked at me expectantly for a while, then said, hesitantly, "Please don't wait too long, Mister King!"
"Oh," I said. "I was waiting for them to sing it in English."
"They have sung it in English!"
"Oh, sorry!" I felt a complete fool, but everyone laughed and thought it was a good joke.

The concert party was run on professional lines; there were the usual departments: stage management and props, costumes, script writers, actors, directors, and a notice board in the "green room" with calls for rehearsals.

There was an orchestra of talented musicians under a Dutch maestro.

Regular members, of whom I was one, were kept free of outside work parties so that rehearsals and other preparations could be properly attended to. Any work in camp was done on a part-time basis, such as the occasional unloading of a barge or some weeding and watering in a vegetable garden that the Japanese had planted at the riverside.

With two other members of the concert party I spent some quite pleasant hours watering the plants. Pat Fox was one of the three. He was well known in the camp, a good comedian, and of eccentric appearance with the pipe he had made from a curved pipe stem, and a bowl carved from the solid root of a young bamboo. It had two horn-like projections from the base of the bowl. The pipe and the Great War-vintage forage cap with the tiger emblem cap badge of the Royal Leicester Regiment, that he wore gave him a unique appearance. Pat was tall and had a handsome Roman nose. We became good friends.

There were Americans in the camp, survivors from the Houston and other vessels sunk in the Battle of the Coral Sea; and some from the Texas Artillery, taken in Java.

They were friendly types and some joined the concert party. One, in particular, always got a good laugh because his accent was so broad that it sounded like a parody.

I wrote and produced a series of comic sketches and had as a partner a Lancashire lad called Johnny Branchflower. His accent fascinated the Americans, who said they wished they could take Johnny home with them, " Just so folks could listen to his accent!"

Also in my little group was K.O.Thompson, a lanky, laconic, Texan.

"What do your initials stand for?" he was asked.

"They don't mean nuthin'. I'm called K.O. My father was called K.O. Senior. I'm K.O. Junior."

And so he was always simply known as K.O. The name was very inapt, because he was in no way pugilistic.

Our shows were high spots in camp life. The Japanese, who appreciated them as much as our lads did, provided two large pressure lamps which, together with the row of coconut oil footlights gave good stage lighting. There was always an eager and appreciative audience.

Life in general was an improvement on that which we had known in other camps along the river, but even so there was still deprivation and sickness.

It was when I went with the concert party to cheer patients in the sick hut that I found Gunner McConnel T. of my old Battery, the younger brother of McConnel R. The poor lad was in a bad way, having been wounded by shrapnel when Allied planes attacked the train on which he was being brought to the camp. He did not recognise me, and died soon after our visit. His brother, who had bullied him, survived to return to Northern Ireland.

Before long I myself was in the sick hut, struck down by the deadly cerebral malaria, with a temperature of 106° F, and in the next bed-space to me was the little Australian comic; similarly afflicted; he was writhing and raving, making horrible burbling noises, sounding like an idiot, with his tongue lolling out of his mouth.

That is all I remember until I came round days later. Did I make the same sort of spectacle of myself? I will never know. What I do know is that both I and the little Australian recovered at about the same time and were soon "back on the boards" again. Our "work" was a wonderful tonic.

Then I received my first letter from home. It was from my father. It was over two years old and was brief. It told me that all was well at home, that it was written on the eve of his 57th birthday, and urged me to keep my pecker up. I felt a rush of elation as I read that all was well at home, and remained optimistic that the two years that had passed since it was written would not have changed things.

There was another pleasant surprise in store for me. I was crossing the square after a show in which I had just taken part, when someone called "Hello, Badgie," to me.

I was well known in the camp because of my stage work and just replied, "Hello," as I hurried on.

Then I stopped suddenly as realisation struck me. It was Joe! Joe Lowe, my old friend.

"Joe!" I shouted, and rushed back to him and shook his hand vigorously.

"I'll give you hello," he grinned, thinking I had greeted him casually. I had. But only because I had not recognised him at once. Joe was much thinner than the last time I saw him.

A long time had passed since then. He told me that after leaving the Railway Engineers Depot he had gone to a large camp called *Nonkompatong* and had been suffering from a deficiency disease that had caused extremely painful feet; "happy feet" it was known as among the PoWs.

It was good to have his company again. We had shared so many happy times in Singapore. Now we relived them again in our conversation.

I told Joe of my intention of returning to Singapore after the war, which did not seem far off now that our planes were over so often, and how I felt sure that *Sumini* would still be there, waiting for me in the quiet *kampong*. I saw her so regularly in the *ashram* that I did not have the slightest doubt that it could be otherwise.

Of course, I did not tell Joe about my *ashram.* It was something to be kept secret, otherwise the magic would be destroyed.

Weeks passed uneventfully until one evening roll call. For this parade British and Dutch contingents lined up separately. There was usually a mutual, mild dislike between us, except for the odd individual friendship, and this was shown to a small extent in the drill of numbering from the right. Allied prisoners did it in English, the Dutch did it in Dutch.

If a party consisted of Dutch and Allied personnel, then each nationality insisted on shouting out their own numbers, with slightly comical effect, such as: "een, two, dree, four…."etc. But once the Japanese came on parade numbering and drills had to be in Japanese; and counting took a long time as the guards checked and re-checked, making sure that the final totals reported to the commandant were correct.

It was a fine evening. The parade had been standing for over an hour as the counting was done, and now we stood in silence awaiting the arrival of the commandant.

Suddenly the roar of heavy aero engines filled the air as about 20 bombers swooped down out of the sun.

Time froze for a moment, then the Dutch parade broke up as men left the ranks to dash for the safety of rain drains at the sides of the huts.

Having no orders to move the British stood fast. Some of the Dutch saw this stoic display and, shamefaced, began to return to the parade.

Then came the unmistakable whistle of falling bombs and, order or no order, the British line broke as we made a mad dash for the gutters.

At the same time the anti-aircraft battery near the camp began blasting away at the bombers.

I rushed to the drain at the side of my own hut and threw myself down. The drain was roughly 18 inches (45 cm) deep and about the same width and ran along below the eaves of the hut.

The ground heaved and shook, and I could feel the increasing intensity of the shock waves as the bombs fell nearer and nearer. I pressed myself into the earth, expecting the next one to fall on top of me. It was terrifying.

I moved and immediately jumped as my abdomen came in contact with a hot piece of metal, a bomb fragment had fallen by my side. A few inches in front of my head was a jagged shell splinter, about 5 inches (12.5 cm) long; and just in front of that I saw that the trench had closed in along its length, almost to where I lay. Half of the hut had been flattened and on my left only yards away a hut had vanished completely, demolished by the last of the stick of bombs.

Two men were dead, killed by the blast, completely unmarked, in the slit trench they had dug for themselves under the sleeping platform of the doomed hut. (We found their bodies later).

Badly shaken I climbed to my feet. The planes had passed overhead and were making a wide sweep. The A.A. guns were still banging away and a heavy machine-gun, firing down at the planes from the summit of a nearby hill, was spraying bullets into the camp.

Pat Fox was standing close by, his eccentric pipe clenched between his teeth.

"What's happening now, Pat?" I called out to him.

"I think the planes are coming back." Then, "Everyone's going to the other end of the camp!"

As this was the farthest point away from the bridge and the A.A. battery, it seemed the best place to go.

At the far end of the camp a Korean guard had opened a small gate and, waving frantically, was urging the prisoners through.

"All men jungle go! All men jungle go!" he was shouting.

We rushed through and scattered among the scrubby growth.

The sound of the planes died away. They were not coming back. The A.A. guns stopped firing. Dusk was falling and quiet had fallen on the camp.

In small groups we drifted back to the small gate, and there an unwelcome sight met our eyes: all returning prisoners were being made to sit cross-legged on the ground just inside the fence, ringed by a circle of guards with levelled bayonets.

A Japanese officer was beside himself, dancing with rage. He was unusual for a Japanese in that he wore a black beard of thin, straight hair several inches long. He was, naturally, known to the prisoners as Blackbeard, (or Bluebeard) and seemed to possess the nature of that bloodthirsty pirate. He was acting like a demented madman.

The last prisoners were back from the bush and the gate was closed behind them.

Screaming with a rage that must have frightened the guards every bit as much as the prisoners, Blackbeard began raining blows with a thick bamboo down on the unprotected heads and shoulders of the helpless seated figures before him.

He beat frenziedly at the ones in the front row and reached over them to reach those behind. He worked his way along, swinging the club high above his head and bringing it down with all the force he could muster.

BLACKBEARD BEATING PRISONERS

The rain of bangs, buffets and cracks as wood met flesh and bone, crept closer and closer. My flesh crawled in anticipation. I tensed myself for the expected blows.

Then, suddenly, weariness must have overtaken the crazed creature for the blows ceased and were replaced by shouted orders, and we were made to join the other prisoners who were already assembled on the parade ground.

I found myself next to Joe.
"Good lord, Badgie,!" he gasped. "Where've you been? I thought you'd had it. Someone said he'd seen you run across to the hut where the bomb fell, and when you didn't turn up on parade I thought you'd had it!"
I explained what had happened.

Counting and recounting, and counting over and over again by angry, cursing guards went on throughout the night and we were still at attention on the square when dawn broke.

Hours later we were still there, kept until the dead had been found and all men were accounted for.

Then we were kept a few hours longer, presumably as a form of punishment.

At last we were dismissed. My hut was demolished from the far end and up to my bed space. A few bananas that I owned were dangling from one of the shattered roof members.

I retrieved them, ate them, then went along to the theatre. Behind the closed curtains, on the stage 21 bodies were laid out in rows. Some bore wounds, some, including the two recovered from the slit trench under the hut that received a direct hit, showed no signs of injury at all.

News came later of a camp farther down the line where the huts were built in the middle of a marshalling yard where a 100 of our lads had been killed in a similar raid.

The raid on the bridge had two marked effects on us. It had exacerbated the condition of our nerves but had also raised morale as it was positive proof that the war might be drawing nearer to an end. But the possibility of being killed by our own planes, after so much had been suffered for so long, was very worrying.

The picture of Blackbeard thrashing wildly at his helpless prisoners remains stark and ineradicable in my brain, and the thought comes that he should have had someone at his shoulder, as in a Roman triumph, saying "Remember you are only mortal;" for, whatever the perverted sense of power that possessed him that night when he had so many defenceless wretches in his thrall, his mortality must certainly have been brought home to him when, after the war, the noose was placed round his neck and he was about to be executed for war crimes.

BLACK BEARD A.K.A BLUEBEARD

SAMURAI SWORD

It is said that there is a coward at the heart of every bully. This was shown to be true in Blackbeard's case for when the writing on the wall became plain, he shaved off his beard and went among the prisoners to see if he would be recognised.

He was. And it is to be hoped that the knowledge struck fear in his black heart.

The railway bridge appeared to be undamaged by the bombing but the central piers had been damaged and the structure was unsound and therefore unusable.

The strategic value of the railway as a supply route to Burma was lost almost as soon as the line had been completed.

I was not to see later air raids on the bridge at *Tamarkan* camp because I was one of a group sent down to the Isthmus of *Kra*. This journey was made standing in the backs of open lorries, mostly along unmade, rutted roads with frequent dismountings to reduce weight and allow the lorries safe passage across rickety wooden bridges over dry stream beds.

After the years in the jungle the countryside made a welcome change, and was quite different, having villages and agriculture.

Out destination was near a monastery on a flat plain. A massive island of dark rock reared up starkly from the plain, with verdure along the top and a temple building high up on one side.

The main monastery buildings were situated among a small cluster of attractive Thai houses. Within a white wall were a number of stupas of various sizes and over a gateway I was surprised to see the carving of a rabbit.

Amid a setting of banana plants, flowering shrubs and coconut palms there was a large pool with water lilies and shoals of fat carp. Because of the Buddhist law that forbids killing any living creature, we were warned under the threat of dire punishment not to catch the fish.

There was a school with young children who paid scant attention to their teacher because they were so intrigued by us. Some of the Australians diverted the smiling pupils even more by removing their false teeth. The surprise on the young faces at this trick was comical to see.

A saffron robed monk with shaven head came to call at each house and stood quietly at the foot of the ladder until the lady of the house descended to add some rice to the food he already had in his begging bowl. They exchanged bows and the monk departed as silently as he came.

There was an air of peace and tranquillity about that quiet spot, the sense of a community of gentle people living a simple life in a serene and beautiful place. It was a pity to have to leave it, but after an hour or so we set off on foot to our new camp a short distance away.

Our first job was to build more huts and dig a well. Later on we were marched out to the work which was the reason for our being here; it was the clearing of trees and scrub to make dirt airstrips for fighter planes, and lay about seven or eight kilometres away from the camp: a tiring walk after an exhausting day's labour under a tropical sun. Ripe bananas and mangoes in gardens of the houses at the roadside were a tantalising sight for thirsty men, a temptation made worse because we had no chance of getting at them!

Our new camp was unlike any previous ones in that it was enclosed by two high bamboo fences, between the fences ran a deep dry moat, the soil from which had been piled into a bank.

The camp commandant had a little house all to himself close by the compound. It seemed that the Japanese authorities had determined to give the place at least the semblance of a proper PoW camp. Perhaps sensing the end was coming?

There was no concert party established here, so we obtained permission and built ourselves a small stage and lost no time in putting on shows; not nearly so lavish as those at *Tamarkam*, but every bit as much appreciated.

In one of these shows I had a small revenge on the enemy. A heavy shower had filled, almost to the brim, the pit in front of the stage (the soil from which had been used to build up the stage itself). Seeing the water had given me a good idea just before the performance, and I told the other members of the cast my plan.

It involved my sketch The Private Life of Cleopatra. In it I am seen as Cleopatra lying on a divan attended by two slaves. A messenger arrives with bad news, on receipt of which I give the order, "Throw him to the crocodiles!"

The slaves seize the messenger by wrists and ankles, and with a "One — two — heave!" they fling him high into the air above the pit. He falls with arms and legs flailing, gives a loud scream, and hits the water with an almighty splash.

The splash drenches the front row of spectators, which is entirely composed of Japanese, with the commandant in the centre. It happened too unexpectedly for them to leap out of the way. No-one could be blamed; they had, after all chosen the front row for themselves!

THROW HIM TO THE CROCODILES!

It was on this stage, in another of my burlesques, that I assaulted a British officer and got away with it. Having said that let me hasten to add that it was entirely accidental, and it happened this way.

I was Robin Hood and our medical officer was the Sheriff of Nottingham. My merry men and I had entered the castle to rescue Maid Marian and had to fight our way out.

The Sheriff and his men-at-arms each had a large club made from a stout cane with a large padded knob at the end. My outlaws and I were armed with similar clubs.

There were three men a side and we lined up on stage facing each other and bashed away in time to the music of the Anvil Chorus.

In my enthusiasm I missed with the padded knob and landed the cane with a heavy blow and a loud crack on the Sheriff's forehead. I saw his face flush angrily under his ginger hair, and hastily apologised, "Sorry, sir!"

After the show I apologised again, but he had quite recovered his composure by now, and laughed about it.

Then he added, "You know, you were pea green with malaria before the show, but I let you go on because I knew it would be good for you!"

That young medical officer was Hugh deWardener, and he became one of Europe's leading kidney specialists after the war. (I learnt this from a doctor at the hospital where I had my first hip replacement; he had studied under Mr. deWardener in London.)

One morning I was in camp sick with a bout of malaria and was in the hut with two or three other sufferers. There was a strange stillness in the air that day and a weird sort of quiet hung over the area; there were no sounds and no birds flew, the leaves on the trees were motionless in the lifeless air.

The sky was festooned with a low, oppressive grey overcast, and there was an ominous, sulphurous yellow light in the eastern sky.

Then a strange sight met my eyes; in absolute silence trees on the horizon bent over as if a wave were rushing towards the camp. Then, a few minutes later banana plants in the nearby plantation lay flat as if pushed down in my direction by an invisible force.

At once the air was filled with debris and a loud howling arose as if the lid had been lifted off some Buddhist hell and the screams and moans of thousands of tormented souls had escaped into the air.

Then the cause of all this strangeness became apparent. A great wind had struck the camp; we were in the teeth of a typhoon.

Our hut began a serpentine writhing and twisting movement along its entire length like a living thing. At the far end the little monkey clung to a beam in terror.

Acting on the instinct of self preservation, I and two others ran to one of the hut supports and clung to it in a desperate attempt to hold the hut down. It was a gesture as futile as it was foolish. The folly of it struck me as the whole hut began creaking and groaning in danger of imminent collapse.

I shouted to the others, "Get outside — quick!"

We dashed out through the door as, with loud cracking and tearing noises, ties snapped and timbers splintered and the building crashed to the ground.

I flattened myself face down against the earth in the open and felt as if at any moment the terrifying force of the wind would tear me off and hurl me away. Sheer, naked terror gripped me in a sense of utter helplessness against such an awful, elemental power.

Then, in torrents that battered and stung the chilled flesh, the rain beat down.

The hut had collapsed but the roof was intact and was flattened against the ground. I crawled across and dragged myself under it into shelter. I found my blanket and wrapped it around me as violent malarial shivers shook me to the core.

By the time the typhoon passed, havoc had been wreaked in the camp. I had lain in my shelter while the rain beat a deafening tattoo on the attap thatch close above my head, and I have no idea how long it lasted, but sick or not I was rousted out to assist when the returning work parties were set to repairing the damage.

As we worked a rumour circulated which said that the storm was coming back. This was a frightening thought but, thankfully, it did not happen.

It was possible to lose track of days. Sometimes we knew day and date. Often we did not. I remember April 4th. 1945 because it was the eve of my father's birthday and I had mentioned this to a new friend.

The new friend was an Aussie known as Gunboat Smith. His real name was Laurie, but this was too cissified a name for an Aussie, so his mates had nicknamed him after an old-time boxer.

His most outstanding feature was a pair of big ears which stood out from the sides of his head like a pair of open car doors. With a beaky nose and a prominent Adams's apple, and a full set of false teeth (a common feature among Australians at that time), he was certainly no beauty, but he had a happy-go-lucky nature and a devil-may-care streak.

When he learned that the next day was my father's birthday he grinned and said,

"We'll have a little celebration tomorrow, Badgie. I know where I can get some tea and sugar."

"Where?" I asked.

"Never you mind!" he replied, mysteriously, tapping the side of his long nose.

"I'll get some tonight."

The next day I noticed that Gunboat was missing from our working party. No-one knew where he was, but there had been no hue and cry, so he must still be somewhere in camp.

Some days later, when walking past a hut I saw a skeletal figure standing under the eaves, tipping water over himself out of a four gallon kerosene can. It was Gunboat!

I rushed over to him. "Gunboat, where've you been? What happened?" We shook hands warmly.

He grinned ruefully. "I got caught robbing the Japs' store hut. They beat me up a bit and put me in a bamboo cage behind the guard room."

His bony ribs stood out like the bars of a cage.

"Didn't they feed you at all?" I asked.

Gunboat grinned again. "Oh, they gimme a rice ball with some salt in it once a day, and some water to drink."

I did not stop to hear any more, but rushed back to my own hut and returned with the only piece of food that I had. It was a banana, not quite ripe and still a bit green. Gunboat accepted it with a nod and a smile, and ate it.

He made light of his days in the bamboo cage and was perhaps, fortunate that the Japs had been more interested in another prisoner.

While drawing water at the well it was possible to see across the intervening ground and into the guardroom. Tied down on his back to the top of a table was a civilian. It was not possible to see if he was Chinese or Thai, but it was plain to see what was going on.

About four Japanese soldiers, possibly *Kempei Tai,* were standing around him and he was being given the water torture.

The victim is forced to swallow a large quantity of water, then his swollen abdomen is beaten with thin canes. It is known to be excruciatingly painful.

I don't know what the man's fate was, or why he was being tortured, but I do know the depth of loathing and disgust I felt at witnessing this inhuman treatment of a helpless prisoner. I had seen enough brutality to know that the Japs were capable of unbelievable acts of cruelty, but it still revolted me, and I found it inexcusable and unforgivable.

Work on clearing the airstrips was the usual unremitting grind in blazing heat. The long march along the rough road out to the site was exhausting for half-starved men weak from an endless series of malaria attacks and dysentery, and all the other tropical diseases that had afflicted us for the past three years, but the trek back seemed twice as long, and it was always a stumbling column of very weary men that made its way back to the camp.

Thirst tormented us throughout the long, hot days. The full water bottle that each man took out with him had to last all day, but heavy labour and constant sweating often made this difficult, and the blessed relief of a drink and the prospect of a few hours rest made the camp a haven that was always reached gratefully.

Air activity around the area was increasing day by day, and the sound of cannon fire and the heavy crump of bombs as targets were attacked caused both elation and alarm; elation because it could only signify that the war was going badly for the Japanese, and alarm because there was the fear that our camp could become a target. Our nerves were already ragged as a result of poor health and because the memory of what had happened at *Tamarkan* was fresh in our minds.

However, the prospect of the Japs getting their just deserts at last emboldened us to show some defiance of our bullying guards, and orders were obeyed with increasing and sometimes quite open reluctance.

This resulted in the whole camp being assembled for an address by the Commandant. As he mounted a rostrum at the front of the parade, excited whispers circulated among the ranks; he was about to announce the end of the war!

He was not. He had noticed the growing tension among the prisoners and had decided to do something about it.

His opening remark caused some derision and laughter. "You are soldiers. Members of a fist class power." This was in stark contrast to the headline on the front pages of English language newspapers (which we had, of course, been allowed to see) which read, "Britain Third Class Power in the World Today." (this had occurred early in the war!)

The commandant went on to say that as soldiers it was our duty to obey orders, and that he would not hesitate to put down any insurrection in the camp. He had the power to execute any man who did not obey a Japanese order, and would not hesitate to do so. He finished by saying, "Be good soldiers and do your duty."

We were subsequently told that from now on we would take orders from our own NCOs, who would receive them from the Japanese engineers on the job. This seemed a sensible arrangement, and one more sign that the end could be in sight; but in practice the order did not appear to have reached the guards.

It was the end of a long, hot day. We had been working under a really nasty Jap known as Snake Eyes. A small white sergeant of the Indian Army Pay Corps was with us as our Honcho. We had fallen in, preparing to march off when Snake Eyes grunted at me and pointed to where a tree stump lay near the edge of the airstrip. It was obvious that he wanted me to walk the hundred yards or so and move it off the strip.

Bearing in mind the new instructions I called out to the little sergeant, "Have I got to go and move that, or not?"
But the sergeant had removed himself to the rear of the squad, as far as possible away from the Jap's baleful presence.

The next series of events happened in a flash. Snake Eyes whipped his bayonet out of its scabbard, raised it high above his head, turned it back of blade downwards and brought it down on top of my head in a terrific two-handed Kendo chop.

The force and unexpectedness of the blow drove me to the ground on my knees and the steel bayonet rang.

I staggered to my feet and wandered slowly down the airstrip with as much dumb insolence as I could muster, and tossed the offending tree stump to one side.

Angry at the incident I went to a bell tent in which the *Gunso* was sitting at a table writing. I pointed to the top of my head and mimed the Kendo chop. Not knowing the real name of Snake Eyes my complaint meant absolutely nothing to the *Gunso,* who merely looked at me as if I were mad and did nothing. At one time he would have given me a beating on his own account.

I did not think the incident at all funny but there was at least one man in our party who did; it was Buck Ryan, a Queenslander from Brisbane. He had been standing behind me and had burst out laughing when the blow landed on my head. He came to me afterwards and apologised.

"Sorry, Badgie" he said, grinning broadly, "but that bayonet rang like a bloody church bell!"

I have come to the conclusion that I must have a very thick skull!

Sometimes in the course of one of the wearisome, endless days, something would happen to give us all a laugh, and it was so much more enjoyed when it was at our enemies' expense; as it was when a

Jap came to where we were sitting during a ten-minute *yasume* break. There were often silly exchanges such as,
"Nippon number one. England number ten!"
"No. England number one. Nippon number ten!"
Today it was a bit different. The Jap pointed to one of the Aussies and said,
"Ostralia — *kah*?"
"Yup. Australian."
"Ostralia — all finish!"
"Rubbish. Nippon finish!"
 "Ostralia finish. Darwin bom bom. All finish!"
There was a moment's quiet. We all knew Darwin had in fact, been bombed at some time. The Jap looked pleased.
Someone said, "Sydney?"
"Sydaney bom bom. All finish!"
"Melbourne?"
"Melbun bom bom. All finish!"
The Jap did not suspect that he was being lured into a trap.
"Bull shit!"
"Burroo sheet? Bom bom — all finish!"
There was a loud roar of derisive laughter all round and the comic look of stunned amazement on the Jap's face was wonderful to behold.

DARWIN BOM BONI — ALL FINISH !

Nowadays we noticed an increased tenseness about the guards; perhaps they sensed that the fortunes of war had turned against them. We were no longer permitted to have fires in the open after dark, and they were very much on edge when planes were about. Any man found outside a hut during an air raid in the area would be beaten.

One evening a small group was yarning by a small fire between the huts and, realising that it was dusk, hastily began to put the fire out and, at that moment, saw the bulky figure of a Japanese coming towards us. Thinking that we were about to be punished for being late in having a fire, we waited apprehensively as he approached.

It was an officer in casual dress, and hatless. To our surprise, he began talking to us in a friendly manner and in good English. It had become quite dark and the night sky was clear, its deep velvet studied by myriads of stars as bright as diamonds in a jeweller's display, and as beautiful as they can only be in a tropical sky.

Our visitor showed a great interest in the constellations, and a good knowledge of astronomy; in fact his erudition made me feel quite ashamed of my own ignorance.

He named several stars, then pointed to a very bright one.
"I expect you know the name of that one," he said.

As luck would have it, it was the only one I knew.
"Yes. It's Sirius," I said.
"The Dog Star. It is in the constellation of Canis Major," he added.

At that moment a sentry quietly crept up to us in the dark; perhaps thinking that he had caught some prisoners in an unlawful activity, and giving a good bashing would be a welcome diversion to his tour of duty.

He was very close to us before he recognised the officer. He started as if he had been stung, bowed stiffly from the waist, made a hurried apology then sucked in his breath noisily (a sign of great respect to a superior) and withdrew the way he had come.
"These men are peasants," the officer said and continued talking to us, whom he obviously considered not to be peasants!

Perhaps he had felt the need to practise his English. Whatever the reason, his socialising with prisoners was certainly another of the changes taking place around us.

Inevitably, as the completion of the airstrips neared, a number of us were required elsewhere for another assignment. I was one of that number, and wondered where and what it would be.

As camps go this one on the Isthmus of *Kra* had not been the best, but it had certainly not been the worst. The names of those hideous camps, where so many of my friends were buried, passed in a dismal roll call through my mind, with special emphasis on those in the jungle north of *Wampo*.

Would the new camp be like these? Only time would tell, and the time between leaving this camp and arriving at the next was to hold some hardships and suffer from the same lack of organisation that never failed to accompany such undertakings.

We assembled in the chill dark before dawn and spent the inevitable long wait while counting and re-counting went on. But eventually we set off on a series of long, hot marches with no provision for regular food supplies en route, and nights spent sleeping in the open, on the ground, until we arrived at a small station, the equivalent of a wayside halt at home.

After a period of waiting which afforded us a welcome rest, an engine puffed up drawing a number of little wooden carriages. Not imagining for one moment that we would be travelling in such civilised transport, it came as a great surprise when we were ordered aboard. The compartments were very small and the seats were of wood, but it seemed like luxury to us and we enjoyed the pleasure of watching the countryside, from the unglazed windows, as it rolled past.

After an hour or so the train stopped and we were ordered out. We had reached a wide river and the huge bridge that spanned it had been completely destroyed by Allied bombing. Its shattered mass of grey girders reared up in places, like enormous triangles, high above the swirling yellow waters, and in others, dipped to water level. It resembled the skeleton ruin of some colossal dinosaur; upright in parts, canted over drunkenly in others. Our pleasure at seeing the destruction was dampened a bit when we learned we had to walk across it.

The girders were narrow and the ascents and descents over the triangles made for a hair-raising experience, especially at the highest points where my vertigo made me very nervous indeed, and I was very conscious of the great drop down to where the river rushed over the smashed piers far below. It was a great relief to reach the far side safely.

We formed up to march off again, still with no idea of where we were heading, except that we were moving northward on yet another long, tiring march.

In the heat of the day, at a halt, while we were sprawled in exhausted abandon in the dirt at the roadside I heard a guard moving along among the prisoners and stopping by each group to ask, "*Nihon go wakarimasu kah?*" (Do you understand Japanese?) He was met with puzzlement and the shaking of heads at every enquiry. Then he was standing over me where I lay, and asked the same question. It was a phrase that I understood, and I replied, " *Nihon go wakarimasen.*" (I do not understand {or speak} Japanese.") At which he said something which I did not understand but which I assumed must mean, "But you are speaking to me in Japanese!"

Then he asked, "*Marai go wakarimasu kah?*" (Do you speak Malay?)

"*Hai. Marai go wakarimasu.*" (Yes. I do speak Malay).
He then began to talk to me in fluent Malay, and told me that he had lived for seven years in Java, and had been conscripted when the Japs invaded the Dutch East Indies.

His name was *Wihara*, he was a thin, apprehensive little man and his attitude was almost one of diffidence. He possessed the reddest, most sticking-out ears of any I ever saw in his race. I was to see them looking even redder later on.

PTE. WIHARA

There was no interpreter with our party, and no British officer, the senior rank was a rather young and nervous R.S.M. who seemed quite unable to communicate with the Japanese in charge of the column. *Wihara* had been sent to find a Japanese speaker among the prisoners, and had found none. So I was to become the interpreter and any interchange of information had to take place with four parties present; the Japanese officer to *Wihara* in Japanese; *Wihara* to me in Malay; I to the R.S.M. in English; then vice versa as required. It was a long drawn out, tedious business but it worked.

Our next stretch took us through little villages where the local population turned out to enjoy the spectacle.
This never failed to have a strange effect on the little frog-like guard who normally traipsed along beside the column trailing a rifle and bayonet that looked too big for him.

   On entering a village he would become transformed and would puff himself up like the frog he resembled, and literally strut, rifle on shoulder, in overweening pride, as if he had only just captured the whole bunch of us single handed. On leaving the village behind he would deflate as quickly as he had inflated.

   Eventually we came to another railway station and were paraded on the platform where a young Japanese lieutenant was in charge. He had a fearsome reputation among some of the prisoners, but I had never seen him before. It seemed to have a strange effect on him when he saw me. Perhaps it was my rather unusual appearance for I was wearing my homemade "forage cap" and had a smart silver-topped swagger cane tucked under one arm. The cane was part of the gear belonging to our concert party. He seemed to assume that I was an officer, which made me rather worried because he had been barking out orders and, not being understood, had handed out slaps all around. He was pleased when Pte. *Wihara* told him I could speak Malay, as he spoke quite a lot himself.
"Where did you learn it?" he asked.
 "I learnt it from a book," I replied.
 "No. No, you learnt it at Raffles College," he insisted, and my denials could not convince him otherwise.

   Between us we were able to restore some order on the crowded platform, and shortly afterwards a locomotive hauling a long train pulled in.
"Tell the men to get on the train," he ordered.
"How many carriages ?" I asked.
For some reason his face lit up at the word "Carriages". Perhaps it was a new one for his vocabulary.
He repeated the word, "Carriages. Carriages."
They were, in fact, wooden box cars. He allocated a number for our party and we climbed aboard. There was more room than we had been accustomed to, and two guards travelled with us in each wagon. The locomotive blew its whistle and we were on our way.

Our next stop was Bangkok and here we endured an anxious wait in the midst of a devastated goods yard, expecting the bombers to come over at any moment. From there we moved on to the docks, where we dismounted and were put in a large godown to spend the night.

As we settled in there was an angry shouting in Japanese, accompanied by the unmistakable thwack of fist striking flesh.

I looked across to where the noises were coming from, fully expecting to see a PoW in trouble; but this time it was different.

An irate *Gunso* had our guards lined up in front of him over by the steel grille that enclosed the front of the godown.

The object of his rage was the unfortunate Private *Wihara*, at whom the *Gunso* vomited a stream of harsh words. He landed a heavy blow on the left side of *Wihara's* head, which knocked his head to one side and sent his cap flying off to the right front. *Wihara* quickly bent down, picked up the cap and replaced it on his head, snapping back smartly to the position of attention.

Bang! A blow to the right ear. Off flew the cap in the opposite direction, and again it was retrieved.

Poor *Wihara's* ears grew redder and redder under the rain of blows and abuse, and, by the time the *Gunso* moved on, poor *Wihara's* ears, illuminated by the light that came through the grille, were like the scarlet disc of the Rising Sun, one on each side of his head.

PTE. WIHARA UPSETS THE GUNSO (SERGEANT)

I felt very sorry for this inoffensive Japanese private, who seemed so different to the rest. He came to me shortly afterwards with his head bowed to hide the fact that he had been weeping. It was clear that he felt deeply ashamed at his public humiliation.

I don't know what, if anything, he had done to deserve his beating. I tried to commiserate with him but he turned his face away. For a moment or two it looked as if he were about to say something by way of explanation, but seemed to think better of it and wandered off to be alone with his flame-red ears and misery.

The concrete floor of the godown was not an inviting bed, so I looked around and found a large heap of sand; spread my strip of canvas on it and lay down to sleep.

When I awoke next morning it was already dawn, and above my head daylight was streaming down through a large, gaping hole in the roof.

With a great shock I suddenly realised that I had been sleeping on a pile of sand that was covering an unexploded bomb. Judging from the size of the hole it had made, the bomb was a really big one.

I hurriedly got up and moved away from the spot, not that it would have made much difference. Had the bomb gone off in that enclosed space not many of us would have survived.

Because of the likelihood of there being an Allied air raid at any time, we were very relieved to leave the godown and the battered dockland area and set off once more.

Again we travelled in box cars with two guards in each. But this time the doors on one side were kept shut and the two guards usurped the open door, which they kept to themselves.

The journey was uneventful until about midday, when the train stopped, for no apparent reason, in open countryside. It remained stationary for a long time, and we baked slowly in the oven of the wagons while the guards sat with their legs dangling at the open doorway.

A quiet settled over the wagons and the lulling, sleepy puff-puffing of the locomotive was the only sound to disturb the hot silence.

The peace was abruptly terminated by the hoarse shouts of "*Skorgi! Skorgi!*" (Planes! Planes!) and there was a mad scramble as the guards leapt down from the wagons to run some distance away and fling themselves flat on the ochre-coloured ground.

We crowded the open doors of the wagons, ready to do the same if necessary, and to see what was happening. Then we saw a lone plane, quite high overhead. At the same moment the bomb bay doors opened a cloud of pamphlets fell, like autumn leaves, in a twirling, fluttering stream.

We laughed with relief; our embarrassed guards rejoined us, and the train rattled off again on its journey.

It was night when the train stopped. Outside in the dark, Japanese voices were shouting. The doors that had been locked on that side of the wagons were rolled back, and we were ordered out, to raucous cries of *"Tenko! Tenko!"*

Men were being pushed about, slapped and screamed at by guards who seemed on the verge of hysteria. We hurried to form up in some sort of order.

The nervousness of the Japs could have been due to the fear of losing some prisoners in the darkness, and it took several attempts before they were satisfied that the head-count was correct.

In column of fours we began a march along a rough un-made road. I was with *Wihara* at the rear, and we soon found it was not the best place to be.

In the godown on the docks we had been given a meal of rice and stew. Both the size of the ration and the quality of the stew had been much better than usual. There had actually been meat in the stew, and lots of beans. Lots of beans! It had been eaten with relish!

Now the results of that unusually rich meal were becoming manifest. A ragged chorus of trumps of varying tonalities was arising from the ranks; sounding as if a number of the talented Slasher Harrises (of the camp fire concert type) was present and producing a prodigious selection of variations on the Trumpet Voluntary.

Wihara held his nose and gave the Japanese equivalent of "Phew!" Then he said, "Ask if anyone needs to benjo!" (go to the latrine).

I shouted his query to the malodorous marchers, but nobody wanted to take advantage of the offer, and the column continued its smelly march into the night.

Hours passed as on and on we marched in a seemingly endless trek. The occasional all too short a break gave us a welcome rest, but in no time at all we would be ordered to our feet again and it took great effort to force weary limbs forward once more.

We became more and more exhausted as mile after mile was passed, with nothing to mark the way other than the telephone poles that loomed out of the darkness at the roadside.

Then, about midnight, guards and PoWs alike lay down dog-tired on the stony surface of the road and fell fast asleep.

It was daylight when we awoke and no time was lost in getting the march started again.

Around us lay a flat landscape of rice paddies, with here and there a small palm-thatched house set within its own group of fruit trees and banana plants.

Ahead the road disappeared in the distance, with no discernible end. Time dissolved into a limbo of pain, where sheer will power kept a man moving under the increasing affliction of aching bodies, and bare feet rubbed sore by the course, gritty surface of the road. No provision of food or water had been made, and the lack of these added to the hardships of the march.

Far off, a range of mountains became visible on the western horizon and as we neared them it became possible to make out a cluster of shapes on the plain below.

The shapes resolved themselves, eventually, into attap huts set in the unmistakable layout of a prison camp.

At long last, we were nearly there! We had, it seems covered 40 miles in that interminable march. What sort of state were we in that a prison camp could be a welcome sight?

The camp was surrounded by a water filled-moat, in which some prisoners were working, up to their thighs in the yellow water. A timber bridge crossed the moat to a gateway in the fence inside which a guardroom was situated.

The picture of that camp remains clear in my recollection, but I have completely forgotten the name of it. (It was near the French Indo-China border).

The events that were to take place there, however, were momentous ones, and these do remain very clear, in my memory.

There were many friends in the camp that I was very pleased to be united with, and there was a mixture of British, Australian and a few American troops.

The buildings were of the usual type but the latrines were outstanding; the best yet! Because it was not possible to dig more than a foot or so down without striking water, the latrines had been built up with a high earth bank; they were covered-in, had proper squat holes, and attap roofs with side walls and good ventilation. Quite civilised, in fact, luxurious!

The moat had more than its fair share of leeches, as we soon discovered when working in it; but by now we were well able to deal with these.

We also discovered that we smelt badly, for when we passed local people on the road while marching out to work, they turned their heads away and held their noses. Soap had been a rarity for a long time!

I went deaf in this camp. It became apparent when someone would start talking to me and I could see his lips moving but was unable to make out his words.

I reported to the M.O., an elderly man who tested me by whispering words and watching my reaction. Perhaps he formed the opinion that I was malingering in an attempt to be excused work, because he did nothing, nor did he give me any information about my condition. So I was left to make the best of things and get on with life as well as I was able.

A cure for my deafness came from an unexpected quarter later on. About a week after seeing the M.O. I stubbed my bare foot on a splinter of bamboo that was sticking out of the ground. It was about 2 inches (5cm) long, and twice as thick as a tooth pick. I hobbled round to the medical hut where an orderly drew it out with a pair of tweezers; as he did so a stream of blood jetted out, narrowly missing him, possibly cleansing the puncture as it did so, for I had no further trouble with it. The accident had a fortunate outcome, because the orderly had noticed my deafness; looked into my ears and decided to try a remedy of his own.

"Hang on a minute, mate," he said. "I might be able to do something about that for you!"

He put some drops from a pipette into each ear; these produced an instant fizzing and popping noise, and in no time at all I could hear perfectly well. I had my hearing back, for which I was very relieved and thankful. The drops were, I believe, peroxide; and my ears had been blocked by wax.

Apart from the M.O.s there were no officers in this camp. The Japs had decided to separate them from the other ranks, and for the first time we had none with us. It seemed another indicator to the likelihood that some part of the Geneva Convention was at last being observed. Not that the officers were far away; they had a camp of their own about half a mile away along the road in the direction of the mountains.

The main purpose of our work now was the making of tunnels into these mountains. The tunnels were cut into the solid rock and there were a number of them set in at various angles, each about 10 metres deep by 2 metres in height and width, circular in section. They were apparently to be used as last stand, suicide defensive positions, such as were used on some of the Pacific Islands, and would have to be eliminated one by one by any attacking force. A very difficult task.

The tools supplied for the work were quite unsuitable. Instead of light miners' picks there were ordinary, heavy road pick-axes and shovels. After an hour or so an ordinary pick-axe felt like a ton weight and exhaustion set in; and the frantic urging and bullying of the Japanese engineers rivalled that of the awful Speedo gangs.

It was a relief, one day, when I was detailed with a small party of men for a different job. Around the mountains, hidden securely amid the dense jungle foliage were scattered many attap huts, the quarters for a division of fighting troops.

We were taken by one of them into the forest off one side of the road, and followed a narrow path for a hundred yards or so to emerge at a small clearing in which there was a rectangular pit. The excavation was about 10 metres long, 2 metres wide and 2 metres deep. It was not quite finished and we were ordered in to remove the last layer of soil from the bottom and toss it out on to the large pile to one side of the pit.

Our supervisor was a surly, ill-favoured individual, and when the work was finished I asked him the purpose of the pit.

While digging out, the lads had speculated as to what use it would be put to. The favourite suggestion was that it was a tank trap. This seemed nonsense to me, in view of the terrain; so I decided to ask the guard.

At first he declined to answer, but when I persisted he looked at me with a sneer on his evil face; pointed to the pit and then at us and made a machine-gunning motion with his rifle and bayonet. He was telling me that it was a mass grave for the PoWs.

This confirmed the rumour that we had heard, to the effect that the Japanese High Command had ordered that in the event of one Allied soldier invading the sacred soil of Japan, all PoWs were to be killed. After the war this became known to be a fact; and I have always been convinced that the atom bomb saved our lives and those of countless others in bringing the war to a sudden end.

There was no air activity in this area and we had had some relief from the daily fear of being killed by our own planes so close to the possible end of our imprisonment; an anxiety that was now replaced by the knowledge of what the Japanese intended for us. It was a disturbing thought aggravated by not knowing where or when it would happen.

The next day I was back working again in one of the tunnels; but now not only did I find the walk from the camp very difficult but it had become almost impossible to swing the heavy pick-axe. The cause of my debility became obvious when I turned yellow with jaundice and had a ghastly pair of dirty orange eyes.

Life in camp went on unchanged until one morning, about an hour after *tenko*, work parties, who had been kept in camp instead of marching out as usual, were dismissed and all personnel were ordered to assemble on the parade ground.

The air was electric with rumours as we waited; then the camp R.S.M. appeared with the camp commandant at his side.

"Gentlemen," he began, much to our surprise, for he had never used that term before.

"Gentlemen, the war is over. Japan has surrendered — ". He got no further.

A wild roar of cheering rent the air, and instantly flags appeared, as if from nowhere: waving wildly from the ends of bamboo poles were the Union Jack; the Australian ensign; the Scottish lion. How these had escaped detection during the multitudinous spot searches that had been made over the past month, it is not possible to say .

As I saw the Union Jack rise proudly above the excited men a shock like a bolt of electricity hit me in the chest; I was choked with an emotion and a profound feeling of relief too deep, too fundamental to adequately describe.

I was moved to the very depth of my being and felt an overwhelming urge to weep, but could not do so among so many ecstatic men.

Spontaneously the whole, jubilant mob burst into "God Save the King"; (British and Australians shared the same anthem then.)

The Americans made an attempt to sing "The Star Spangled Banner", but there were few of them and some did not know all the words, so it petered out to some good-natured jeers from the crowd. Some of them sat on the ground, laying out pieces of coloured material in an attempt to make the Stars and Stripes; but I never saw it hoisted, so perhaps they had not been able to do it.

The Japanese Emperor had accepted the Allied terms of surrender on
August 14th, 1945; and we remained in the camp for some weeks after that.

The camp commandant asked us to take down our flags, otherwise he could not guarantee our safety. The division of fully armed fighting troops nearby represented a very real threat. The flags were taken down and hung inside the huts.

Japanese soldiers continued to guard the camp but did not interfere with us in any way. Some of our officers came into the camp and gave us all the latest news, including that of the atom bomb.

The senior British officer went to the nearest Thai village and with promissory notes obtained a supply of meat for the camp. A big disappointment to me, because in the throes of hepatitis, I was unable to eat any of it.

Gunboat Smith went to the same village and came back with a supply of *lauk* (a potent Thai rice spirit) on which he became maudlin drunk.

Snuffy Craig organised a concert in which most of the sketches were about homecoming and ranged from the ludicrous to the lewd.

Sometime after the elation that followed the news of victory, things began to change as the outside world began to find the scattered prison camps.

Rice sacks were laid out at one side of the camp to spell out the message :
P.O.W.s 2,000, and later a large plane flew over and dropped large bales. We were very careful to keep well out of the way of these, for they hit the ground with force and bounced wildly. The plane had the badge of the airborne forces painted on the side of its fuselage, and we cheered wildly as it swept past.

Later on a smaller type of aircraft flew over and dropped a parachutist, a lanky American master sergeant, who was grabbed by eager hands and carried shoulder high to the stage of the theatre, where he was given three rousing cheers and someone shouted, " Speech ! Speech! "

" Speech ?" said the startled sergeant. " Goddamit, ah'm a goddam hill billy from Noo York. I can't make no goddam speech. All I know is we gotta get you guys outa here pretty damn quickly. You've been in these hell camps long enough!"

The plane had circled and now dropped a second parachute. This time the parachutist landed on the roof of one of the huts. As he gingerly scrambled down it he was cheered wildly and excited hands reached to help him. The sight of the mob seemed to terrify him, for he yelled out,

" Hey, you guys, I'm a lootenant ! I'm a lootenant !"

But he was grabbed anyway, and carried in triumph around the camp.

Sometime later a strange sight met our eyes when, early one morning an old, clapped out flat-top lorry drove across the bridge into the camp. Ignoring the Japanese guard completely, sitting bolt upright on a chair on the back of the vehicle, was an archetypal British officer. He was wearing a round, paratrooper's helmet, had a fair, drooping moustache, and a monacle in his eye: looked neither to left nor right and had his hands resting on a shooting stick between his knees.

It seems he had come to get things moving, for the next day a number of civilian lorries arrived, and the first party left the camp, and I was among them.

In true Army fashion units were to move out in order of seniority, and the Royal Regiment of Artillery being the senior regiment was first to go.

Still in our rags we climbed into the backs of the lorries and drove off down the long and bumpy roads to Bangkok.

In Bangkok we were lodged in one of the university buildings. Young Thai cadets in uniform gathered around us, eager to practise their English. One came up to me and said very precisely, " In England there are many oak trees !" I assured him that indeed there were !

We bathed in the filthy river, then went out to look at the city. Crowds of friendly, smiling Thai's followed wherever we went. We were bare foot and in rags, and I was still yellow, but already feeling much better.

On the 2nd September we were driven to the airport and housed in a hanger. Ghurka soldiers were on guard duty, a very welcome sight; civilian workers were painting out the Rising Sun on some fighter planes and replacing it with Thai colours.

Night fell. We lay on the concrete floor, but were too excited to sleep. I met several old friends there, among them was Sergeant Timber Woods of the Field Artillery, whose guns had fired from the beaches in Singapore. This plucky man had lost both his legs to tropical ulcers and had been fitted with bamboo stumps. He moved about briskly on crude crutches and spoke cheerfully of his determination to walk down the gangplank when we reached England. Which he eventually did.

But there was bad news, too. I was told that Frankie Bowler, the sky-larking friend from my home town, the morale booster of earlier prison camp days, was dead. He had lived long enough to hear that the war was over but had died of blackwater fever while waiting for an aircraft to evacuate him. A bitter irony.

The next day, September 3, exactly 6 years after the war had started (and also my mother's birthday!) we were flown out of Siam and landed at *Prome* airport near *Rangoon* in Burma. We had made it, at last!

Below us, in the green jungle, we left behind a dead comrade for every sleeper of that accursed railway.

Monsoons would wash unfelt over their graves, and mosquitoes would sing unheard above their heads; but their memory would live on, and I would always remember them as they were when young; with bright faces and hope in their hearts.

In *Rangoon* events followed rapidly one after the other. My party was sent by mistake to an Indian hospital where we stayed for some days until we learned that British ex-PoWs were in barracks nearby. We immediately transferred ourselves there; wrote our first letters home; were amazed at the luxury and variety of the comforts of civilisation available; could draw what pay we wanted; saw our first film for 3 ½ years; were issued with jungle green clothing, and had two visits from V.I.Ps.

The first was from Lady Mountbatten, small and neat and wearing a smart uniform with a kind of tricorn hat. We had no idea who she was!

The second was Lord Louis Mountbatten, marching up briskly, bounding up onto a dais, gold braided cap at a rakish angle, handsome as a film star in Navy whites, beckoning us in closer, giving a crisp, short speech ending with the words,
"And I believe you have a special message for the Koreans!"
A great roar of approval greeted this remark; but most of the Koreans got off scot free and were repatriated as a subjugated people freed from Japanese tyranny.

Then we waited. It was strange to have no restrictions, no guards, and no hard labour. We had a lot of catching up to do. There was a blank of 3½ years in our knowledge of what had gone on in the world, and about the progress of the war.

We all longed for news of our families at home, and how things were in England. I also wanted news of *Sumini,* but there was no way of getting it. It would have to wait until after I got home and could contact Singapore.

It was possible to walk out of barracks unmolested, and very soon I hitch-hiked to *Rangoon* and experienced the pleasure of wandering freely around the streets.

The city had a drab, run down appearance and an air of neglect. Families were living on the pavements and the people were not at all like the smiling Thais.

I saw a young woman with a toddler on her hip, and each was smoking "on a whacking great cheroot". Just as Kipling wrote. I also saw the *Sule Pagoda* with its gold-leafed roof, but I missed the great *Shwee Dagon* — an experience which should have been a must; a neglect I have always regretted.

At last the great day arrived: we were ferried by landing craft out to where a large ship lay at anchor. It was the M.V. Boissevain, a Dutch vessel under the command of Captain J.D.A.Janssen, with a mixed crew of Indonesians, under Dutch and British officers.

It was a sleek ship of graceful lines, a passenger/cargo vessel with one large funnel and derricks on deck fore and aft. It was a beautiful craft — the ship that was to take us home, and as I clambered excitedly up the ladder at her side to me it really did seem the stuff of dreams.

The Dream Ship

It was in the hangar at Bangkok airfield that I received news of a Gunner from my old Battery whom I had not seen for some time. He was one of those characters that is never forgotten. I first got to know him in the barrack room on the island of Belakang Mati that had so impressed me with its spaciousness and beautiful views of padang and sea. His name was Len Fog, a Yorkshire man who stood five foot six feet tall, with a full head of dark crinkly hair that contrasted strongly with a pair of light blue eyes and a perfect set of white teeth. He had a ready dry wit and seemed to look upon army life with a kind of detached and sardonic amusement. Of sober habits, neat with possessions and impeccable in dress he often whistled one favourite tune- The Dark Town Strutters' Ball. This he did melodiously with a lively, jazzy, beat and always the full version with a catchy. and possibly original bridge. I never hear it or sing it myself without remembering him.

We were moved to our war station at Buona Vista at the same time. At the age of seventeen and a half years I stopped being a trumpeter and joined the ranks with the rank of Gunner, and a friendly sort of rivalry developed between us. When a guard duty was mounted the

smartest turnout on parade was rewarded with selection for the post of Attending Man, or The Stick, as it was called by the men. the man selected by the inspecting officer would
be dismissed from the parade before the guard marched off, and was not required to do sentry duty but was present in the guard room to relieve any man who fell sick. He could wear casual dress, would collect tea and meals from the cookhouse and performed a few other light duties. Understandbly this was a desirable concession and competition for it was keen.

Len would win on all his guard details and I would win on mine. Len's turnout was always faultless and so was mine – thanks to all I had learned from Sammy Mayo.

The crunch came, as it were, on the infrequent occasions when Len and I were on the same detail. At such times the guard mounting parade was played to a packed gallery as all the Battery personnel free to do so would watch from the sidelines. Bets were laid as to which of us would be chosen. Len and I both had our share of triumphs and disappointments, but I should certainly say no more of this!

We were never more than acquaintances. Len was a mature man and I was still a callow youth, but I was left with an abiding respect for him. Our `Stick` rivalry ended when I received my first promotion and Len remained a Gunner. About this time we were both recommended for officer training, and were waiting to go on the next intake at the local OCTU. Len was most emphatic that he did not want to go, but I was very keen, in fact, eager (albeit nervous) to take the opportunity. Unfortunately, circumstances changed drastically when the Japanese arrived and for me, as for Len, it was never to be. After being transported to Siam to work on the railroad we were in the same camp for a while then our paths went different ways as we were moved from camp to camp. I saw and heard no more of Len until the end of the war when I met in the hangar the same man that brought me news of Frankie Bowler. " Did you hear about Len Fog," I was asked.

"No," I said. "What happened to him?"

"I saw him upcountry a few months ago. He was in a terrible state in the latrines, suffering from dysentery. He'd had both his legs off. He looked up at me and said, `Ah've fookin' 'ad it, mate. The next time we heard he was dead."

This was a great shock to me. The vivid mental image conjured up by these few, stark words evoked a poor, filthy, emaciated and demoralised wretch who had once been that dapper, stolid Yorkshire man. It was a profound and traumatic shock and it disturbs me to this day, Such a sad and cruel fate to die, helpless and far from home and in complete and utter desolation.

CHAPTER 10   Homecoming

The Boissevain was a fast ship and her main aim was to get us home as soon as possible. The time spent aboard was very pleasant. Food was plain but plentiful and we all gained weight rapidly. Ship's officers did everything in their power to make things enjoyable for us.

Pat Fox and I were befriended by the assistant purser, a young Scot by the name of Dougie Forbes, perhaps "adopted" would be a better term, for we shared his comfortable cabin for the whole of the voyage. With only two bunk beds in it Pat and I took turn and turn about at sleeping on the floor, which, of course, was no hardship to us!

There was an endless series of parties given by the ship's officers, at which duty-free drink flowed freely.

Down below in one of the holds a few of the crew got together with their guitars, one of which was an electric Hawaiian guitar, to sing Malay songs. They made me very welcome and it gave me a chance to practise my Malay and join in the singing.

They taught me the words to *Pengawan Sulu* (The River Sulu). I liked the melody very much, and thought the lyrics very poetic, and learned only much later that the words were subversive. It was all allusion, but clearly understood by native speakers. The movement for independence from Dutch rule was already strong at the time.

There were ship's concerts which kept us happily occupied with rehearsals and prop making, and the shows were a welcome diversion for the troops, especially since we now had a real live woman in the cast, an attractive nursing sister — the only woman aboard, and, as such, an excitingly exotic creature to all! In many ways it was like old times, with Taffy Long and his faithful old accordion, Pat Fox, and I on the same bill.

In Colombo harbour, Ceylon, all ships in port saluted us with a cacophony of hoots, whoops and blasts from their sirens.
It was now all of seven years since I had seen the German liner flaunting its large Nazi ensign from its stern in this very same port.
We were long enough in port to collect some mail and were then on our way again.
It was while we were sailing up the Red Sea that my nerves betrayed their, unexpectedly, shattered condition. I happened to be on deck when, without warning, there was a series of terrifying explosions. I flung myself down flat in the scuppers quaking with fear, in an instinctive reaction.
Were we under attack? — but the war was over! Had we run into a mine field? No. The ship's heavy anti-aircraft battery was having firing practice. It was a surprise to me that I was nowhere near as well as I imagined.
At Port Said we saw German prisoners of war working on the dockside. They looked bronzed and healthy, well-fed and well-clothed. It was galling to reflect on the difference between their treatment and our own.
We were kitted-out with khaki battledress (the first time we had seen it) which felt very rough to the skin after the light tropical clothing. There was no shore leave, and we were soon on our way again.

I had never forgotten my bad seasickness all through the Bay of Biscay on the voyage to the Far East all those years ago, and was dreading the repetition of it, but I need not have worried, we sailed up the Irish Sea to Liverpool in mill-pond-calm all the way.
On the docks at Liverpool the Mayor gave us a civic reception, bands played, a Ladies Committee provided refreshments and some bad mannered men among us dumped their rice pudding into the water as a sign of what they felt about rice, and greatly embarrassing the poor ladies, who had thought it would be a treat.
From the docks we were driven in convoy through streets lined with cheering people. How strange they looked with faces so white

and cheeks so red. How wonderful it was to see them and hear their wild enthusiasm. They were greeting us like returning heroes — which we certainly did not feel ourselves to be.

Suddenly the cheering changed to a loud booing. A convoy of German PoWs had become interspersed with our own! "Hooray!" and then "Booo!— Hooray!— Booo" the cheers and jeers (very good natured ones I must add) greeted each lorry according to its contents; and there was the happy sound of the vast crowd laughing at its own joke.

We spent the night at a nearby army camp and were issued with all necessities there, including army boots; we had been in gym shoes on board the Boissevain, and the hard leather of the heavy boots reduced my heels to red rawness in a very short space of time. We were free to go out on the town, and all did so. I remembered going to a huge cinema and seeing "The Picture of Dorian Gray". When the awful portrait was flashed on the screen the uninhibited Liverpool audience gave a great hoot of derision, and again, laughed loudly at themselves.

Within a day or two, all formalities completed, we were all sent home on leave.

The train pulled into a little country station. On the platform stood a solitary figure, an elderly man. Through the carriage window I called, "Excuse me. Is this Horam?"

"Yes this is Horam," the old gentleman replied.

Then came recognition — "Dad!" I pulled my two bulging kit bags down from the luggage rack and hurled them out onto the platform. One contained my entire Army kit, the other was full of bars of chocolate, cartons of cigarettes and bottles of spirits. All very short in war time. All bought duty-free aboard ship, and all passed unchecked through Customs.

From the station it was a short walk up the hill to the Horam Hotel, and there in the lounge bar my mother waited.

She looked very tiny as she rose to embrace me. The war years had left their mark on her, and both she and my father looked much older.

With four sons and a daughter in the forces there had been more than enough worry for one small lady to bear; and now she knew at last we had all come through the war safely, but only she could know how much joy that meant to her.

We went happily down the road to a modest, semi-detached, rented house near the foot of the hill.

As we entered, the warm fug from an old kitchen range filled the room. There were familiar things around me; things that had not changed since childhood.

I was home — at last!

Life became a series of reunions as my brothers and sisters came to visit in the ensuing days; all older; all changed; and my time was spent happily until, all too soon it was time to leave.

The Army proved to be very insensitive to its returned PoWs. We were all assembled in a camp near Devizes in Wiltshire. Here we were assessed for physical fitness by turning us out in gym shorts and vests, in freezing November cold, for a cross-country run down winding, frost-white lanes, and over frozen fields.

Later on we were stripped of non-substantive ranks, having been told that time spent in a prisoner of war camp does not count towards substantiation; and were posted out to different units in various parts of the country.

I was now parted from friends with whom I had served and shared experiences with for a period of seven years. It was like being cut off from a close family, and in the years that followed I was to meet only two of them again. A fish out of water would have been better orientated than I was at this time.

It seemed a completely different army that I rejoined. The uniforms were different; the drills were different, and the standards were different. I was different too. I was greatly changed by the terrible experiences in the Japanese prison camps and would never be the same again. The scars on my body healed, but those to my mind never will. The memories will return time and time again through the years, as they must for all those men who survived those awful times.

After a spell in an ugly camp of Nissen huts near Coventry, I was posted to the Field Artillery School at Larkhill. There, in a draughty wooden hut, sitting near a coke stove with my front roasting and my back freezing, I wrote to a Eurasian friend in Singapore asking him if he would go to *Geylang Serai* for news of *Sumini* and to tell her of my survival.

At last, after an unbearable wait, a letter with a Singapore postmark arrived. I tore it open and my hopes were high.

The writer came straight to the point, after the conventional opening :

"I called at 699Q *Geylang Serai* and the people there told me that *Sumini* was dead. She died of starvation during the Japanese occupation."

It was a terrible shock. I was devastated. I had been so certain that I would return to the *kampong* one day and find her waiting for me among the thatched houses and palm trees. Poor *Sumini*; how she must have suffered. It seemed so cruel.

I had lost the pieces of the little ring she had given me, the amulet had rotted away, as had the only photograph, and I had no souvenir, nothing to remember her by. I had a feeling of irreparable loss; and yet — there was still my *ashram,* and in that enchanted plot *Sumini* remains forever young and beautiful, loving and gentle, awaiting me in the little alcove, on her golden mats.

To me she will never be dust in *Bidadari* Cemetery; and the wonder is that whenever I pass through the wicket gate in the white wall, and wander the sinuous path through the perfumed garden to seek her, I am no longer the crabbed and creaking old man who writes these words, but the young and eager boy who called her name at the *tingkap* window and kissed her sweet lips in the long ago.

> Ah, Moon of my delight who know'st no wane,
>
> The Moon of Heav'n is rising once again:
>
> How oft hereafter rising shall she look
>
> Through this same Garden after me — in vain!

Life served up more, in fact a series, of disappointments. I was again recommended for a commission; the Colonel approved it but while waiting to go to the O.C.T.U. an order came from R.A.

Records to the effect that I had been posted to the Field Artillery School in error and was ordered to return to the holding unit near Coventry.

The usual Army muddle! At the holding unit they had no information concerning the O.C.T.U. posting and I languished for weeks, doing fatigues or travelling about the country on escort duty; bringing in arrested absentees, and once taking a batch of German prisoners who had arrived from a camp in the USA to a PoW camp somewhere up north.

Doreen, the girl who had been my pen friend and childhood acquaintance wrote to me. We met a few times and had a brief engagement, but were unsuited and she broke it off to return to her erstwhile boyfriend.

Before this, things had turned sour at home. Far East PoWs had 3½ years back pay due to them. The administration obviously took a long time and it was January, 1946 before we received notification that we were to receive the money. The rates of pay were very low in those days and my back-pay was to amount to about £370. We were to receive it in the form of Post Office Savings Books, but these had not yet been sent out.

My father imagined that the amount should have been much greater, and I felt that he believed I was lying when I told him how much (or how little!) it was.

"I thought you would have got much more, Jack," he said.

Perhaps he had been deceived by the wording on the little Japanese card which said,

"I am working for pay."

I had already given a sum of money out of my leave pay but he felt that it was not enough, was unable to believe I had not yet received the back-pay, and could not wait for a share.

His rancour festered and one evening, when several family members were present, it burst out in a blazing row.

He accused me of meanness and ingratitude.

"We've kept you for 25 years!" he stormed, ignoring the fact that I had left home at 15 to join the Army and had not yet reached my 24th birthday.

Angry words flew back and forth across the room until he ordered me out of the house.

"Get out!" he shouted. "Get out of this house!"

"Oh no," I replied. "You're not throwing me out. I'm leaving of my own accord."

My poor mother was in tears. The happy home-coming was in tatters.

"Don't go, Jackie," she pleaded. "Please don't go!"

It was heart-rending but I could not bear to stay in that house a moment longer.

"Don't cry Mum," I said, pained by the anguish on her face.

"I'll come back to see you from time to time."

Then I collected my case and left. Outside on the pavement I heard footsteps hurrying up behind me in the dark. I turned and saw my brother, Dick coming towards me. I set down my case and put up my fists, thinking he was about to attack me; but he was not. Instead he laid a hand on my forearm.

"Come back Jack," he pleaded. "Come back and tomorrow this will all be forgotten."

"No it won't, Dick," I said. "Not by me it won't."

He stood and watched as I walked away.

I walked through the night to my sister's house in Heathfield, about seven miles away, glad that the darkness was hiding the tears that were running down my face.

It was a shattering time for me. Nothing was going right. I was adrift like a ship without a rudder; my only home was a barrack room. I was terribly unsettled.

My beloved *Sumini* was dead; Doreen had jilted me; and my father had turned on me; my parental home was lost.

I was back to square one in my Army career; Gunner King again, a stranger among strangers with every new posting. The only connection I had now with anything approaching a normal life was through my brothers and sisters, and it was while I was spending some leave with my sister, Trixie, that an event occurred that was to change my life completely; and it happened on the railway station of my old home town of Eastbourne.

The scene: a platform on Eastbourne railway station.

The players: John Clark, Audrey, myself.

John is an old friend; he is short and fair with faded blue eyes and a rather large nose.

Audrey is a very attractive young woman with a mass of gleaming, chestnut hair of natural waves, an eye-catching, slim figure and a bright smile.

<u>Private Ffitch</u>

They are standing by the open door of a carriage. Audrey is seeing him off. I walk up to them and a three-way conversation follows. It is interrupted by the guard's whistle; the train is about to leave. John enters the carriage first. As I follow him through the door Audrey calls cheekily to me from the platform,
"You can take me to the pictures, if you like !"
She waves goodbye from the platform as the train pulls out. John, an LAC in the RAF, is in uniform and is returning to his unit. I am going to the station about 1½ miles away where I am spending my leave at my sister's house.

   John settles back in his seat and eyes me, speculatively, then says, "Did you hear what she said?"

I laughed lightly and replied, "Yes, but she didn't mean it."
"She did, you know," he said with a gruff, ironic emphasis.
(I did not learn until much later that John and Audrey were unofficially engaged. They had only shaken hands on parting! Nor did I know, until Audrey later told me, that she had gone straight home from the station and said to her mother, "I've met the man I'm going to marry!")

I was passing my time wandering around on my own, so the next day I decided to test the validity of the impromptu invitation and called at Audrey's house.

The cold grey days of winter were past and May was warm and sunny; we spent every possible moment in each other's company, walking, swimming and dancing. The summer passed in a golden glow. Audrey left the ATS at the end of her service. I got away at weekends whenever possible, and after a whirlwind and passionate courtship we were married in a redbrick church on September 14th, 1946 and left for a honeymoon at Ilfracombe in Devon.

I had lost a friend but found a wonderful wife!

CHAPTER 11   Post-War / Emigration

I stayed on in the Army, and the years that followed would fill another book; here, in order to leave time and space for another great change that took place in my life later on, they will be condensed into a synopsis.

Audrey proved a loving wife, as steady as I am erratic; always a good companion and an excellent mother to my three fine sons. We all shared happy times in married quarters in various places; and despite several changes of schools, all three boys grew up to be clever and well-educated, and, in time married and gave us eight lovely grandchildren, seven girls and one boy. But that is looking far ahead.

After some ups and downs I reached the substantive rank of sergeant. Sat for, and passed, the First Class Certificate of Education (and found that I could do mathematics after all!)

There was a communist guerilla war going on in Malaya, and in the belief that my jungle lore and Malay language would be useful, I volunteered for the Malayan Scouts, a commando unit. The Army, being what it is, posted me to Hong Kong.

Hong Kong 1950

The troopship docked at Singapore but no-one was allowed ashore because the Bertha Hertog riots were taking place and some Europeans had been murdered in the city.

I was very disappointed to be deprived of a visit, but some months later I passed through Singapore again on my way back to England to attend a Long Gunnery Staff Course.

There was a day or two to wait for an RAF flight and I went to look for *Bayu's* house where I had spent so many happy hours.

The area beyond the New World amusement park appeared to be unchanged. Leaving the lighted streets, I turned down the short lane to where the house stood. The place was dark and deserted. The house had gone; *Bayu*, the jolly Javanese woman was gone, as were the pious husband and little *Eh Nun*; the tiny room where *Sumini* and I had cradled each other while the bombs rained down, was gone. It was as if none of it had ever really been.

An air of desolation enveloped me, and I wondered at the imponderable nature of time that can eradicate tangible things, yet leave intangible things such as sights, sounds and touches to remain indelible in the memory, to return, unsummoned, time and time again.

I returned to England, went to Wales for my gunnery course, passed successfully and was promoted to Warrant Officer and remained some years as an instructor on the School staff's radar wing.

There followed a period on the experimental ranges at Pendine Sands, Pembrokeshire where there are miles of beautiful sands and lovely headlands, and where our third son, Steve was born; in a bungalow on the dunes overlooking the sea.

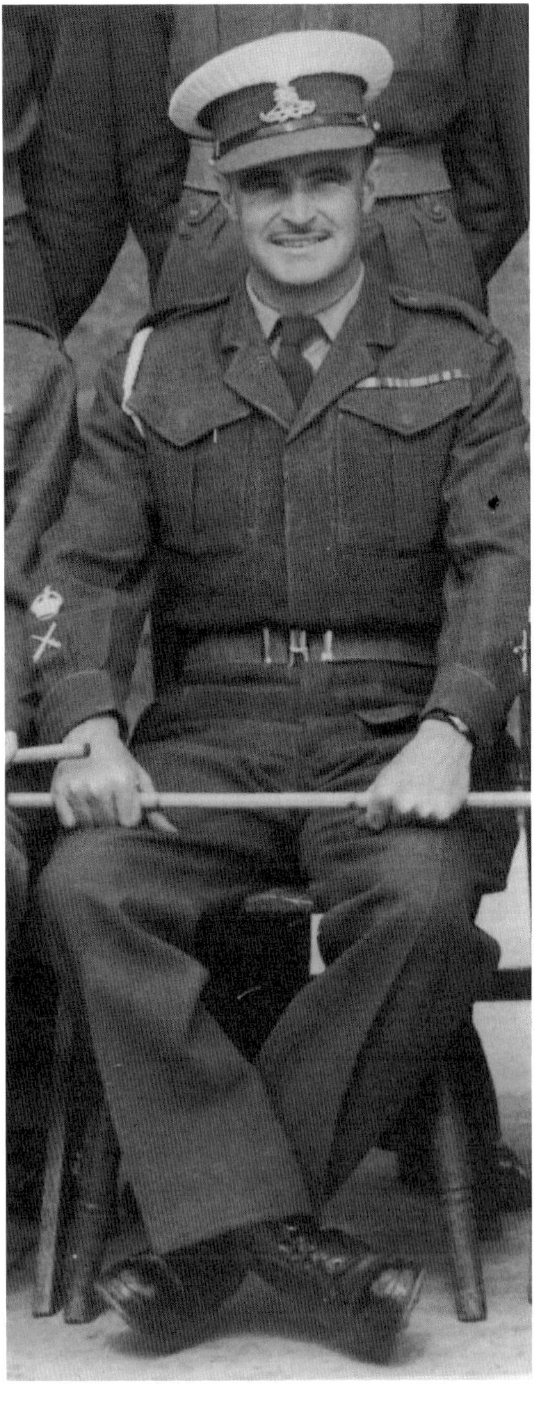

Radar Wing

Then I joined the British Army of the Rhine in occupied West Germany. Here David (Number one son), went to a boarding school on the windswept quayside at Bremerhaven; Richard (number two son) went to the Army school at Delmenhorst; and Steve (number three son) stayed at home in our luxurious married quarters, being too young to go to school.

In my 25th year of service I left the Army. It was time to settle down. I took out a mortgage I could ill afford, on a newly-built, 3 bedroom, semi-detached house in Eastbourne, on the edge of the wasteland that had been my playground as a boy.

The only relation I had left in this area was my sister, Trixie. My parents had died within two weeks of each other during my service in Germany. My mother died of a stroke while I was hurrying home to see her. My quarrel with my father had been patched up some years before, but our relationship was never close again. Both were buried in the same grave in the quiet of Old Heathfield churchyard, a peaceful spot in lush Sussex Countryside.

We moved into the new house. Furnishing from scratch ate up all my savings and Army gratuity and 3½ years followed during which I tried various jobs, all poorly paid; felt completely disorientated by civilian life; suffered an increase in the attacks of arthritis that had begun while in Germany; had periods of black depression, and generally felt that my ship of life really had run up on a reef.

Then, worse still, at a time when I was unemployed, Richard was knocked down while crossing the road. David came to me with the news while I was working in the back garden. I rushed to the hospital and found Richard in great pain. He had sustained a fractured femur and a hair line fracture of the skull; his leg was in traction and, because the accident had happened soon after lunch, could not be given an anaesthetic. I was shocked by the agony on his little face and sank down to the floor at his bed side. A nurse put smelling salts under my nose.

A metal plate was needed to repair Richard's fractured femur, and it remains in place to this day.

On leaving the Army, I had wanted to emigrate to Australia; but Audrey was unwilling. Three and a half years later, when the boys were expressing similar desires, she said;
" Oh well, if you all want to go, we might as well do it."

I was delighted, and needed no second bidding. I contacted Australia House in London and things began to happen.
Medical inspections were arranged and an interview was attended; we were officially accepted as suitable assisted passage immigrants and visions of a long sea voyage in the sunshine of tropical seas began to dance in my head. But, as so often in life things turned out differently!

On the afternoon of June 16th, 1965 I was at work as exports department supervisor at a pharmaceutical products factory when I was contacted by a G.P.O. representative
who had first called at the house before finding me at the factory. He carried a message asking me to ring Australia House, which I did at 4.10p.m.

Australia House offered me a flight on July 17th. Visions of the sea voyage evaporated immediately, but, suddenly, the future looked brighter.

Our nice modern house sold very quickly, to a couple from London who agreed to allow us to remain in it until the day we left. The one sad thing was that we had to leave behind Toby, a lovely little brown mongrel dog that had become one of the family. The happy thing was that the new owners were delighted to adopt him, and Toby retained his own familiar home with his cosy bed under a cabinet in the kitchen.

On the afternoon of Friday, 16th July I was still at work in the pharmaceutical factory. On Saturday, 17th July we left the house in the morning, with Toby looking unhappy, as if he sensed what was happening, and were seen off by a small family group at London Airport (Heathrow). Take-off was at 3.25p.m., and a new chapter in all our lives had begun.

CHAPTER 12   Townsville, Australia

I had chosen the City of Townsville as our destination because it seemed ideal for a number of reasons: it was a town of almost 60,000 inhabitants, offering good prospects of employment, having industries; sugar and copper terminals, a meat processing plant; road, rail and air communications, a port and excellent school facilities, which included a college of Brisbane University (which later became James Cook University in its own right).

Very important, too, was the fact that it was on the coast. The thought of sunshine and sea was appealing; the harsh conditions of an out-back township were not!

I arranged the transfer of my money to a branch of the National Bank of Australia (it sounded such a grand name!). I wrote to the mayor asking to be put in touch with a reputable estate agent; and bought an old cabin trunk for the things we wanted to take with us to our new life.

Our aircraft was a prop/jet optimistically referred to as The Whispering Giant — which it certainly was not; it was very noisy. Stops were made at Istanbul, Bombay and Singapore, all of short duration, and we landed at Darwin on Monday, 19th July at approximately 7a.m. in fine weather.

An official sprayed us and the cabin before we were allowed to leave the aircraft and go to a sparklingly clean lounge where rowdy immigrant children at once began, unchecked, to slide up and down a handsome, polished hardwood floor.

We enjoyed a break and a meal before resuming our flight to Brisbane. It was dark when we arrived and a violent storm was raging, forcing the aircraft to circle a long time before landing.

There was a welcoming party from the Immigration Authority. Carefully avoiding a jet of water from a leak in the roof, an official apologised,

"Sorry I can't say "Welcome to Sunny Queensland" today!"

We had emigrated under the terms of what was called The Nest Egg Scheme, in which a certain sum of capital was needed before an assisted passage could be granted. Under these conditions a family had to be self-supporting on arrival, and no accommodation was provided. A family had to look after itself.

Guided through the rain swept streets of Brisbane by a helpful member of the welcoming delegation, we booked in at an old-fashioned hotel called the Atcherley Private Hotel, which appeared to be locked in a time warp of 50 years before. We learned that a murder had been committed there some time previously, and for all we knew perhaps in one of the very rooms we occupied! The dining room was closed and no food was available in the hotel, so, hungry as we were, we went out into the shining wet streets in search of something to eat.

Most premises appeared to be closed and the best we could manage to find was a dim sim roll in a small shop. From nearby the sounds of a discotheque emerged from the steps of a dimly lit cellar. Feeling very tired now, we returned to our rooms to try to get some sleep.

There was the choice of a flight or a train journey to Townsville. Having had enough of the long flight from London, and expecting that the train would provide a scenic and interesting journey, we opted to go by rail.

The helpful official called to escort us to the station the next day and told us that we were to travel on the Sunlander Express, and apologised for having been unable to book a sleeper. We dismissed that lightly (blissfully ignorant of how long the journey would take) believing that we would be in Townsville the next morning, and we departed from Brisbane at 9.30p.m. on Tuesday, 20th July.

The "express" chugged along at 40m.p.h. stopping at station after tiny station, throughout the night, all through the next day and the following night and we did not arrive at our destination until arriving exhausted at 5.45a.m. on Thursday, 22nd July.

The journey of a thousand miles had not produced the scenic beauties we had hoped for; instead for hour after tedious hour we rolled through sun-parched countryside of stark, ring-barked trees. Of animal life we saw little other than two kangaroos that bounded away through yellow dust at the approach of our train.

The carriage seats were comfortable, but there was a desperate desire to lie down. The food in the dining car was excellent, and the huge breakfast steaks were so generous that enough nourishment was provided for a whole day.

At one station along the way an Aborigine entered the carriage. He was poorly dressed in dark, shabby clothing and wore a broad-brimmed felt bush hat. He was carrying a parcel wrapped in newspaper. He took a seat and unwrapped the newspaper. A strong smell of sea food filled the carriage as he began to eat some enormous prawns. A large Aussie making his way along the aisle, stopped by the black passenger, looked down at him and remarked: "You got too much food there, Jackie!"

There was a brief pause, then came the answer: "Yes. That's my trouble. I got too much food and not enough friends!"

I felt that in that one brief phrase he had expressed a deep sadness, and had made an illuminating comment on the condition of his people in Australia at that time.

At long last a board bearing the name Townsville met our tired eyes. In bright morning sunshine we tumbled out on to the platform and gazed about us at a rather unprepossessing sight: peeling paint; rust holes in a corrugated iron roof; a parcels office that looked as if it were built of old packing crates; and a fading war-time poster that warned the enemy might be listening; all in a brooding air of quiet neglect.

In the station yard I asked a reluctant taxi driver if he would take us to a hotel. He looked very neat in a light short-sleeved shirt, shorts and knee-length stockings.

"Yer won't get in without a booking, mate," he warned. "It's the height of the holiday season."

Reluctantly he agreed to try. We clambered aboard. I looked about as we cruised around. There was not a soul to be seen. I had expected to see crowds!

The taxi stopped at a white-painted wooden building. After a wait of several minutes a middle-aged woman answered the bell. The driver spoke briefly. The woman looked at us and shook her head. Without further bidding we were driven back to the seats at the front of the station.

"I told yer, mate. There's nowhere!" The cab drove off and we were left on our own.

We sat down on one of the seats and pondered our situation. Steve, small, tired little boy that he was then, began to cry quietly. But it was a really beautiful morning. The sun shone brightly on the ochre rocks and dull green shrubbery of the great mass of Castle Hill that reared its bulk over the city of white-painted wooden buildings with verandas and red, corrugated iron roofs.

We seemed to be the only people around, then I saw a lone figure approaching. I went to him and asked if he knew if there was anywhere I could find accommodation for my family. He was very friendly.

"There's a place down there, mate," he said, pointing down the road and into the distance, "But there's mainly black fellers there and it wouldn't be nice for your family."

He thought for a while then added, "Or you could try the People's Palace. You might be able to get in there."

It was nearby. He told me how to find it and, gathering up our bags, and feeling more hopeful we set off to try our luck.

The People's Palace was a sprawling gothic building with a long white frontage and a tall central tower. It was raised on piers and had a portico over the entrance with a flight of steps leading up from street level on either side.

It was the Australian winter, of course, and all but two of the windows along the front were closed. To us it seemed like a glorious summer day!

After the brilliant white sunshine outside, the interior looked quite dark and was pleasantly cool. A man came to answer the bell at the desk inside the door. He was polite and helpful, and I realised for the first time that we were in a Salvation Army establishment.

"We haven't got anything at the moment," he said . My heart sank. "But," he added, "I can have two family rooms ready for you shortly if you would like to wait a bit." My spirits revived.

Two rooms had been hastily tidied. David and Richard shared a room along the corridor from the one into which Audrey, Steve and I were shown. Above our door hung a large loudspeaker, and next door was a washroom and toilet block.

We climbed thankfully into our beds and fell asleep. It seemed only minutes later that we were jolted wide awake by loud hammering from the toilet block where workmen were demolishing a wall. Then the loud speaker blared into life with all the majesty and fervour of a Salvation Army Citadel band and massed choir in a rendition of: Shall We Gather at the River, followed by: We Shall Meet on that Far Distant Shore; and an announcement that breakfast would be served in the dining hall. (A few months later the Palace was sold for £5 at auction!)

Audrey sat up, groaning, urged Steve and me to get dressed, and said that we must go out.

Along the corridor two very sleepy boys were roused and got dressed, and out we went into the sunlit streets.

Being English, we carried raincoats — we were not to see real rain for many months! Also our brisk pace must have seemed very eccentric to the people ambling so slowly along the way. We had much to learn.

With eyes glowing like coals I registered at the Labour Exchange; saw the bank manager, and was surprised to find that the branch with the grandiose name was really quite small; called on the house agent, who had a hard business man's face and a pair of cold, calculating eyes, which unhappily reminded me of the unpleasant boss I had worked for on first leaving school.

An employee drove us out to view the house which was in an area known as North Ward, one of the oldest parts of the city, situated along the strand. We returned to the office to arrange financial matters.

During our absence the estate agent had called in the owner of the property, a tall, taciturn elderly man. He demanded 6 months' rent in advance, with an option to buy. He also wanted me to sign an agreement not to hold drunken parties. I bridled at this and angrily said that we were a respectable family, and it was an unreasonable demand. The agent persuaded him to see reason and we signed a 6 months' agreement.

We returned to the People's Palace which was now quiet, climbed wearily into our beds and settled down to a much needed sleep.

The next day we went to look at the seafront, and in the evening climbed to the top of Castle Hill to admire the view. It was a lovely evening and the view was magnificent, if not quite up to the claim of a notice board that stated, with typical Aussie reticence: The Finest View In The World!

During the next week there was much to do: we looked around the town; saw the famous Strand Fountain; did shopping, bought furniture and beds (the house was unfurnished) and went to have another look at the house.

On Monday we left the People's Palace, and moved in. Gas, electricity and telephone were all on.

The bank manager, on learning that I was looking for work, advised me to apply at the Townsville Electricity Board, which was just around the corner in the next street.

"They sometimes take people on," he said.

In a tall, modern building with air conditioning I was interviewed by a panel of engineers. After reading my references in private, I was called into the room, where they asked me a great number of questions. Then I was told that there was no vacancy at the moment but an employee would be retiring in 3 months' time. They explained the position and salary and asked if I would be interested. If I was, I could start the following Monday. I could hardly believe my luck, the salary was double the amount I had been earning at home and the hours were better. The retiring employee would show me the routine.

At the house in North Ward we were awaiting delivery of the furniture. Hours passed and we were still waiting. I telephoned the shop and detected a note of panic in the man's voice when he said, "What number is your house?"

I told him and he told me that the delivery had been made to a house down the road, and had been left in the front yard because no-one was at home. He promised to come at once.

We hurried along and found the beds being carried into the house. The shop keeper looked hot and harassed. The people in the house claimed that when they found the furniture in the yard they had thought that friends had decided to come and stay with them unexpectedly and had sent their beds on ahead.

It was so improbable an excuse that it sounded really funny, and from it we learned a valuable lesson: when goods "fall off the back of a lorry" in Australia they do not stay on the ground for very long!

The house was old, and very old-fashioned. Built of timber and on low wooden piers for coolness, it had a corrugated iron roof with a steep pitch; a trellised veranda across the front and along one side; one large bedroom; a central room; a very small bedroom, and an annexe at the back that contained a bathroom and toilet. It was painted dark green throughout inside and had a gloomy air.

It stood in a quarter-acre square of sandy ground, with some mature mango trees, one or two shrubs and had a tumble down, doorless garage at one side.

The rent was expensive; well in excess of what I had been paying for the mortgage back home, but was typical for the district.

We settled in as best we could, with Steve in the tiny bedroom and David and Richard on the veranda. It felt very basic and quite primitive after our modern house in Eastbourne.

I heard a shout from the small bedroom where Audrey was putting things away.

"Quick! Come and see these beautiful big golden brown beetles."

I hurried along and there on a shelf in the cupboard were two enormous brown cockroaches. Once I had told her what they were, Audrey no longer thought them beautiful.

There were lots of them about. Our hot water came from an ancient gas geyser in the bathroom and of a morning when we took a shower the burner would blast into action with a minor explosion that never failed to dislodge several of the creatures which would plop down with a soot shower into the bath beneath.

Far more attractive than those unwelcome house guests were the brilliant green and orange parrots which descended on the mango trees in the garden and feasted on the ripe fruit on the branches and which lay around on the ground. The bright colours became perfect camouflage against the leaves, green skins and orange flesh of the fruits they were eating.

Evenings produced a spectacle worthy of an early horror movie. Against the scarlet flame of a dying sunset sky and the midnight purple silhouette of Castle Hill, hundreds of giant fruit bats, flying foxes with a wing span of four to five feet, left their roosts among the trees on the mountainside and fanned out in a great skein to feast in gardens on the fruits that the parrots had so recently left.

One evening I went outside to put some mango skins in the dustbin. It was pitch dark and the bats were quarrelling noisily in the tree above my head. Audrey and Richard became very alarmed and felt sure that I was being attacked; but the bats are, of course, quite harmless.

FRUIT BATS OVER NORTH WARD, TOWNSVILLE, QLD.   JK

   Townsville was founded by an Englishman, Robert Towns, in 1868, who raised cattle. It stands at the mouth of the Ross River which was its main water supply until a pipeline was installed from the reservoir at Mount Spec, about 70 miles north. It lies within the tropics, so the sun passes overhead twice each year. The summer months are very hot and heavy rains can occur. The winter months are delightful, dry, with warm sunny days and cool evenings and nights.
The Strand is beautiful with lawns and palm trees and flowering shrubs, a fine swimming pool and sandy beach. An artificial waterfall cascades down a rocky bluff and a handsome ornamental fountain is illuminated at night.
   Winter is, of course, the tourist season and visitors are attracted from southern parts of Australia and many parts of the world.
   The town was growing fast all the time we were there and continues to do so.
   I began my work at TREB on 9th August and travelled by bus to the town centre. On my first journey in the elderly vehicle I looked down and, to my great surprise, saw the road surface rushing past — there were holes in the floor boards!

My work place was not to be the large air conditioned building that contained showrooms and the main offices, but a sprawling one-storey wooden building near the bridge that spanned the Ross River. Cool sea breezes swept in through open windows and tossed about in a merry dance any papers that were not anchored down under a motley collection of objects and stones of various sizes.

There was a friendly, easy-going atmosphere in which everyone was on first name terms, as the section head kindly pointed out to me after a day or two of "Mr. Pearse", "Mr. King".

I soon abandoned my suit for a short-sleeved shirt, shorts and knee-stockings, the same as every one else. It seemed rather strange to me that with this relaxed approach to dress it was de rigeur to wear a tie.

Money arrived from an endowment policy I had surrendered in order to obtain the amount of Nest Egg capital required, and on the following Saturday morning I went out early and bought a used Ford Zephyr station wagon; the first car I had been able to afford since serving in Germany. We were mobile again as a family, and it was a good feeling!

The weeks went by with sunshine every day and we got out and about to see all the local sights. David, Steve, Richard and I went bush walking and saw a pale brown snake with darker patches, it was about three feet long and quite ignored us. We kept our distance, not knowing what it was! There were large termite hills everywhere, not quite as big as those I had chopped down in the jungle; and at one stage Steve was, unwittingly giving a frog a ride on his back.

We drove out to Mount Stuart to enjoy the marvellous views from the summit, the vast panorama of mountains, plains and Coral Sea. By the roadside we found chillies and tomatoes growing in the grass — evidence of past picnics.

We swam in the Kokoda Memorial pool on the seafront; drove two miles out of town to Pallarenda where there were lovely sandy beaches, a shark-proof swimming enclosure (like the *pagars* on *Belakang Mati*), and stands of bougainvillaea with masses of crimson and purple blossoms against which we had photographs taken, and generally behaved like tourists on an exotic holiday.

Late one afternoon I decided to explore a tract of wild land near the town. Local people called it the Common and it was a sort of nature reserve of sandy tracts and bush. Audrey, Steve and I set off in the Zephyr and for a while cruised about along narrow tracks between crackle-dry grasses and dry yellow trees. Then, attempting a rise in the terrain, the car's back wheels spun and failed to grip. I had struck a pocket of ultra-fine sand that the locals called bull dust.

All the techniques learned in the Army for freeing bogged vehicles failed to work in this case. It was getting late so I decided to go for help taking Audrey and Steve with me.

I had reckoned without the swiftness with which night falls in the tropics. In no time at all it was dusk and before we had gone very far it was dark. It was Stygian darkness, an impenetrable black wall that made it impossible to see any distance in front at all. There was no moon and we were in a very difficult situation We joined hands and cautiously made our way along as best we could, stumbling now and again over some root or a hole in the ground.

Suddenly we were surrounded by fireflies, they sparkled every bush with diamond flashes, and danced in the air around us. In the velvety darkness it made a breath-takingly beautiful spectacle.

I headed, hopefully, in the general direction from which we had come, but I was very aware how easy it is to go round in circles under such circumstances. So it was with relief that I saw lights ahead. They came from an old people's home and beyond it lay the road. We crossed a shallow ditch to reach it and set off down the road home. It was not long before we were picked up by a young couple in a car and given a lift to the house — for which we were very grateful.

I rose at dawn the next day and set off with David and a spade to cycle out into the bush to dig out the car. We almost managed to succeed but were beaten by time, and rushed home filthy and sweating by 8a.m. with just enough time for a quick shower and breakfast before leaving for school and office.

At work the same morning I told a friend about the incident and how I had had to leave the car.

He looked worried. "You don't want to leave it there, John," he said. "By the time you get back to it some-one will have had the wheels off it!"

I was now more worried than he was. From the engineer in charge of the department I obtained permission to use one of the company's utility trucks and drove out with my colleague to the common where we were able to pull the Zephyr out of the sand trap.

Our boxes arrived from England containing winter clothing that we were never to use in Townsville.

David and Richard, looking very smart in their tropical school uniform of light grey, short-sleeved shirts, shorts, socks and felt hats, were attending Pimlico State High School, about five or six miles away the other side of Castle Hill.

Steve was attending a junior school nearby, which had a balding , pear-shaped headmaster and spacious, pleasant grounds in which huge old banyan fig trees grew.

When he first joined the school Steve looked rather forlorn, sitting on a bench at the side of the playground while other children rushed shrieking about in an excited turmoil, like small schoolchildren everywhere; but in a few days he had been accepted and rushed straight off to join the melee.

SCHOOL UNIFORMS. TOWNSVILLE

By September I had decided that the gloomy old house was not for us. Attractive modern dwellings were being built in various parts of the city to cope with the rapidly increasing population, and we drove around looking at properties.

Eventually we chose a 3 bedroom design that featured two verandas at the front. I saw Mr. Merril, our helpful bank manager, to discuss finance.

First, it was necessary to purchase a plot of land. There was a very efficient grapevine in Townsville and word spread with wild-fire speed when a sale was in the offing, so much so that one day when I got home from the office I learned that an agent had called at the house in North Ward and had taken Audrey out to see a piece of land in a suburb called Gulliver (after a one-time town councillor). That evening I went there with the agent.

It was in an ideal location; in front, across a few acres of grassland , was the school that David and Richard were attending, and there was a fine view of Mount Stuart.

A huge wooden building was across the road to the left of the plot, which the agent assured me was to be demolished.

At the rear of the plot was what I took to be a lumber yard; but, in fact, someone was building his own house there and was living in a shack at the back, temporarily.

The piece of ground was roughly triangular, with a very wide frontage, tapering to a point at the back. It was a rough patch of lumps and bumps, rather like rice field bunds, with Chinee apple trees, and some small eucalypts. I decided to buy it, and, after formalities at a solicitor's office, I became the owner of a small piece of Australia.

In October, with valuable help from the three boys, I began clearing it. First the bushes were burnt. The neighbours did not seem to mind, in fact, one insisted on helping by bringing old motor tyres in order to burn out Chinee apple trees, which are very difficult to kill and resist normal surface burning. Dense clouds of oily smoke blacked out the sun, making me very nervous, but my helper insisted that it was the only way to kill the roots, and nobody would object. To my surprise nobody did!

I contacted the builder of the type of house we liked and arranged for the work to start.

In the meantime we continued to enjoy outings; a memorable one being our first visit to Magnetic Island.

Wrongly believing that it had affected his compass, Captain Cook named it Magnetical Island. It lies about 5 miles off Townsville in Cleveland Bay; is about 20 square miles in area with 1638 feet high

Mount Cook at its centre. There is a wide variety of trees, mimosa bushes and wild life that includes parrots, kookaburras, many species of birds, and some koala bears. At the time there were some small settlements around the bays, but it has seen more development since. The place names had a distinctly Australian flavour; Picnic Bay, Nelly Bay, Arcadia, Ticklebelly bay, and Horseshoe Bay. A launch service runs regularly from Townsville, and a quaint old bus gives scenic tours. It has the picturesque quality of a Japanese tea plate scene and is a pleasant place to visit.

   We crossed on a beautiful morning over a flat-calm, very blue sea, landed at Picnic Bay and walked to Nelly Bay where we swam off some rocks in crystal-clear water, keeping a wary eye open for sharks, and not going out much further than a yard offshore. A feature of the island was the massive granite rocks that abounded everywhere, and it was sad to see that graffiti vandals had been at work on some of them.

MAGNETIC ISLAND TOURS

We monitored progress on the new house from time to time. The concrete piers (tall ones) were in place and two sides were on.

On the sides of the town buses there was an advertisement for a zoo that boasted "The Biggest Crocodile In Captivity". We decided to see it and drove a few miles out of town on a hot, sticky day in November. It was also very windy.

We found the zoo at the end of a track that led into a salt pan area. It was a depressing place beset by flies. Sad-looking animals languished in shabby cages, and we came upon one cage above which hung a notice which said "Reesus" (sic). The next cage was labelled "More Reesus" (sic). What a visitor would make of it if he went round the zoo from the other direction and came upon "More Reesus" first, I don't know.

In another cage a tired elderly male lion yawned to reveal almost toothless gums.

We went to an enclosure at the edge of the salt marsh. It had a low mesh fence around it and a notice announcing , "Tiger The Largest Crocodile In Captivity".

An untidy-looking man nearby looked as if he might have something to do with the zoo.
"Where's the crocodile?" I asked.
"Oh, that escaped some years ago, mate. It's probably out there in the marsh somewhere!"

When I spoke to people at work, telling them my unfavourable impression of the zoo, I was told that it had been a menagerie, part of a travelling circus, that had broken down in that spot and just stayed where it was. This explained the reason why some of the cages looked just that: old circus wagons.

A year or so later the place was taken over by a young German couple who worked hard and made many improvements. However, much of the original stock had died and replacements had been difficult to obtain.

The next time we went to see the house it was November. The sewage connection was being made. This was a plus, for up to this time the suburb had been on the "dunny" system; an outhouse with a sanitary bucket, as in the Far East.

There had been a good shower of rain, the ground was nicely dampened and a fine fresh scent filled the air.

In December heavy rain fell during the night and hundreds of large frogs appeared on the roads. To the boys' joy the long school holidays began — 7 glorious weeks of leisure!

The expenses of buying the car, furniture, the land and paying a large deposit on the house as well as school expenses had just about exhausted my bank balance, so I had to get to work making bits and pieces for the new house and renovating some second hand pieces of furniture.

At work my department moved from the old wooden building into a new air-conditioned premises in Sturt Street in the town centre.

The new house had been completed and we could now move in. On Wednesday 22nd December, 1965, early in the morning I borrowed an ancient flat-top lorry from the builder, for the removal. Instead of trafficators the lorry had a bracket on the driver's side to which was hinged a wooden arm, on the end of which was the tin cut-out shape of a hand, painted red. A pull on the lever in the cab raised the arm and hand to the horizontal position to indicate a right turn, and to the vertical to indicate a left turn or a halt. It was possible to pinch the skin of the hand in the mechanism — which, of course, I did!

Between us we loaded the lorry and David and Richard came with me to the new house where I backed up to the veranda where the furniture could be conveniently lifted in over the rail.

Back to the old house for another load and Audrey and Steve, and we were all in the new place by 1p.m.

On Saturday we celebrated our first Christmas in Australia, and on New Year's day I wrote the following in my diary;

Summary of year: cold start — coldest hours spent speeding through night on scooter to typing sessions*, and over hills with Steve to Hove and back. Moved house 14,000 miles (approx.) to Australia. Hot weather at time of writing.

Advances: new house, new 23inch T.V., large estate wagon, easier job, larger salary. Boys' dream realised: right near school.

Set backs: higher cost of living. Delay with insect screens.

(* Explanatory note: in England I had been teaching touch-typing courses on a part time-basis. The mention of a delay with insect screens refers to the fact that I had ordered screens to be fitted over the windows of the new house but had been let down on a delivery date).

The new year of 1966 started with much work to do in the garden which, now rain fell more frequently, had begun to resemble a quagmire and the long ridge that ran across it, and which had bent my Dutch hoe during early attempts at levelling, now proved as easily sliced as Christmas pudding, which it resembled in its rich dark colour and texture. I removed it and used it to fill in low spots.

I had bought a load of topsoil which I spread around the yard and some of which I used to build up the level under the house.

Friends and neighbours came with plants and buffalo grass, a broad bladed, heat-resistant grass that grew well in poor soil, and among the plants received were: eight rosella bushes, seven pineapple suckers, paw paws, frangipani and oleanders. A friend from work gave me four Bowen Special mangoes. They were delicious, very sweet and juicy and of a less fibrous texture than the wild variety that proved so attractive to the parrots and bats in the garden at North Ward.

We were given so many plants that, had all survived, we would have had a veritable botanic garden around the house, but dogs roamed free at nights, as did the odd cat, and these trampled many of the delicate shoots. The wind, which could be quite strong at times also accounted for several casualties. A coconut which was showing great promise out in the front of the house fell victim to a small child just when the sprout had started to grow.

As it was, a sufficient quantity of trees, plants and shrubs survived and eventually made a pleasant, park-like setting for the house.

When heavy rain fell great puddles formed and overnight became packed to capacity with mating frogs which filled the air with noise, and nights became a deafening chorus of croaks, booms, creeks, carracks; high notes, low notes, some like a rattle of machine gun fire; others ; pings and pongs, a bewildering and seemingly endless variety.

In a very short space of time the puddles would be deserted except for the masses of spawn left behind, and within days this would become tadpoles, really big ones
which, in turn, would sprout limbs and be hopping off as tiny frogs. The speed of this cycle was truly amazing

At this time, too, under the house could be found little green tree frogs, beautiful creatures gleaming like enamelled toys, clinging with miniature suckered feet onto the concrete pillars.

At night the windows had to be closed against the hordes of flying insects which would otherwise have been attracted into the room by the lights. When insect screens were eventually fitted we were able to keep the windows open and a solid crush of insects, thick as a doormat, would form against the mesh, with no chance of escape until the lights were switched off.

There was a rich variety of flora and fauna around the city and its environs. There were snakes, poisonous and non-poisonous; spiders red-back and funnel web, both very poisonous; lizards, and many bird species, large and small: ground doves, crows, black-backed ibis, parrots and cockatoos, to name but a few.

Among the insects that came into our bedroom before the screens were in place was a beetle about ½ inch long which resembled a piece of jewellery with an iridescent pattern of red, green and blue on its shield-shaped back, as luminous as light through a stained glass window. There was also a rhinoceros beetle, big enough and heavy enough to knock a man's eye out!

Summers in Townsville were very hot, with high humidity, and rain fell with the intensity of a monsoon. Road surfaces in places quickly disintegrated into pot holes, some small, some the size of bathtubs; and the earth strips along the sides could become treacherously soft. When driving home one afternoon for the first time in the Wet, I saw a small car that had sunk up to its axles at the side of the road. It was a sight that made me quite uneasy, and I was relieved to find that I was able to drive off the road and across the run-in to under the house where I parked the car safely.

Later in the year, with back-aching labour, but with useful help from the boys, I cemented the whole area beneath the house, and made cement tracks for the run-in.

We now had very useful extra space which became: a garage, laundry, work and play area with bench and a table tennis table. It was shady, airy, and as cool as we could make it. A beautiful flowering creeper formed a screen at the end where the afternoon sun shone in, and flowering shrubs enclosed the sides.

In January and February temperatures were in the high 90's F (30's C), and on February 13th, 1969 a 30 year record of 109°F (43.5°C) was reached. During these months nights were sweat-soaked and uncomfortable, and nights were noisy. The houses, being of light construction, and with windows open, kept out very little noise. The local inhabitants, being exposed to it since birth, seemed quite inured to it.

Milk was delivered from an old lorry that would clatter about in the small hours with the jingle-jangle, chinking and clanking of bottle against bottle augmented by the rattles from its ancient churns.

We paid for our milk by leaving the cash in an empty bottle outside the house once a week. Inevitably, after a while it was stolen. We learned that thieves would target a road in different areas of the city from time to time. In an effort to fool the thief, and under the illusion that he would not strike again so soon, I put a note in the bottle explaining to the milkman where I had hidden the money, when payment was next due. The next morning the milkman had left a note for me, which read

"Oh, dear. I'm afraid the thief has read your note and found the money."

(As I had had to double up on the payment to cover the previous theft, the amount was now considerable, and the milkman generously offered to go halves on the amount owed. Afterwards we were able to pay by cheque — to our great relief).

This affair had made me determined to catch the thief, and the next time payment was due I sat under the house in darkness holding a heavy piece of timber — but no thief appeared (which was probably as well!).

A beer lorry was another source of unwelcome night noises. Australians (due to the climate?) are great beer drinkers, and the beer lorry always chose the roadside outside our bedroom window to halt and re-arrange the night's collection of bottle-filled crates. This procedure always took a long time, always in the wee small hours, and added its own orchestra of chinks and clinks to the barking of free-roaming dogs.

There was, however, one silent service in the city — the "Garbos". This was the local name for the garbage collectors. There were strict restrictions on what could be placed in dustbins, and in practice this meant that very little other than paper could be disposed of. The Garbos, wiry men in brief cotton shorts and singlets, would hop over the garden fences from house to house, carrying a sack into which they would empty the contents of each dustbin.

Every now and then they would go to an open-top truck, which always parked outside our house, and tip the contents of their sacks onto the pile of rubbish already in the back.

When the wind blew, which it often did, much of the paper they had recently collected would dance away to festoon the fences they had just hopped over.

With the coming of the rain, yellow grasses and khaki scrub turned green very quickly, and the first time this happened we went to the top of Castle Hill purely to enjoy the greening of Townsville. It had been transformed, and would remain so until the Wet ended.

We were now well settled in our new house, and life took on an orderly routine. All three sons were studying hard; Audrey was fully occupied at home looking after all of us (washing and ironing had to be done daily, with at least two changes of clothing each day.)

I was the librarian and Design Branch Clerk, two jobs in one which entailed ordering and circulating books, checking all design estimates for accuracy, and keeping records and checking computer cards.

My fellow workers were a very friendly and helpful company and the atmosphere in the office was very pleasant.

As in any year, there were bright as well as dull periods. David and Richard took part in amateur dramatics and appeared in various productions, notably "Lady Precious Scream, and the Gypsy Baron (David played a comic role in this and got good laughs!) Richard made an impressive Hamlet in a modern dress production. Performed at a theatre in the town centre, all of these shows were well supported and received good write-ups in the local newspaper.

I felt the urge to take up writing and had completed a novel of 60,000 words by November.

Our second Christmas in Townsville was ushered in on a happy note when on the 23rd of December David's examination results were published in the local press and we were delighted to learn that he had matriculated in all six subjects with very good grades. A toast was drunk by us all to celebrate his well-deserved success.

Once the wet season passed, the days again became Arcadian, dry and sunny; over the months a rare shower might occur, and, now we were acclimatised, in the evenings or when the wind blew, it could feel cold. At such times we would wrap our dressing gowns around us to watch television.

One morning we awoke to find the world swathed in a thick white mist that layered the ground up to the height of the verandas, and houses, trees, and hills swam above it like islands in the sea.

When grass everywhere had dried to desiccated tinder, small fires would creep along verges of garden fence or footpath with raptors in the air above, ready to swoop down on lizards or whatever small prey was fleeing the burning.

Sometimes a dust storm would blot out the landscape in a thick red fog. But these days were rare and, in the main, life held a rich variety of compensations in the form of plenty of swimming and outings.

To the north of the city lay Saunders Beach with its lovely curving sweep of sand, where we picnicked in the shade of casuarina trees beside a sparkling blue sea.

There was no telling what could be found on that quiet beach. It had a few beach huts tucked away among the trees, but the shore itself was often deserted, and we were often completely alone, exploring the tide edge for shells and such. One day, to our great surprise, we came upon about half a dozen sawfish of various sizes, the biggest about three feet long. Obviously discarded by a fisherman, they appeared to be quite fresh, and it was fascinating to be given a close up view of these strange creatures with a row of sharp teeth at the sides of the flat protruding nose.

About 70 miles north along the Bruce Highway, we often visited a place where a little crystal creek flowed out of the mountains to wind through an area of rain forest.

From our tent, pitched on the creek bank close to the water and out of the shade where mosquitoes pestered, we could slip straight into the shallow stream for a cool swim, or paddle on airbeds up the creek between tall royal palms, feeling like explorers, and completely away from civilisation in the beautiful tranquillity.

David and Richard went skin diving at times to enjoy the colourful marine life off Magnetic Island.
Audrey joined a launch party on a trip to see the Great Barrier reef, which was about 70 miles out from Townsville. Unfortunately the reef was under water when they got there, but at the end of the day she returned home, tired, bronzed and very happy. Apparently it had been a jolly party on board and not until the white launch tied up at the wharf did they discover that the liveliest passenger on board was a clergyman, who had not been averse to telling his share of, not always polite, jokes!

As David and Richard had their own circle of friends, so Steve had his. The boy, known as Cee Dubb (from his initials, which were C. W.) was a kind of Australian Huckleberry Finn. The two boys were dissimilar but inseparable.

Early, very early one morning, at daybreak, in fact, we were woken by a strange scraping noise advancing from down the road. It grew louder and louder, then stopped in front of the house.

It was Steve's friend, who was dragging behind him on a small pair of wheels a length of corrugated iron that had been folded down its length to form the crude shape of a boat; closed at bow and stern by folds hammered shut to form a seal.

Steve hurriedly dressed and rushed out to join him and they set off together, hauling the "boat" between them, heading for the part of Ross Creek that lies above the dam.

It was a relief when the awful rattling and scraping sounds died away in the distance.

Later on I drove out to see how the boys were getting on. Cee Dubb was cruising about happily, if somewhat precariously balanced in his strange craft, among the water irises. Steve, unable to keep the boat upright was standing in the shallows, watching.

The location was idyllic, the sun was shining and paper bark trees and eucalypts were reflected in the still water. I went home, leaving them to their pleasant pursuit, and determined to build a boat for Steve, which I did shortly afterwards, making it extra wide as a safety factor. When eventually it was used on Ross Creek, the little craft, and the place in which it was sailed, were the realisation of my own dreams as a small boy when I sailed my tin bath on the marshes at Eastbourne.

STEVE'S FIRST BOAT

Despite advances and salary increases at work, money was always tight, and in order to augment the budget Audrey got work as a nurses' aide at Townsville General Hospital. It was shift work that entailed my driving her to and from the hospital at awkward hours. At weekends I would do the housework and ironing in order to help out a bit. Audrey enjoyed her work in the thoracic ward until a new matron arrived in the form of a Chinese dragon lady. Her fire-breathing soon made her very unpopular with the staff and when she ordered Audrey to do permanent night shifts, which she was not contracted to do, Audrey gave in her notice and left.
We were very pleased to have her at home with us again!

For winning the "Youth of the Year" finals, Richard was presented, by his headmaster with a cheque for $20, a book "100 Great Modern Lives", plus an expenses-paid holiday down south to Brisbane and other places.
On December 21st, 1967 we learned that he had matriculated with excellent grades in all subjects and had been awarded a Commonwealth Scholarship.

Not to be out-done, Steve brought home his school report which showed him to be first in his class, with A's in all academic subjects.

These results were, naturally, a source of great pride to me, more so since the boys had achieved them by their own application with no parental dragooning at all!

A legacy from the WW2 years existed in the form of a disused airfield on the edge of town. Rough as it was, it proved an ideal place for driving lessons, and here I gave David and Richard instruction. Both ultimately passed their driving tests.

During the year I wrote twelve works; 2 novels, 3 short stories, 1 children's story and 6 poems. Some work was sent off and received rejection slips, albeit getting encouraging comments from editors, and one brickbat. A short story written in a style I thought suitable for a woman's magazine was accepted and a cheque was sent to Mrs. J.P.King.

It seemed that I could write successfully — as a woman!

At Christmas, 1967 a present from the boys of a small set of oil paints, and some simple instructions, started me painting. I had made some abortive efforts before but in the absence of guidance had not made any progress. Now I took it up with enthusiasm and soon began to produce saleable work and had sold 13 paintings by the end of the year. It became a self-financing hobby and a useful, if small, addition to my income.

One end under the house became a studio. I took part in local exhibitions and a store in the town centre gave me the use of one whole window on the main street in which to exhibit my work. Audrey, Steve and I motored all the way up to Cairns, 200 miles north, to take part in an exhibition. It was an interesting drive with a great change taking place in the countryside when we left the dry and monotonous area north of Townsville and passed through emerald green sugar cane fields where raw red paddocks made a strong contrast and mountainous scenery lifted high above the plain. Cairns was an interesting little town, much greener than Townsville and we spent the night at a comfortable caravan park before returning home the next day .

Among the cartoons that I produced for the Electricity Board's house magazine was one I did of a new sub-station. The drawing was shown on local television and in the evening of its transmission I was very much looking forward to seeing it. However, at the very moment it was shown, our television picture was shattered by interference patterns and we could see nothing. Steve and I were the only ones who did not think it funny; the others thought it hilarious! Luckily the illustration was shown again at a later date and we were able to see it properly.

Time passed and our lives followed a quiet course. The two older boys were now at university, setting off in morning sunshine with their brief cases to walk across the grassy area to the building so near at hand.

Steve was now at the senior school next door. Our situation was very convenient and our existence was very comfortable. I had paid off my overdraft at the bank and things were generally very quiet — and then the "Girls" entered our lives.

The "Girls" were six white pullets, ordered from Brisbane and arrived by train. At the apex of our triangular yard I had built a hen house on stilts; enclosed the area with chicken wire mesh and planted a screen of oleanders, rose of sharon, and bananas.

For many months the girls supplied us with eggs, save one which laid shell-less eggs which provided a treat for any of the others that happened to be under the hen house when the shell-less egg burst on the floor slats and dripped down through them.

THE "GIRLS" IN THE COMPOST

In the fullness of time no more eggs were laid and, in an ordinary Australian yard, the birds would have become Sunday dinners. But by now the hens had developed individual, if eccentric, characters and we could not bear to part with them. Each one had been given a name based on its appearance and personality.
"Hats" for one with a large comb; "Spoons" had big pendulous wattles; "Cocky Tail" — and so on They were let out of their run each day and would take off like racehorses, and dash madly right round the house to the compost heap (they never learnt the most direct route) where they would scratch happily for the fat white witchetty grubs. When frogs were about they would be eagerly seized, and it was a common sight to see a hen, with a frog's leg dangling from its beak, being hotly pursued about the yard by all the others.

The "Girls" idyllic life was to end dramatically later on. When we left Townsville we gave them to a lady in North Ward who had a kind of pet's sanctuary in her back garden, which was kept in a wild state, rather like a small jungle, and in which we thought the Girls would end their days happily. Sadly this was not to be, for in the year following our departure the poor things were blown away in a cyclone.

One day Steve and a friend were playing under the house next door when they spotted a snake and called out to me. I hurried across and saw a brownish reptile about three feet long, overhead on a ledge under the floorboards of the house above. I raked it out and killed it. When I described the snake at work the next day I was told it was most probably a carpet snake — quite harmless and welcome in many homes because it would eat pests. With help from Steve, I skinned it and it eventually became a hat band.

Art work, which produced rewards, took over from writing, which did not. Apart from one short story, and several articles for the TREB magazine, I had had nothing published, so I stopped writing and devoted my efforts to painting, which I enjoyed.

I had always been looking at the world with a painter's eye as two extracts from my diary will prove.
Purple passages they may be, but I believe they prove my point:

"May 23rd Monday. The evening skies have been very beautiful for the past few days. Being cloudless the gorgeous colours have blended with a delicate subtlety and above the brilliant lower layers the fine sliver of a sickle moon has lain on its back in a field of purple dusk, a lone star high above it, and then the brilliant spangles of celestial fires in the deep blue belt of the night overhead."
"July 23, Saturday:

The western sky is glorious — a welt of gleaming gold across the horizon, the black silhouette of Mount Louisa tree edged, and a solitary palm sharp against the changing hues of evening. Then as the deep purple rolls down like a final curtain, the last red blaze beyond the black mountain peaks resembles Pompei drowning in a holocaust of flame."

The hot, wet summer is very different to the halcyon winter days here. Extremes can occur, ranging from drought conditions, when brown water can spout from the taps and the earth fractures into a myriad of cracks, and all that was green becomes desiccated; to torrential rain that turns the roads below Castle Hill into cataracts; to an unexpected blast of wind that ripped part of the roof from a neighbour's house; to the cyclone that will strike the city from time to time; and to the most violent hailstorm I had ever seen.

The afternoon sky was a surging mass of swirling clouds and unusual colours. A powder-blue cloud hung overhead, cheek by jowl with a luminous pink one, both surrounded by an ominous black mass.

Then came a sudden roar, like that made by an express train coming out of a tunnel. The din approached across the roof tops from the north, and in an instant the area around our house became an amazing sight. Hailstones crashed down in a dense grey barrage, battering the ground and bouncing several feet into the air. The sound of their smashing impact on the roof became deafening, and the stones varied in size from golf to cricket ball, and whereas some were perfectly spherical, others were spiked with points and angles like roughly shaped stars.

For the first time, I realised the good sense in having an iron roof in this part of the world. Some new houses were being given aluminium roofs, and some clay tiles. The iron roofs of the city escaped undamaged; aluminium ones were badly dented, and clay ones were shattered. I had learned a new respect for our iron roof!
Time passed. It was now our fifth year in Townsville. Letters from home and the enervating, hot, sticky nights of the wet seasons had begun to arouse a touch of home-sickness and nostalgia for an English country lane and a breath of really fresh air. Nostalgia expunges memories of the realities of cold, grey wet days; so, one day, when Audrey came to me in the garden and suggested we go home, I at once agreed.
In such a casual manner are life's important decisions made.

From there it was a short step to travel agents for brochures and information. Many months were to pass before we set sail but in order to obtain a berth in a liner plying the Pacific/Panama route it was necessary to make an early booking.

I asked David and Richard if they wanted to come with us, but they were, of course, continuing their studies at university and wisely opted to remain.

During the months before departure all preparations were made and the house was put on the market. All went smoothly and shortly before I was due to leave I was given a pleasant surprise at work when the whole of the Design Branch staff assembled in the yard to have a group photograph taken and I was given the seat of honour in the centre of the front row. I was also presented with gold cuff-links, set with Lightning Ridge opals, and a matching tie clip, and a book about Queensland.

On Sunday 29th December, 1970 I ferried David's and Richard's possessions to the house in South Townsville, where the boys were to have lodgings with Mrs. Reynolds, the mother of Dianne — David's girlfriend. This took several trips in the Zephyr. The boys ate their last tea at home with us before departing that evening to their new accommodation. It was the first break-up of our close little family.

November 27th was Steve's last day at school and my last day at the office. Here I had another surprise, I walked in the door to find that my desk had been cleared of all official things and was, instead, heaped with frangipani blossoms, poinciana, laburnum, bananas, an orange, a pineapple topped by a Sturt's desert pea, a large ripe yellow paw paw, balloons, streamers and crepe paper, while across the front of the bookshelves a large Bon Voyage streamer had been stretched.

Photographs were taken of me seated at the desk and I was interviewed for an article in the staff magazine.

I was touched by this generous display of affection, such as I had never seen before, nor was I ever likely to find such warmth from colleagues again.

On Wednesday 2nd December, with help from Steve, the last pieces of furniture to be sold were moved to under the house. I drove Audrey and Steve to the luxury motel on the Strand where accommodation had been booked, then returned to the house to clean the rooms and close doors and windows.

I sat alone beneath the house. Buyers came for the last pieces of furniture.

After the rush and bustle of the past days, a sense of emptiness came over me, and an intense awareness that an era was coming to a close, a chapter ending and a new uncertainty beginning. Then, unbidden, there came to my mind a Malay proverb:
(equivalent to East, West, Home's best)

"Hujan emas di negeri orang.
Hujan batu di negeri kita.
Baik juga negeri kita"

(Golden rain in other lands,
Hailstones in ours.
But still our land is good.)

Two days of luxury living followed at the Caravilla Motel on the Strand; Then on Friday 4th December David, Richard and Dianne came to Townsville airport to see us off.

It was time to leave. We all shook hands and at this moment the irrevocable nature of the step we were taking struck me with full force.

As I released Richard's hand he looked down at the ground as if deeply moved. Suddenly I felt the awful wrench of parting and had to turn away because my eyes filled with tears that I was powerless to prevent.

The aircraft was a blur. At the top of the steps I turned to wave farewell, and suffered again at the sight of the small group left behind, standing on the tarmac looking very young and vulnerable. The years have not faded that image, and they never will.

CHAPTER 13   Voyage Home

Sydney was greener than the city we had left; bigger, louder and noisier — especially around the hotel in the King's Cross area in which we stayed overnight.

To pass the time next morning we took a ferry across the hustling harbour and walked in hot sunshine to North Head, pestered by raisin-sized flies that dotted our white clothing in a polka dot pattern. A visit to the Taronga Zoo followed — a great improvement on the one at the edge of the salt pan in Townsville — and in the afternoon of Saturday 5th December we joined a motley crowd queuing to board the RMS Ellinis, a Greek passenger liner, for the voyage home.

In our stateroom on the promenade deck we found more tokens of the generosity and kindness of the friends we had left: a lovely bouquet with a good wishes card, and a large box of chocolates.

The RMS Ellinis was elderly, broad in the beam, and she wallowed. When the pilot launch left us outside Sydney Heads the night was dark and a heavy ocean swell was running. The chill air soon made us desert the deck for the warmth and comfort of our cabin.

I had chosen the Pacific route home because of the interesting ports of call on the way, and had (optimistically, it turned out) booked tours at each of them.

Three days out from Sydney the rugged mountain peaks of New Zealand's South Island appeared off the starboard beam and three magnificent killer whales could be seen quite close in to our ship. Later the mountains of the North Island came into view off the port side. A pilot boat met us and we were taken into the spacious harbour at Wellington which was surrounded by mountains, with houses clinging to the steep slopes.

Because the ship was late in arriving (this was to be a regular occurrence) our tour was cancelled, so we wandered about the waterfront and along a rather drab and old-fashioned main street and gained the impression of a place that was several years behind the times.

Heavy seas were running when we set sail again, there was a brisk cool breeze blowing and the decks were deserted except for a few hardy souls, and even these had sought out sheltered corners.

A lifeboat drill was held in the ballroom where men, women, babes in arms and children were packed in a solid mass, orange lifejackets were donned and the children created a head-splitting din by blowing on the whistles.

Audrey and Steve felt ill after this experience and returned to the cabin.

Steve had, in fact, felt unwell since the ship left Sydney Heads and seldom visited the dining saloon; but during the greater part of the voyage existed mainly on chocolate wafer biscuits and apples which we brought to the cabin.

Once the cold, windy weather was left behind and we sailed through calmer waters he got out and about more, to beat me at games of shuffle board and admire the ocean view and any wild life that appeared.

Thursday 10th December was the day of David and Dianne's marriage and we sent a ship's telegram to wish them happiness. This was the day, also, that we crossed the International Date Line and celebrations were held to mark the event; and we had another Thursday — this is something that I still find hard to grasp!

Now we were heading for Tahiti, that romantic isle being the main reason for my choice of route. The island had always fascinated me because of its association with the H.M..S Bounty mutineers and with the painter Paul Gauguin. What follows is what I wrote there during our short visit;

"Today we are in Tahiti. It is Sunday 13th December, 1970. The temperature is 78°F (26°C). There is a light breeze. The sea is calm and very blue.

At about six o'clock this morning the sun rose over the fantastic ruggedness of this volcanic mass. It is green from the shore to the tops of its razor-ridged pinnacles, and the brilliant sunlight spilled light and shade and drew a thin mist from the deep valleys.

Papeete was in shadow for a while, then emerged, iron-roofed and rusting into the sunlight, looking like the South Sea island port of a thousand stories that it is.

The town is small and has been spared the despoiling horror of high-rise buildings. There are some new buildings of modest dimensions and raw gaps among the old veranda-ed, wooden colonial-style houses, where construction is going on. But it is still very much as Paul Gauguin would have seen it.

Island schooners are moored in the harbour and the unchanging mountain hangs over it in primeval beauty.

The town, only a street or two back from the clean and orderly dock area, seems to be drowning in greenery. Our ship, a great white cliff against the wharf, makes a good vantage point from which to view the scene. Toy churches, white walled and red-roofed, point small spires at the ragged clouds snagged on the peak above.

French naval vessels, with rust on bows and anchor ports, nod drowsily at their moorings near the breakwater.

A lazy sea creams quietly over the reef, and across 12 miles of calm sea the moonscape shape of the island of Moorea stands misty grey against the sky. It is unbelievably rugged. From a flat, narrow plain near sea level it soars up to a jagged peak, to dip down and up again like a dinosaur's spine, rising and falling, flaring up to a tip-over Matterhorn of a peak, with a crest like a crumpled horn. Then, more ruggedness and another great peak, before plunging down at the northern end to a flat coastal strip once more.

With the day, the town comes to life and Tahitians begin to move about a row of small souvenir stalls on the quay. Tourist buses assemble, with bright red flowers decorating the areas between unglazed side windows. Inside and out the little buses are very clean, the seats hard and covered with masonite, and each driver seems to have picked a different radio programme; and the loud music is definitely not Polynesian! An elderly woman, in a bright sarong and wearing a straw hat completely covered with creamy white tiare Tahiti blossoms, wanders among the buses.

We take a tour. Corrugated iron roofs give way to native palm thatch, and each small house is near-hidden behind its tall hedge of hibiscus plants, bright green and with a myriad of scarlet blossoms. There are flowers everywhere; pink, white, yellow, red and gold, and an abundance of fruit trees: mangoes, paw paws, bananas and breadfruit. The lushness saturates the senses and all is bathed in the gold of morning sunshine, and the raw red-brown of the fecund volcanic soil glows wherever the ground has been disturbed.

At the tomb of King Pomare the Fifth, the last king of Tahiti, we are down on the flat, narrow coastal plain. The mausoleum has a gloomy air, it is a melancholy pile of dark, local rock topped with coral. On a flat slab that rests on the coral there is a stone sculpture in the shape of an absinthe bottle — a tribute to his alleged alcoholism; it strikes me as being tawdry and out of place. The faded red doors of the tomb bear the brass initials: P.V. It all looks poor and neglected, and ferns sprout up the sides of the structure with roots sunk between the stones. Nearby a group of native boys troop along carrying a banner which proclaims "Polynesia Francais". Others play bare-foot football on a dusty clearing.

Through a screen of casuarina trees and coconut palms the sea is a Gauguin painting: a strip of ultramarine blue, the white bar of the reef and the emerald lagoon within.

Beside a winding, high-rising road a new hotel, built to blend with its surroundings, has the tall, sweeping curve of a Polynesian ceremonial roof with wooden tiles, and overlooks a panorama of scenic beauty that takes in the curve of a palm-fringed bay, the long swing of a reef and a view of distant Moorea.

On Moorea a mushroom-shaped cloud has hooked the highest peak and hangs there, growing larger every minute.

Now we are down at Point Venus where a little rectangular-sided lighthouse barely lifts its lantern above encircling palms. The ground is a carpet of golden-yellow blossoms, like miniature sun-flowers. From here Captain Cook made observations for the transit of Venus in 1787, and here, repainted and restored, stands the memorial erected by him.

At the side of a tiny stream, where it flows into the sea, is another memorial. It is in the form of three massive pillars of rain forest timber and commemorates the visits of the first three Europeans to visit Tahiti: Wallis, 1785, who claimed it for England; Bougainville,

1786, who claimed it for France (not knowing, it was said, of the prior claim); and Captain Cook, 1787, (who went on to discover Australia.)

Present on this occasion was Lieutenant William Bligh R.N. who was to return later on H.M.S. Bounty to collect breadfruit.
The most famous mutiny of all time followed!

Here we swim in the lagoon, undressing on fine black sand, which is really a rich, dark brown. The water is warm and as clear as glass, and the waves play tricks as they sweep in, rising over the shallows in the sandy floor, disappearing where it deepens. Coming straight in through the gap in the reef at one moment, surging up from the opposite end at another, and at times moving outwards from the shore in the most capricious way.

There are Chinese children in the water, golden-skinned Tahitians and Europeans. Along the sand, small houses peep out from enveloping hibiscus bushes and coconut palms.

It is warm .It is beautiful. It is heavenly. It proves hard to brush the dark sand from our feet as we dress. It is hard to leave this idyllic place.

Our last view of Tahiti is from the deck of our ship as the sun dips westward. Moorea is a dark silhouette on a shimmering sea and its coastal plain is misting with distance.

In the fading light, Tahiti's peaks become more rugged as they float past. The valleys darken and deepen, and the greenery along the ridges stands out in razor sharpness as they twist and zig-zag up to the savage peaks.

A warm breeze blows from the indigo sea and wave crests sparkle the vast emptiness ahead, while Tahiti drowses in the sunset glow."

Day followed tranquil day as we sailed the 4,463 miles of ocean that lie between Tahiti and Balboa at the entrance to the Panama Canal, and life on board followed the normal pattern of an ocean liner: deck games, runs and exercises for the energetic, lazy hours in deck chairs, fancy meals in the dining saloon where Greek waiters dressed in national costume for special occasions; bingo games where prizes snowballed and greedy players actually fought each other for front row seats. Some seats in the bar were permanently occupied by card enthusiasts who seemed never to go on deck during the whole voyage.

Just before noon on Sunday 20th, December the Equator was crossed. To mark the event a really sumptuous buffet was laid out on tables that almost stretched the entire length of the promenade deck. The ceremony marking crossing of the line was carried out the next day with all the usual amusing antics, including duckings, on the swimming pool deck.

We were now 560 miles away from Panama; my hip was painful (from exercise sessions); Steve's little portable radio that he had bought on board ship, now began receiving programmes from North and Central America; and we saw a vast school of dolphins stretching in line abreast for about a mile on both sides of the ship, making a spectacular ballet, leaping right out of the water. Many flying fish appeared, and we passed close by a cargo ship which was heading south — the first sight of human existence since leaving Tahiti.

On December 23rd the ship (not surprisingly) arrived late at Panama and we were unable to go ashore. I had been looking forward to visiting the cathedral to see the great golden reredos that the priests had painted black to deceive Captain Henry Morgan during his sacking of the city in 1671.

Here my hip, as it had done only occasionally in Townsville, had become so painful as to cause me to drop out of the on-board exercise sessions.

As we had neared land chocolate brown cormorants in large numbers, white-breasted, with primrose legs and eye rings, dived around the ship for small fish disturbed by our passage.

From the sea Panama City looked fair, with tall, pastel coloured buildings gleaming against a back drop of ragged jungle green mountains. The ship passed under a handsome bridge and entered the Miraflores lock at about 6p.m., and we watched the operation of the busy little locomotives on the lock side. Darkness fell as we left the lock and lights came on along the canal.

From the deck we monitored our progress from lock to lock up to Gatun lake, which supplies all the water for their operation.

The lake, set among mountain peaks and jungle, was very murky and the air was hot and fetid with the smell of decaying vegetation. The surrounding dense jungle and the marks made by pickaxes down the rock faces of the deep cuttings, through which the canal passed, painfully reminded me of similar cuttings made for the railway, with such terrible human cost, during my days as a prisoner of war of the Japanese in Thailand.

Steve had been on deck without a break since first light, fascinated by all that went on. We arrived at Christobal at the Atlantic end of the canal at 1 a.m. and were allowed ashore for a walk. Not that there was much to see, for tough looking security guards made sure that we did not leave the docks. We finally retired to bed at 2 a.m.

We awoke when the ship was in the Caribbean en route to New York, tossing and pitching in a rough sea that grew worse as the day went on. A complete contrast to the calm, blue Pacific, this sea was angry, grey and windswept under heavy overcast. It was difficult to walk on the decks and many passengers became unwell.

On Christmas day the sea was calmer and there was a gala dinner in the festooned lounge with waiters in black clothing and crimson neckerchiefs and cummerbunds.

Now the sea becomes rougher and the temperature falls lower and lower. Icy slush coats the decks. Passengers don warm clothing. As we near New York there is a great crush in the lounge to complete immigration formalities.

We pass the familiar shape of the Statue of Liberty as we sail up the Hudson River, have trouble docking and — arrive late! The day brightens and we have the full benefit of a view of the fabulous sky line, so well known from so many films. There is snow. The tour we had booked has to be curtailed because of our late arrival, and we miss out on a visit to Ellis Island and the Statue of Liberty, but we do get driven by coach around the city, where steam rises from street gratings; the sky scrapers look impossibly immense from down below; and human derelicts huddle on the sidewalks of the Bowery, and we pass the distressing sight of a man, with blood streaming from his head, lying on the pavement ignored by passers-by.

The cold bites through to my bones, despite the two shirts, two woollen pullovers, jacket and coat I am wearing. We walk around Chinatown with our guide, and in a temple, which is also a souvenir shop, I buy a small wooden carving of *Ho Toi*, the Chinese god of good fortune, which stands to this day on a shelf in our living room, his arms stretched above his long-eared, bald head, with a happy smile on his chubby, cheerful face and ample stomach that has to be rubbed for good luck, and is, of course, highly polished!

The wild Atlantic is crossed in stormy weather that sets furniture in our cabin sliding about the floor, and the air is filled with crashes and bangs as the same thing happens all over the ship. The ship's siren signals the new year in and the seas grow mountainous.

In the library an elderly lady is seated in an armchair, one of several roped securely in one corner.

"I'm safe here!" she tells me, jokingly. A moment later, armchair and occupant are tipped upside down on the floor.

In the ballroom a mass of excited, shrieking children is lying tangled together like a huge carpet, sliding up and down the length of the polished floor with the pitching and tossing of the ship.

The violent bucking and dipping, heaving and twisting motions of our old lady of the seas makes it impossible for meals to be served in the dining saloon, and toast with a boiled egg is served at the door to any passenger intrepid enough to make the hazardous descent down the companionways.

Monday 4th January sees us finishing our packing and baggage is removed to assembly points by stewards.

At about 9 p.m. in stormy blackness and sleet showers the Bishop Rock lighthouse is passed on the port beam.

It is 7 a. m. on Tuesday 5th January, 1971. I am standing alone on deck in wintry cold. Lights can be seen on shore, and there is the winking of the Needles lighthouse.

Instantly, a memory floods back of the same scene in the dusk of 33 years before, and a boy setting out on a troopship for that fateful voyage to the Far East.

The world and I — how changed we both are now!

A pilot comes aboard and RMS Ellinis is at a berth by 10 a.m.

On the quayside in the grey morning light a lone woman is peering up at the promenade deck. After a while she returns to the shelter of a building close by, then returns again to resume her scrutiny. Suddenly, I recognise my oldest sister, Dolly, we wave excitedly at each other. Then more people join her, it is a family group come to welcome us back.

We have returned to England and home. Hard times lie ahead and adjustment to climate and conditions proves difficult; but there is happiness when first Richard returns, followed later by David, and our family is reunited.

The Magic Shadow Show is drawing to a close and as the phantom figures flicker and fade I would like to leave the reader with another thought from the Rubáiyát of Omar Khayyám :

Ah, make the most of what we yet may spend.
Before we too into the dust descend;
Dust into dust, and under dust, to lie
Sans wine, sans song, sans singer,
and —— sans end !

THE END

Printed in Poland
by Amazon Fulfillment
Poland Sp. z o.o., Wrocław